Off the
Beaten Path®

minnesota

Help Us Keep This Guide Up to Date

Every effort has been made by the author and editors to make this guide as accurate and useful as possible. However, many changes can occur after a guide is published—establishments close, phone numbers change, hiking trails are rerouted, facilities come under new management, etc.

We would love to hear from you concerning your experiences with this guide and how you feel it could be improved and be kept up to date. While we may not be able to respond to all comments and suggestions, we'll take them to heart, and we'll make certain to share them with the author. Please send your comments and suggestions to the following address:

The Globe Pequot Press
Reader Response/Editorial Department
P.O. Box 480
Guilford, CT 06437

Or you may e-mail us at: editorial@GlobePequot.com

Thanks for your input, and happy travels!

INSIDERS'GUIDE®

OFF THE BEATEN PATH® SERIES

Off the
SEVENTH EDITION
Beaten Path®

minnesota

A GUIDE TO UNIQUE PLACES

MARK WEINBERGER

INSIDERS'GUIDE®

GUILFORD, CONNECTICUT
AN IMPRINT OF THE GLOBE PEQUOT PRESS

The prices, rates, and hours listed in this guidebook
were confirmed at press time. We recommend,
however, that you call establishments to obtain
current information before traveling.

To buy books in quantity for corporate use
or incentives, call **(800) 962–0973, ext. 4551,**
or e-mail **premiums@GlobePequot.com.**

INSIDERS' GUIDE®

Text design by Linda Loiewski
Maps created by Equator Graphics © The Globe Pequot Press
Illustrations by Carole Drong
Spot photography throughout © MedioImages/Alamy

ISSN 1542-4170
ISBN 0-7627-3528-7

Manufactured in the United States of America
Seventh Edition/First Printing

To my wife, Lisa, one of those rare spouses who is not afraid to be an honest editor. And to my children, Matthew and Alexandra, with whom I look forward to sharing many trips in the future.

MINNESOTA

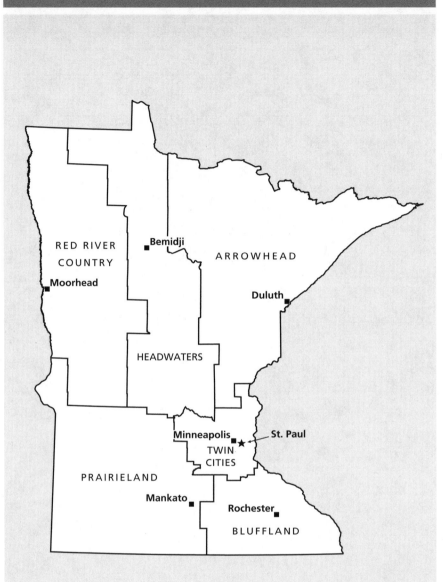

RED RIVER
COUNTRY

Bemidji

ARROWHEAD

Moorhead

Duluth

HEADWATERS

Minneapolis St. Paul

TWIN
CITIES

PRAIRIELAND

Mankato

Rochester

BLUFFLAND

Contents

Introduction

Generally speaking, the interstate highway system has been good for our country. It has made motor vehicle travel faster, safer, and much easier to get from point A to point B and beyond. It's scary to think of where our standard of living would be if we didn't have thousands of miles of interstate crisscrossing our country.

But we pay a price for all the convenience that interstates have brought us. As more miles of concrete sprang from the countryside, the travel habits of Americans changed. Instead of the leisurely trip where the drive was part of the experience, the multiple lanes of concrete caused us to begin treating the driving portion as strictly utilitarian. Got to get there as soon as possible, can't stop, got to make time.

As our travel habits changed, ubiquity became the feature most valued by travelers and truckers. McDonald's and Wendy's replaced Mom's Place and Al's Diner as the favorite haunts of hungry drivers, and generic convenience stores usurped the position occupied by the full-service, get-your-oil-checked-and-windows-washed gas station.

Which brings us to *Minnesota Off the Beaten Path*. This book encourages the reader to turn off the impersonal interstates and travel the back roads that define our state. Leave the fast lanes to explore the rolling prairie country of the south and west where Plains Indians and massive herds of buffalo once lived in harmony. Take a two-lane ribbon of blacktop through lake country as it winds through tunnels of greenery and past thousands of large and small watery gems. Follow intimate country lanes in southeastern Minnesota through narrow ravines and around regal bluffs. Seek the unique in the Twin Cities of St. Paul and Minneapolis.

When you leave the interstates, time seems to slow, especially when you find yourself behind a piece of farm equipment. This slower pace provides the time to explore the lands of the Vikings, stoic Norwegian and German farmers, miners, lumberjacks, and fur traders. And though you can find some unique and even some undiscovered sites close to the interstates and major highways, to truly taste the local flavor of each region, you must reach beyond and explore the minor highways and county roads.

Stray even slightly from the beaten path in such an environment, and there's no telling *where* you might wind up. It could be in a squat canvas tent observing the bizarre courtship rituals of the prairie chicken. Or it could be enjoying an incomparable Mississippi River sunset from the roof of a chartered houseboat. But no matter how unexpected the turn of events, if the people around you are refreshingly civil and sometimes use quaint expressions like "Uff-da" and "You betcha," know that you aren't really lost—you're just somewhere off the beaten path in Minnesota.

The more than 300 destinations described in this book were selected following extensive firsthand field research. They reflect the breadth of attractions that Minnesota offers those travelers willing to venture down the back roads that radiate through our farmland and forests. There are sites of historical, geological, and archaeological interest; novel recreational opportunities; unusual restaurants, taverns, shops, and country inns; unique events and festivals; buildings of special architectural significance; compelling tours; fascinating museums and art galleries; and those occasional phenomena that refuse to be pigeonholed. As much as possible, these areas of interest have been represented equally in each region of the state. Consult the index if you are having trouble locating a specific destination in the text.

More than any state, Minnesota occupies a large geographical transition zone. From west to east, the landscape changes from prairie to hardwood forest. And from south to north it goes from prairie and hardwood forest to bogs and pine forest. Besides the obvious differences in landscape, the climate changes—often dramatically—along these lines of geographical demarcation.

Rainfall increases as you drive from west to east in Minnesota, which helps nurture the lush forests, streams, and lakes of this often ravine-riven landscape. While driving north, it's easy to see the effect of cooler temperatures and thinner soil as farms shrink in size, conifers become the dominant tree, and rock becomes an omnipresent feature of the topography. And to completely mix up the climatic equation, Lake Superior acts as a giant air conditioner in the summer, often causing dramatic temperature differences along its spectacular shores.

The Twin Cities chapter, which includes Minneapolis and St. Paul, occupies some choice Minnesota landscape. Located along the banks of the Mississippi, the state's largest cities also lie close to two other major rivers, the St. Croix and Minnesota. The region has many lakes, scenic parks bordering the rivers, and cultural attractions. Fun seekers could start their day canoeing the wild upper St. Croix and end it with a play at either the Guthrie or Ordway Theater. From nature lover to culture lover all in one day.

Bluffland runs southeast of the Twin Cities along the Mississippi and is a land of deep valleys, clear trout streams, and imposing limestone bluffs. Glaciers didn't scour this area as they did much of Minnesota. Instead of ice, torrents of meltwater from massive glacial lakes sculpted the broad Mississippi Valley, countless ravines, and caves. Small towns nestle between river and bluff, and picturesque views await the traveler around every curve or crest of a hill.

Prairieland covers a large chunk of southwestern and western Minnesota. This is the type of landscape many people drive through and call boring, and that's unfortunate. By putting on the blinders, these travelers miss the essence of this region. Rolling farm fields stretch around you for miles, oases of hardwoods provide shelter for wildlife during harsh winters and scorching summer days, and historical significance abounds in the settlement of the prairies. It's both a harsh region where winters are often brutal, and a nurturing one where wildflowers and fields of small grain coexist under gentle summer breezes.

Red River Country includes the part of Minnesota once covered by Glacial Lake Agassiz, a body of water that at one time or another covered an area larger than all the Great Lakes combined. As you enter this region in northwestern Minnesota, you'll quickly see the legacy of this enormous lake—a landscape so flat that highway overpasses offer the only relief. As the lake receded it also left behind incredibly rich soil that has led to this region becoming one of the most productive agricultural areas in the world. Featureless, prone to flooding because of the shallow river channels and tabletop flat surroundings, and located in a region of harsh weather extremes, Red River Country has always exacted a toll on inhabitants lured by the promise of productive land.

In the form of lakes, rivers, swamps, and bogs, water best defines the Headwaters region. And though much of the region sports a thick carpet of pine forest, it's the lakes that draw people. Lake Itasca is perhaps the best-known body of water in this area because the Mississippi River begins its impressive journey from this humble lake. Besides this famous body of water, visitors to the area will find thousands of lakes dotted with hundreds of resorts. As you drive from south to north, the landscape changes gradually from sand plains and farmland with scattered lakes to sand, forest, and more lakes, and finally to peat and sand with thick forest and lakes and swamps around every curve in the road or clearing in the woods.

The Arrowhead region covers the northeastern part of Minnesota and is an area of vast forests, clear lakes, fast-flowing rivers, and the highest hills in the state. But the attraction that best defines this region and occupies a special place in the hearts of native Minnesotans lies in its farthest northeast corner. Lake Superior, with its 150 miles of Minnesota shoreline, dominates this part of the state. As the largest freshwater lake in the world, Superior exerts its influence over the north shore. During the summer, temperatures may run 20 to 30 degrees cooler along the lake than just a few miles inland, and in the winter the big lake helps keep the bitter cold from invading the shoreline. The soaring cliffs, rocky shore, and narrow canyons make this region the most unique landscape in Minnesota.

At the end of each chapter, you will find phone numbers for chambers of commerce for most of the cities or towns featured in that chapter, Web site addresses (where available), and a list of motels and restaurants. For general information on the state, or to receive an excellent travel guide, contact the Minnesota Office of Tourism at one of the following phone numbers: Toll-free at (800) 657–3700, in the Twin Cities at (651) 296–5029, or TTY Relay Service for the Deaf at (800) 627–3529. If you're hooked up to the Internet, the Web site is: www.exploreminnesota.com and the e-mail address is: explore@state.mn.us. *The Explore Minnesota Travel Guide* has an extensive listing of 151 chambers of commerce and good descriptions of each region in Minnesota.

Except where indicated otherwise, prices in the text are described in general terms according to the following rough guidelines. Meals in restaurants are deemed inexpensive or modest if under $10, moderately priced if $10 to $20, and expensive if over $20. Accommodations are listed as modest or inexpensive if under $40, moderately priced if $40 to $100, and expensive if over $100. Admission prices are termed token, modest, or inexpensive if under $5; moderately priced if $5 to $20; and expensive if above $20.

At the end of each chapter, you will find a short list of scenic roads to try. While I have probably missed a few, some of those listed will take you even farther off the beaten path and may lead you to even more scenic routes through the ever-changing landscapes of Minnesota.

Minnesota Facts

MINNESOTA OFFICE OF TOURISM

(800) 657–3700
(800) 627–3529 (TTY Relay Service for the Deaf)
(651) 296–2800 (fax)
www.exploreminnesota.com

CLIMATE

Minnesota has four distinct seasons. Summer highs average in the upper seventies to mid-eighties, with winter temperatures averaging from the low teens to twenties. The southern part of the state usually has about fifteen to twenty days of temperatures at or above ninety degrees, with the north rarely getting that warm. Winter can see temperatures as cold as thirty below zero, with several cold snaps of minus ten to minus twenty common throughout most of the state.

Autumn features cool mornings with warmer days and lower humidity than much of the summer. Spring features gradually warmer days and a dramatic growth of plants and trees. However, it has been known to snow in May.

NEWSPAPERS

St. Paul Pioneer Press
345 Cedar Street
St. Paul, MN 55101
www.twincities.com

Minneapolis Star Tribune
425 Portland Avenue South
Minneapolis, MN 55415
(612) 673-4000
www.startribune.com

Duluth News Tribune
424 West First Street
Duluth, MN 55802
www.duluthsuperior.com

Rochester Post Bulletin
18 First Avenue South
Rochester, MN 55904
www.postbulletin.com

Twin Cities

While most visitors to the Twin Cities area will not notice or care much about its geography, this part of Minnesota offers some striking contrasts. In a distance of about 50 miles, the landscape changes from rolling prairie now covered with sub-divisions to shady ravines that cut through the steep, forested hills along the St. Croix River bordering Wisconsin.

In a state blessed with an abundance of lakes and rivers, it's no surprise that the Twin Cities owes much of its existence to water. Both Minneapolis (known as the City of Lakes) and St. Paul sit on the Mississippi and evolved as grain-and-lumber milling centers. Between the two cities, the Minnesota River ends its journey from the South Dakota border and meets the Mississippi at historic Fort Snelling. Southeast of the Twin Cities the third major river of this region, the scenic St. Croix, joins the others near Hastings.

The rivers offer many options both in and away from the mainstream. In a day you could visit Fort Snelling, stroll or cycle along the popular River Road trails, and leave the cities behind to enjoy a quiet afternoon in the St. Croix River towns of Afton, Stillwater, Marine on St. Croix, or Taylors Falls.

The St. Croix River National Scenic Waterway lies only 25 miles from the Twin Cites. The lower section of the St. Croix,

TWIN CITIES

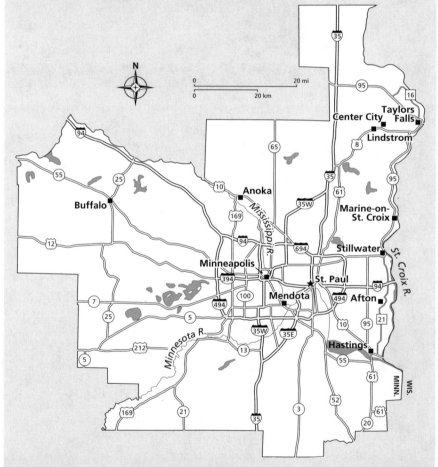

from Stillwater to its junction with the Mississippi River, is by far the busiest section of the river, especially on weekends when it seems as if every over-sized yacht in the area is cruising the river. North of Stillwater the river is much shallower, and canoes outnumber powerboats by a large margin. The river flows through a varied landscape on its journey south, with the most spectac-ular features starting with a narrow canyon at Taylors Falls and continuing through tall, thickly forested bluffs to the Mississippi. After you spend some time visiting the lakes and rivers of the Twin Cities area, you'll quickly under-stand why residents have such an affinity with water.

Washington County

As the skinniest county in Minnesota, Washington County borders the St. Croix River for about 40 miles, from the mouth at the Mississippi north to near Tay-lors Falls. Although the county is filling up as the Twin Cities expand eastward, it's still easy to find peaceful areas to visit, especially along the river. From St. Paul and Minneapolis, Interstate 94 and State Highway 36 provide the most direct routes to the St. Croix, while State Highway 95 follows the river from its mouth at the Mississippi to Taylors Falls.

Afton, a quiet little river town only about thirty minutes from the Twin Cities, at times feels as if it's several hours removed from the city. If you're hun-gry while in Afton, be sure to stop at *Lerk's Bar,* which sits on the main road through town and serves a good old-fashioned fried burger with onions. To walk into Lerk's across the creaky wood floor is to take a step back in time to the days before fast food and fast everything. During the busy summer months, boaters on the nearby St. Croix River phone in orders from the river and pick them up at the town dock.

If you haven't stuffed yourself at Lerk's, walk the half block to *Selma's Ice Cream Shop,* which occupies the site of a Civil War arsenal. Selma's features

AUTHOR'S FAVORITES

Afton State Park,
(651) 436–5391

Historic Fort Snelling,
St. Paul,
(612) 726–1171

St. Croix River National Scenic Waterway
(Twin Cities region section runs from Taylors Falls to near Hastings)

exotic flavors for ice-cream connoisseurs and a wide variety of candy and other assorted sweets. As with Lerk's, the wood floor creaks as you walk about perusing the sugary treats. But unlike Lerk's, Selma's floor hasn't received a coat of paint lately, and the gaps in the planks make it look as if it hasn't changed in one hundred years. You may wish the walk was longer between the two eateries so you would have a chance of wearing off the Lerk's burger before tackling a double rocky road ice-cream cone.

During the summer, **Afton** is a popular destination for boaters who ply the river and bicyclists who cruise the quiet county roads. Although this area is scenic during the summer, it shows off its beauty during autumn, when the oaks and maples put on their best colors. The hills of Europe may have been alive with the sound of music, but the hills of the St. Croix Valley come alive with spectacular colors in the fall. Climbing south out of town, scenic County Road 21 takes you to **Afton State Park** and the last section of the St. Croix River before it joins the Mississippi. Although it's only 20 miles from the Twin Cites, Afton State Park feels as if it's a hundred miles away from any metropolitan area. Located atop a bluff along the St. Croix River, the park has miles of hiking trails that wind and climb through thick stands of hardwood trees divided up by ravines and prairie. When the snow falls, the park grooms several miles of some of the most challenging cross-country ski trails in the area.

Driving north from Afton on Highway 95 brings you to the historic river town of Stillwater, which hugs the St. Croix as it hangs from the steep hill-

We Speak for the Trees

The residents of Afton have a reputation for being protective of their turf. While some may call it a case of "not in my backyard," residents have passed tough zoning laws pertaining to residential and commercial development.

In a case that epitomizes their protectiveness, several years ago Washington County wanted to rebuild County Road 21 south of Afton. While the narrow, winding road was due for some improvements, the county wanted to eliminate the curves and run it nearly ruler-straight from town to the state park. They also wanted to remove hundreds of gorgeous hardwoods that form a dense green canopy over the road.

Outsiders joined residents who lived along the road and those who didn't to fight the county. Hand-painted signs accusing county planners of a variety of sins, most to do with cutting down trees and ruining the character of the St. Croix Valley, appeared along the road. Eventually the county backed down, and though they widened the road and softened some of the sharpest curves, it retained much of its scenic quality. In this case the residents of Afton proved that sometimes you *can* fight city hall.

Turkey Sighting

Several years ago, while bicycling with friends along peaceful County Road 21 near Afton, we saw a large, dark object moving slowly across the road. Thinking it was a large cat or dog, we kept riding along.

As we closed in on the animal, it suddenly became apparent that this was no domesticated pet. In fact, it was a huge wild turkey ambling across the road, the first any of us had ever seen in the area. It surprised us to see one of these reclusive birds within minutes of the busy eastern suburbs of the Twin Cities.

Since that first sighting, I've found a small flock near Afton State Park and a large one in the northern part of the county. All my encounters with wild turkeys have come from the seat of a bicycle, reason enough to park the car and pedal along the quiet roads of eastern Washington County.

sides and marks the line between the quiet upper and the busy lower St. Croix River.

They say that Minnesota was born at the charming Washington County seat of **Stillwater,** where in 1848 a cadre of visionary pioneer settlers gathered to proclaim Minnesota's territorial status. Out of the wilderness they dispatched a fur trader named Henry Hastings Sibley to convince the U.S. Congress of their legitimacy. The following year Sibley won official recognition on behalf of his group, and Minnesota was on the map.

More than a century and a half later, Stillwater persists as a living museum of nineteenth-century history and architecture that is blessed with one of the loveliest settings imaginable. Nestled in a pocket formed in the bluffs of the St. Croix River on the outside of a bend, the town centers on a commercial district of antiques shops, boutiques, and restaurants in historic buildings that line an attractive riverside park. The waterfront is alive with boat traffic spring through autumn, when, across the river, Wisconsin's undeveloped wooded shoreline explodes in fall color. Any one of the steep streets leading uphill from the center of town passes well-preserved residences, churches, and buildings representing numerous Victorian architectural styles (call the chamber of commerce at 651–439–7700 for information on **walking and auto tours** of Stillwater's historic buildings).

The **Minnesota Zephyr,** a late-1940s dining train, cruises railroad tracks that parallel the beautiful St. Croix River for a distance before climbing atop the bluff to travel through a rolling pastoral landscape. While taking in the view, passengers can enjoy fillet of flounder, game hen, or prime rib as the centerpiece of an expensive five-course meal. The Zephyr operates year-round (thanks to a new winterized depot) on weekend evenings. Weekday evenings are added to the schedule when weekends fill up. Call (651) 430–3000 well in advance to make reservations.

For those wishing to learn more about Stillwater's history, a visit is in order to the residence of the former warden's territorial prison, which now serves as the **Washington County Historical Society.** You'll find this 1850s-era stone structure at 602 North Main Street, Stillwater, in a little canyon known as Battle Hollow; legend has it that two warring Dakota and Ojibway chiefs fought a duel to the death at this spot. Guides at the museum will lead you through a variety of exhibits concerning Stillwater's early prominence as a lumber town, life in the penitentiary, and other aspects of county history. A small fee is charged for admission to the museum, which is open Tuesday, Thursday, Saturday, and Sunday, May through October, or by special arrangement. Call (651) 439–5956 for more information or visit www.wchsmn.org.

As Minnesota 95 runs north out of Stillwater, it climbs a deep, wooded ravine and follows the edge of the St. Croix Valley to the quiet little village of Marine-on-St. Croix. Like most towns along the river, Marine enjoyed early prosperity from the logging boom of the last half of the nineteenth century, resulting in the construction of a number of stately historic homes. Among them is one outstanding example of the Greek Revival style, a bed-and-breakfast establishment named after its builder, Asa Parker, a founder of one of Marine's lumber mills. The warmth of the fireplace, hospitality, and delicious full breakfasts prepared by the owners of the **Asa Parker House,** 17500 St. Croix Trail North, (651–433–5248), combine for a soothing retreat. Several rooms have beautiful views of the valley, and all offer antique decorations, tasteful wall coverings, private baths, and the small touches—fresh flowers, potpourri—that make for a memorable stay. Prices are moderate to expensive. For more information and reservations, call (651) 433–5248.

If you don't feel like making the drive from Marine-on-St. Croix back to Stillwater for lunch, a local eatery may well suit your tastes. Facing the Marine town square on Main Street is the hole-in-the-wall **Voyageur Cafe,** which serves inexpensive sandwiches on homemade bread, soups, and other tasty items made of fresh ingredients.

Chisago County

From Stillwater, if you follow Highway 95 north you'll gradually climb from the banks of the St. Croix and cross into Chisago County. Although the highway follows the St. Croix River to Taylors Falls, you won't see it until you're on Highway 8 and dropping back into the river valley. When you do see the St.

Croix again, you will know that it was worth the wait. The road hugs a cliff high above the valley, and you'll have a spectacular view of the river and the impressive hills across the border in Wisconsin.

Although Chisago County is close to the Twin Cities, it shares characteristics with northern and southern Minnesota. Lakes dot the farmland that covers most of the county, and these pastoral scenes could pass for almost any county to the south. But this gently rolling landscape gives way to thick forest, steep hills, and exposed rock cliffs along the St. Croix River, giving the area a much more northern feel.

Minnesota's logging boom came early to the St. Croix River Valley. The grand bluffs and the valleys of the St. Croix's tributaries, thick with giant white and red pine, were the first areas in the state to suffer the effects of the sawyer's blade. By the mid-1850s, with each spring runoff the river became a highway of logs, each stamped with the distinctive mark of the company whose workers had felled it, all bound for the sawmills of Stillwater.

When these huge log booms reached *Taylors Falls,* however, they often ran into trouble. The river here enters the St. Croix Dalles, a constricted, steep-walled basalt canyon with a sharp, ninety-degree bend at its center. The Dalles was the site of some truly spectacular logjams (check out the pictures on the walls of Taylors Falls's Chisago House Restaurant) that kept river workers busy for weeks as they sought to keep the logs moving by whatever means was necessary—including, at times, large charges of dynamite.

Lava Flows and Glaciers Melt

Long before humans arrived in Chisago County, glacial activity shaped the landscape, leaving behind morainal hills, glacial outwash, and depressions that eventually became lakes. While the glaciers melted, the Glacial St. Croix River flowed through the region as it drained glacial lakes in the Lake Superior Basin. These torrents of meltwater carved out the St. Croix Dalles, now the site of Interstate Park, the second Minnesota state park. As impressive a feat as this was, it's hard to imagine the event that preceded it.

Eons ago, a large fracture in the earth's crust developed across the central United States, stretching from Kansas, through southeastern Minnesota, to Lake Superior and beyond. Thousands of individual flows of basalt lava streamed from this large crack to form a layer of rock more than 20,000 feet thick. Today visitors can see a few of these lava flows at Interstate Park, courtesy of the rivers that poured from the melting glaciers. For casual observers, it's easier to see the terraces carved into the cliffs by the ancient river and the abundant potholes scoured into the rock floor by pebbles and sand grains carried in the strong current.

In an accommodating gesture to the boisterous loggers who frequented Taylors Falls each spring, the community erected a jail as one of the early public buildings. Built in 1856, this stone structure afforded an easy escape to anyone sober enough to climb over the top of the cell wall. The fact that it apparently served its function for twenty-nine years may be a testament to the sorry state of its occupants, but for whatever reason, in 1885 the town finally decided to invest $311 in the construction of a newer and more secure facility. It is this building, the **Historic Taylors Falls Jail,** that now houses a more genteel breed of inmate as one of the state's most unusual bed-and-breakfast establishments.

Julie and Al Kunz, who keep an eye on the lockup from their home next door, have tastefully restored the building in keeping with its original two-by-four cribbing construction, in which the exterior walls were formed by securing the boards sandwich-style on top of one another. The building rents for moderate to expensive rates (guests cook their own breakfasts) and, with the sofa bed in the living area, can sleep four. Write the Kunzes at 102 Government Road, Taylors Falls 55084, or call (651) 465–3112 for reservations.

If you can swing a pass from the warden, you'll find plenty of engaging distractions in and around Taylors Falls. Just a block away from the jail is the entrance to **Interstate State Park,** where there are hiking trails through the Dalles, with its fantastic water-sculpted rock formations. Rock climbers from the Twin Cities frequent this area, as do kayakers who come to frolic in the rapids just downstream of the Route 8 highway bridge. An excursion boat offers rides downstream in summer, and the park has a canoe-rental facility as well.

To get a feel for the world inhabited by the town's early residents, you can tour the historic **W.H.C. Folsom House,** located just a block up Government Road from the jail. This 1855 Greek Revival home of a local logger, general-store owner, and state politician is the most significant building in the town's Angel Hill District, which has been listed in its entirety on the National Register of Historic Places. Almost all the furnishings in the house are original. The half-hour guided tour reveals many day-to-day details of the family's life while at the same time providing a glimpse into a particular point in history. The family was touched by the Civil War, as is evidenced by the blue-and-gray uniform on display that was worn by William Folsom's son, Wyman. A local newspaper on a desk in the library interprets the significance of the assassination of President Lincoln. Tours are given daily, for a modest fee, from Memorial Day to mid-October; for more information call (651) 465–3125.

If you find yourself thirsty or craving a good cup of coffee after roaming around Taylors Falls, you won't have to go far. **Coffee Talk,** 479 Bench Street, (651) 465–6700, is a beautifully restored Victorian house on the main street on

In the Company of Eagles

Last winter while driving along County Road 16 north of Taylors Falls to Wild Mountain ski area early on a Sunday morning, for some reason I looked up and found myself rewarded with a clear view of a bald eagle perched near the top of a tree a few yards from the road. My tired brain suddenly sprang to life as the sight of the spectacular bird woke me up more than the cup of strong coffee I was working on. As usual I didn't have my camera, but the image of this majestic bird stayed with me as if I had snapped a photo of it. Upon reaching the ski area, my mood had brightened considerably from earlier in the morning as I shared my experience with some skiing companions. Although bald-eagle sightings along the St. Croix River have become more common in recent years, seeing one in person still gets this city boy's adrenaline pumping.

the northern edge of downtown. This cozy shop serves a wide variety of coffee drinks, from flavored lattes to a good strong cup of java, and has small tables strategically placed on both floors of this grand old house. It's a great place to kick back and read a book, talk, or just relax and stare out at the St. Croix River Valley.

As you drive west on Highway 8 and leave the St. Croix River Valley, you'll come to a group of small towns that sit on a chain of lakes. One large lake called Ki Chi Saga (now Chisago) by Ojibway Indians originally covered this area, but railroads filled in some of the narrow and shallow places in the lake for rail beds, thereby forming the current group of lakes.

Today *Center City* stands out as perhaps the most historic of the Chisago Lakes towns. It is home to Chisago Lake Lutheran Church, which was organized as a congregation in 1854, and is one of the three oldest Lutheran churches in Minnesota. The congregation built the current church in 1889, and it sits on the site of the original one, which was built in 1856. From the church you can stroll along the Summit Avenue National Historic District, 2 blocks of distinctive late nineteenth- and early twentieth-century homes overlooking North Center Lake.

Center City doesn't have much of a downtown, but neighboring *Lindstrom* and *Chisago City* have more shops and restaurants. Chisago City, the smaller of the two, has several antiques shops and a new mall area that contains, among other businesses, a coffee shop and a unique gift shop. Lindstrom has a more vibrant downtown and consequently has a wider array of shops. Lake Boulevard, the main street through the heart of town, has enough shops to keep most power shoppers and browsers happy for several hours; included are galleries, a gift shop, and a bookstore. Hungry and thirsty shoppers (or travelers) should include a stop at *Many Voices Bookseller & Coffeehouse,*

12805 Lake Boulevard, (651) 213–6604. Lindstrom's water tower, painted to look like a giant tea kettle, has become a tourist attraction. It's easy to find, and, of course, there's no charge for viewing it. For more information call the chamber of commerce at (651) 257–1177.

Ramsey County

St. Paul had its start as a ragged frontier settlement clustered about a tavern on the banks of the Mississippi. The proprietor of this saloon was a notoriously uncouth and licentious sixty-year-old ex-voyageur known as Pig's Eye Parrant. After one of his customers successfully used "Pig's Eye" as a return mailing address on a letter, this flattering name fell into use in reference to the settlement as a whole. Then in 1840 the Catholic Church sent a missionary to serve the needs of the area's settlers and the soldiers at nearby Fort Snelling. Father Lucian Galtier built a log chapel in honor of St. Paul near Parrant's saloon and eventually succeeded in promoting the use of this Christian name instead of the decidedly heathen one already in service.

From these humble beginnings, St. Paul's location at the head of navigation on the Mississippi River resulted in decades of explosive growth, as huge numbers of settlers streamed upriver from St. Louis to stake their claims on the northern frontier. Territorial status was achieved a mere nine years after Galtier's arrival, and Minnesota found itself under the leadership of a young Pennsylvanian named Alexander Ramsey, who served as Minnesota's first territorial governor and second state governor. Today the *Alexander Ramsey House,* at 265 South Exchange Street, provides some fascinating glimpses into this remarkable era of St. Paul's and Minnesota's infancy.

Your tour of the fifteen-room, French Second Empire–style limestone mansion begins in the carriage house/gift shop with a video program on the governor's career. Then a costumed guide leads you into the outer parlor, where, had you been a female acquaintance of Mrs. (Anna) Ramsey and of proper standing, you might have paid a highly ritualized "call." Staying no more than fifteen to twenty minutes and being careful to discuss only the appropriate topics (politics and religion were taboo), you would then have been free to proceed to your next stop confident that Minnesota's First Lady was obliged to return the favor of your visit. The governor, however, dispensed with this formality by ushering his male guests via a side door to his second-floor office, where you can bet that discussions of politics and other contentious subjects were the rule.

The exquisitely preserved house, which remained within the family until it was willed to the Minnesota Historical Society in the 1960s, retains almost all

Alexander Ramsey House

of its original furnishings and many of the innovations (such as running hot water upstairs) that made it a noteworthy structure in its time. Tours last an hour and are given for a small fee daily, except for Sunday and Monday, April through December. A special Victorian Christmas celebration is held each year from Thanksgiving to New Year's. For more information call (651) 296–8760.

To preserve the Victorian spell cast by the atmosphere of the Ramsey House, you need do no more than cross the street to 276 South Exchange Street, where the elegant ***Forepaugh's Restaurant*** serves fine French cuisine in the former home of one of the Ramseys' acquaintances. The grand, two-story, Italianate structure has been lavishly decorated in the spirit of the late 1800s, when it was built for Joseph Forepaugh, owner of the largest wholesale dry-goods dealership in the Northwest. Prices are moderate to expensive. For reservations call (651) 224–5606.

In the very early 1900s, St. Paul police chief John O'Connor set up a system that provided a safe haven for criminals of all types, provided they obeyed the laws while in the city. Though O'Connor stepped down from his post in 1920, his system remained in place. The result was that, from the late '20s to mid-'30s, during the heyday of Prohibition and the Depression, St. Paul served as "home safe home" to some of the most notorious gangsters of the twentieth century.

The ***Wabasha Street Caves/Down in History Tours*** at 215 Wabasha Street South, St. Paul (651–224–1191, www.wabashastreetcaves.com) is located on the site of the famous underground nightclub, The Castle Royal. This event center offers Down in History Tours (the St. Paul Gangster Tours, the Historic Cave Tour, and the Ghosts and Graves Tour, Mill City Mobs Tour, Twin Town Tacky Tour, and The Rivers and Roots Tour), swing dance music nights, and seasonal theater.

As one of the more popular activities, *St. Paul Gangster Tours* provide an outstanding way to learn about this era. A couple of costumed guides host the two-hour tour to the city's most famous gangster hangouts and hideaways. You'll see the apartment complex where John Dillinger shot it out with St. Paul's finest and the sites of the Hamm and Bremer kidnappings. You'll also visit the post office where the Barker Gang pulled off the Swift Payroll Robbery. All the while your guides will regale you with stories about the likes of "Baby Face" Nelson, "Machine Gun" Kelly, and Alvin "Creepy" Karpis.

The Memorial Concourse of the *St. Paul City Hall and Ramsey County Courthouse* has been well preserved as an Art Deco masterpiece and as one of the capital city's most noted architectural landmarks. Entering the narrow, three-story room feels a little like entering a hallowed chamber in the city of Oz. Very dark blue Belgian marble on the walls creates a mysteriously somber atmosphere. A mirrored ceiling reflects your every move and lends even greater apparent stature to the *Vision of Peace* statue that stands at the far end of the room. Made of sixty tons of luminous white onyx by Swedish sculptor Carl Milles, the 36-foot statue depicts five Native Americans in a spiritual ceremony, with a common godlike vision—of Peace—rising among them. The St. Paul City Hall and Ramsey County Courthouse, 15 West Kellogg Avenue in downtown St. Paul, is open to the public, free of charge.

Learning through hands-on exploration of some of the most unlikely objects is the key to fun at the *Children's Museum,* situated in downtown St. Paul. Don't be fooled by the name of this place, either—many adults, as well as kids, will enjoy filming one another in a television studio with real video cameras or operating a large electromagnetic crane.

The Children's Museum regularly holds special events involving its own theatrical troupe and in cooperation with other arts and educational programs in the Twin Cities. There is also a gift shop full of creative surprises. The museum is open Tuesday through Saturday year-round for a modest admission fee. It is located at 10 West Seventh Street, St. Paul. For information on special events, call (651) 225–6000, or visit the Web site at www.mcm.org.

If you had a model railroad as a child, or even if you didn't, the *Twin City Model Railroad Museum* should make it on your list of sites to visit in St. Paul. Visitors will find a 3,000-square-foot O-scale operating model of railroads in Minnesota during the 1930s to 1950s, a collection of railroad art, and a history wall. The museum is located in the Bandana Square shopping mall (a renovated railroad repair shop) at 1021 Bandana Boulevard East (651–647–9628, www.tcmrm.org).

For those who like their trains life-size as well as pint-size, the *Minnesota Transportation Museum,* 193 Pennsylvania Avenue East, St. Paul

TOP ANNUAL EVENTS IN THE TWIN CITIES

St. Paul Winter Carnival,
late January,
(651) 223–4710,
winter-carnival.com

Grand Old Day,
St. Paul, early June,
(651) 297–6985

Karl Oskar Days,
Lindstrom, late June,
(651) 257–8087

Rivertown Days,
Hastings, mid-July,
(651) 437–6775

Wannigan Days,
Taylors Falls, mid-July,
(651) 465–4405

Aquatennial,
Minneapolis, late July,
(651) 661–4700

Lumberjack Days,
Stillwater, late July,
(651) 439–7700

(651–228–0263, www.mtmuseum.org), is another fun place to visit. Besides a restored roundhouse at this location, the museum also has steam- and diesel-powered trains in Osceola, Wisconsin (35 miles northeast of St. Paul), vintage streetcars at Lake Harriet in Minneapolis, and a restored steamboat on Lake Minnetonka.

Traffic on University Avenue—one of the first roadways to connect Minneapolis and St. Paul—has always run thick and fast, which is a pity, because many people zip by the ***Russian Piroshki and Teahouse*** never knowing what they've missed. When Nikolai Alenov opened this modest take-out place in 1978, it was one of the first Russian fast-food restaurants in the country. Since then, his mother's recipe for piroshki, or Russian hamburgers—heavenly dumplings filled with ground beef, rice, and spices that are either deep-fried or baked—has attracted a loyal clientele of office workers and neighbors. Nikolai also serves borscht, stuffed cabbage rolls, and, of course, Russian tea, all at very inexpensive prices. A couple of tables have recently been added if you'd prefer to eat in. To find this humble establishment, which is open Tuesday through Friday for lunch and early dinners, keep your eyes peeled for the sign at 1758 University Avenue, St. Paul, on the south side of the street, just east of Fairview. Call (651) 646–4144.

Another slice of regional history has been well preserved on the grounds of the Luther Seminary in the quiet neighborhood of St. Anthony Park. Here, tucked behind several classroom and administration buildings on top of a hill, is an attractive log building, the **Old Muskego Church,** which stands as a living monument to the first organized Norwegian Lutheran congregation in the New World.

As the door to the lovely old church swings open, there is an aroma of aged red oak and walnut that is as strong as frankincense. One's attention is drawn immediately to the front of the chancel, where, in simplicity and grace, a solid walnut, five-sided altar sits below a turret-shaped pulpit, whose prominence in the building reflects the importance of the spoken Word in the worship of the day. The straight-backed pews, the rough-hewn benches on the balcony, and the grim portraits of some of the early pastors convey something of the life these settlers led. Having chosen a swampy site for their community near Milwaukee, Wisconsin, the settlers experienced a staggering incidence of death by cholera during the first few years (1843 to 1847). But the settlement finally prospered, producing the country's first two Norwegian newspapers, the first elected officials of Norwegian descent, and even a Civil War hero. The church was moved to its present site in 1904 and was added to the National Register of Historic Places in 1974. The building is open for self-guided tours daily, requiring only that you check in at the Seminary Information Desk in the Olson Campus Center building on the southeast corner of Hendon Avenue and Fulham Street.

The St. Paul campus of the University of Minnesota was developed originally as a "farm school," and the study of agricultural science is still a primary activity there. But within the School of Home Economics in the attractive McNeal Hall (1985 Buford Avenue) is an unusual exhibition dedicated to common objects of human design—clothing, textiles, household items, and decorative arts. Exhibits at the small **Goldstein Gallery** change every two to three months and cover a broad range of themes, from underwear making to the history of inventions by women. The gallery is open daily, free of charge; for information on current exhibits, call (612) 624–7434.

As the expanding populations of the Twin Cities pushed the city limits ever closer to each other around the turn of the twentieth century, the Herman Gibbs family on the northern perimeter of this "interurban zone" adapted their farming practices to the growing urban market. By planting a greater variety of fruits and vegetables and by rushing their fresh produce to the farmers' market each day, they joined ranks with a little-known agricultural tradition called the urban-fringe farm. The farmhouse, with its original furnishings, and the outbuildings used by the Gibbs family have been preserved as the **Gibbs Farm Museum,** located at Larpenteur and Cleveland Avenues in Falcon Heights, where the clock has been set back to 1901.

Guided tours of the farm begin with a short slide show and then lead through a one-room schoolhouse, two barns, and the house, where something's frequently cooking on the wood stove in the summer kitchen. On Sundays staff and volunteers in period dress provide demonstrations of such tasks as candle dipping, butter churning, doll making, and quilting, to name only a few. The educational practices of the time are explained by a teacher holding forth at the blackboard. And during special festivals it's not unheard of for staff and volunteers to kick up their heels and dance or to compete in such contests as seeing who can produce the most attractive shawl starting with a mass of uncarded wool. The museum charges a small fee and is open Tuesday through Sunday, planting time through harvest. Call (651) 646–8629 for more information.

"From Urban Places to Country Spaces" is the motto of the recently completed *Gateway Trail,* an old "rail trail" that connects St. Paul to Stillwater, and it couldn't be more accurate. The trail runs for 17.1 miles from Arlington Avenue in St. Paul to Pine Point Park, 5 miles north of Still-

healthyrivalry

Although Minneapolis can easily lay claim to being the bigger and more cosmopolitan of the Twin Cities, it still takes every opportunity to kick sand in the face of St. Paul. When St. Paul received a pro hockey franchise, it didn't take long for Minneapolis to try to lure the team across the river to play in their arena. If the capital city lures a business away from Minneapolis, the bigger city cries foul and carries on about how perpetual underdog St. Paul stole the company.

water. For its first few miles, the trail provides a nice alternative to busy highways as it passes through the communities of East St. Paul, Maplewood, and North St. Paul.

Then, after passing beneath Interstate 694, the Gateway Trail becomes decidedly pastoral as it meanders past many ponds, barns, and marshes in a gently rolling landscape. The primary trail is paved, providing an ideal surface for bicycles and in-line skates. A gravel trail, which can be used by horses and mountain bikes, runs beside it. Steep grades are few and access points many, making the Gateway Trail quite user-friendly. For maps and more information, contact the Minnesota Department of Natural Resources Information Center, 500 Lafayette Road, St. Paul, or call (888) 646–6367; or visit www.dnr.state.mn.us.

If you are one of the many poor souls allergic to domed stadiums and plastic grass, a visit to a *St. Paul Saints* baseball game could be just what the doctor ordered. The Saints, who play forty home games a year at Municipal Stadium (north of Snelling on Energy Park Drive), are members of the Northern League, a six-team independent league, whose teams aren't affiliated with Major League parent clubs. The play is not quite of Major League–caliber, but the games are fast paced, and the between-innings entertainment is at least half the fun. Tickets are inexpensively to moderately priced. For reservations or information call (651) 644–6659.

Dakota County

The same glacial river that carved out the impressive river valleys of the Twin Cities region also shaped the landscape of Dakota County. Outwash, layers of sand and gravel deposited by glacial meltwater, formed the gentle hills of this fertile county that sits south of St. Paul and Minneapolis. The glacial streams deposited mostly sand to the west, forming the Anoka sandplain, an area of dunes and sparse vegetation. The difference in terrain between the two counties provides evidence of the unbelievable power of ice and water.

The geographical hub around which much of Minnesota's history has revolved is the confluence of the Minnesota and Mississippi Rivers. In 1805, two years after the Louisiana Purchase gave the United States access to the Mississippi watershed, the territory surrounding this strategic junction of Minnesota's two largest rivers was obtained through treaty from the Dakota Indians for sixty gallons of whiskey and $2,000 worth of trade goods. The land wasn't occupied by its new owners, however, until fourteen years later, when 200 soldiers spent a miserable winter (40 of them died of scurvy) camped near the site

Swedish Heritage

In a state known for its Scandinavian heritage, the Chisago Lakes towns of Lindstrom and Center City owe a large portion of their history to emigrants from Sweden. This area is the site of the first permanent Swedish settlement in Minnesota (Norbergsholmen, now known by the prosaic name of Center City) and the setting for several historical novels. The emigrants traveled by boat up the St. Croix River to Taylors Falls and walked the final 10 miles west to the lake district, where most started farming.

When historian and author Vilhelm Moberg used this region as a setting in four novels about Swedish migration to America, the area became famous in his homeland. His book, *The Emigrants,* created the local heroes Karl Oskar and Kristina Nilsson, and today these fictional characters stand as statues in downtown Lindstrom.

Other reminders of the area's Swedish ties include historical Glader Cemetery, the fictional burial place of Karl and Kristina, and their fictional home, the Nya Duvemala House. Both sites lie 3 miles south of Lindstrom off County Road 25 on the shore of South Center Lake. The first pioneer was buried in Glader Cemetery in 1855, the last in 1916.

of what was to become Fort Snelling, Minnesota's first military outpost and the Northwest's most remote fort for thirty years (see Hennepin County).

Eventually the Twin Cities sprang up in proximity to this spot—St. Paul a few miles downstream, at the head of navigation on the Mississippi, and Minneapolis at a roughly equal distance upstream on the same river, where the once-magnificent St. Anthony Falls produced waterpower for early industry. But well before either city was established, Minnesota's first permanent white settlement took root in Fort Snelling's protective shadow on the southern banks of the Minnesota-Mississippi confluence.

Mendota (from the Dakota Indian word for "where the waters mingle"), as the town is called now, grew around a fur trading post run by Henry Hastings Sibley of the American Fur Company. A visit to the **Sibley House,** a historic site operated by the Daughters of the American Revolution, reveals much about this pioneer statesman and the era in which he lived.

A year after his arrival in 1834, Sibley and a group of fellow traders and local Indians built the handsome limestone dwelling as a home and business center. As you enter its large entry, a glass wall panel reveals an innovative building process: The interior walls combined river mud, sand, and clay with a latticework of grass and woven willow branches. But despite the primitive materials used in its construction, the Sibley House was an oasis of civility on the frontier. Tasteful period furnishings in every room suggest how lucrative the fur trade was, while providing insight into the lifestyle of the Victorian society to which the Sibleys aspired. A "fainting couch" placed at the top of the stairs was available for tightly corseted ladies who may have arrived upstairs short of breath. In Mrs. Sibley's bedroom a bootjack features a decorative panel positioned so as to have prevented anyone present from glimpsing her emerging ankle.

The Sibley House is adjacent to the **Faribault House,** built by the fur trader Jean Baptiste Faribault and operated now as a museum, with exhibits on the fur trade and the Dakota and Ojibway Indian cultures.

Both houses are open Tuesday through Sunday for a small fee from May through October; they are also open weekends in October, when they are decorated for Christmas. Living-history demonstrations are scheduled occasionally. Both are located along Minnesota 13 on the west end of the town of Mendota. For more information call (651) 452-1596.

Hastings—located about 20 miles downstream of Mendota at the junction of the Mississippi, St. Croix, and Vermillion Rivers—is another community that owes its early existence to the flowing waters at its doorstep. This Dakota County seat of 16,000 retains much charm from its heyday in the second half of the nineteenth century, when water-powered grain mills made the city one of the greatest wheat markets of the Northwest. A drive down the old main street, Second Avenue, reveals many original storefronts still intact.

Another way to enjoy Hastings's rich architectural heritage is to take a self-guided *front-porch tour* of the historic district, following directions in a brochure available from the chamber of commerce at 427 Vermillion Street. In fact the town has become so enthralled by its eclectic porches that on a week-end in early May an annual *Front Porch Festival* is held to rekindle memo-ries of the time when front porches were a focal point of neighborhood social life in America. The festival features house and porch tours, clinics on porch and home reconstruction, horse-and-buggy rides, and historic games. Call (651) 437–6775 for more information.

Two of Hastings's gracious older homes open their doors to visitors as exceptional bed-and-breakfasts operated by Pam and Dick Thorsen. The grand *Thorwood B&B,* the center of the operation, is an 1880 French Second Empire house with a steeple reaching skyward above the roof line. The award-winning Queen Anne–style *Rosewood* dates from the same year. The Thorsens have tastefully renovated both houses in keeping with their original designs while retaining some features that recall their original incarnations as small hospitals.

At Thorwood evidence of a vertical shaft persists from the hospital's primi-tive hand-powered elevator. This "convenience" was unsuitable for use by preg-nant women, who were restricted from unduly exerting themselves on the hand-operated controls. Instead they had to use the stairs. Patients on stretchers were unable to fit into the small enclosure without standing up. The Lullaby Room is popular with some locals who slept there when it served as the hospital nursery.

All of the fifteen rooms at the two B&Bs have private baths, some equipped with double whirlpools, and eleven of them have wood-burning fireplaces. Innovative room service is offered at both establish-ments, including delicious multi-course "hatbox" suppers served in real hatboxes, and extravagant seasonal theme suppers, such as the "Dickens of a Dinner," delivered replete with a hardcover volume of Dickens's prose. Of

the "minneapple"

While Minneapolis has many attributes, including several beautiful urban lakes surrounded by parks and a vibrant downtown, for some reason certain residents and city government officials seem to harbor feelings of insecurity. In an attempt to align their city with New York City, several years ago Minneapolis advertised itself as the "Minne Apple," apparently in an attempt to be recog-nized as the Midwest version of the Big Apple. Go figure. In staying its usual steady course, St. Paul responded by calling itself St. Paul.

course, full breakfasts are provided as well. Rates for lodging and breakfast are moderate to expensive; packages including dinner are expensive. For more information or reservations, call (651) 437–3297 or (888) 846–7966; wwwthor woodinn.com.

What else to do in Hastings? The *LeDuc-Simmons Mansion,* one of the few remaining nineteenth-century Hudson River Gothic Revival dwellings in the country, is worth a stroll by its address at 1629 Vermillion Street. Farther south on Vermillion Street, you will cross the Vermillion River, where just to the east is the beginning of a lovely park around a dramatic waterfall. The ruins of the *Ramsey Mill* can be explored downstream where the river rounds a bend.

Continuing out of town south on Highway 61, in 1 mile you'll see signs for Minnesota's only full-fledged vineyard. The approach to the production facilities of *Alexis Bailly Vineyard* is through a field of more than 6,000 hybrid grapevines that are especially well suited to Minnesota's harsh winter climate. The wine these grapes produce has received national recognition for its excellence. Visitors are welcome to taste-test the Bailly wines and to observe the fermenting process. The vineyard is open free of charge from June through October, Friday through Sunday afternoons. For more information call (651) 437–1413.

Hennepin County

By the late nineteenth century, Minneapolis's flour mills had earned the city a reputation as the flour capital of the world, a reputation dependent on the tremendous waterpower generated by the Falls of St. Anthony. By far the largest drop in the Mississippi's 2,348-mile run to the sea, the falls, with their unstable limestone base, have precipitated some extensive engineering projects over the years. Today they are covered with concrete, and two locks—one 50 and the other 25 feet deep—provide passage for barges, pleasure boats, and an occasional canoe. An observation deck at the *Upper St. Anthony Falls Lock and Dam,* with displays and brochures explaining the operation of the lock and the history of the falls area, is open daily from April through November (a parking area is located near the corner of Portland and Washington Avenues). For information call (612) 333–5336 or (651) 290–5807.

Built between 1819 and 1825 as Minnesota's first permanent structure, *Historic Fort Snelling* still dominates the confluence of the Mississippi and Minnesota Rivers from a prominent bluff several miles downstream of St. Anthony Falls. The fort has been restored to its original appearance and is superbly managed by the Minnesota Historical Society as a popular interpretive center and living-history site. Daily, from May through October, a contingent of soldiers in heavy wool uniforms reenacts with humor and robust spirit the highly

Twin Cities Gorge?

Most visitors to the Twin Cities don't know about it, and for that matter, most residents probably don't either. But thanks to a soft layer of St. Peter sandstone lying beneath hard Platteville limestone and a torrent of meltwater from Glacial Lake Agassiz, the only gorge on the Mississippi River sits between St. Paul and Minneapolis.

Although this gorge isn't in the same league as the great canyons of the western United States, it is still impressive. Unlike the other canyons, however, the Mississippi River gorge lies right in the middle of a metropolitan area of more than two million people. This landmark is ringed by two scenic parkways and pedestrian paths that offer great views of this large gash in the Midwest landscape.

Unlike the bluffs south of the Twin Cities that overlook the Mississippi across an often-broad floodplain, the river runs close to the base of the cliffs through this canyon. The gorge is beautiful any time of year, but autumn is the best time to visit when the thick stands of hardwood trees that line the edge explode into a mix of red, yellow, and orange.

regimented and often tedious life led by the early occupants of this military outpost, which, for all its apparent might, has never seen a moment of fighting. Look for the fort at the junction of Highways 5 and 55 (there are signs on both highways, but don't confuse the historic fort with Fort Snelling State Park, also close by). A small fee is charged for admission to the fort but not to the adjacent interpretive center, where an excellent exhibit space, film-viewing area, and gift shop are open whenever the fort is and on weekdays the rest of the year. Call (612) 726–1171 for more information.

Though he never traveled to the northwestern wilderness, Henry Wadsworth Longfellow helped create in the nation's imagination a highly romantic impression of the Minnesota frontier through his epic 1855 poem, *The Song of Hiawatha*. In particular the story of Hiawatha's courtship of Minnehaha endowed two landmarks with mythical significance: the "shining Big-Sea-Water" of "Gitche Gumee" (Lake Superior) and a waterfall along a small Minneapolis creek from which the lovely maiden received her identity. "From the waterfall he named her, / Minnehaha, Laughing Water" wrote Longfellow, and **Minnehaha Falls** hasn't been the same since. Visitors to the burgeoning metropolis during Longfellow's time flocked to see Minnehaha's laughing waters, which are just as inspiring today, as you can discover for yourself by heading a couple of blocks east on Minnehaha Parkway from the intersection of (what else?) Hiawatha Avenue.

Given what you can see of the **Minneapolis** skyline from afar, you might easily suspect that the entire city has been built within the past ten or fifteen years. While it's true that most buildings with enough stature to be seen from any distance away are new and reflect an innovative variety of current architectural tastes, there is still one remnant of earlier times that now reaches only chest height of its taller neighbors. This is the **Foshay Tower,** an obelisk design inspired by the Washington Monument and built as an ostentatious monument to prosperity on the verge of the stockmarket crash of 1929 by one of the city's more interesting public figures.

Wilber Foshay, a newly rich utility-company owner, spent almost $4 million in the construction of this first skyscraper west of Chicago and then took the trouble to seek two patents on its design so that it would never be duplicated elsewhere. He planned to install himself in a lavish penthouse suite that complemented the building's Art Deco styling with a vaulted entry, rich woodwork, and gold-plated faucets.

For the grand opening of his tower, Foshay invited President Hoover (the war secretary came in his stead), along with every state governor in the country. He also commissioned John Philip Sousa to write a march in honor of the occasion, a work the celebrated composer directed in person.

Two months later Foshay's entire dream crumbled around him in the wake of Black Thursday's stock market plunge. Not only was he unable to pay the bills for the lavish party he had thrown; he was also indicted for mail fraud by the federal government. Foshay spent some time in Leavenworth Prison before being pardoned by President Roosevelt in 1935. He died in a Twin Cities nursing home in 1957, leaving his monument behind for us to visit today. Self-guided tours of the observation deck, which has outstanding views of the cityscape and surrounding countryside, and a small museum devoted to the building's history are available during business hours and on Saturdays for a small fee. You'll find the Foshay Tower by tracing its unmistakable shape to its foundation at 821 Marquette Avenue, Minneapolis. Call (612) 341–2522 for more information.

Another less-celebrated monument to posterity is found in Minneapolis's **American Swedish Institute,** at 2600 Park Avenue, which helped to inspire a movement to preserve Swedish culture that was initiated by the building's first owner, Swan J. Turnblad. This Swedish-born businessman built a thirty-three-room Romanesque château–style castle for himself that was financed by his success as a publisher of America's largest Swedish newspaper, the *Svenska Amerikanska Posten.* He lived in his early-twentieth-century mansion only a relatively short time, donating the building and his collection of Swedish art and historic artifacts to the institute in 1929.

It is an amazing building. The elaborate turrets and carvings of the lime-stone exterior only half prepare you for the incredible woodwork and rich orna-mentation found inside. Eighteen craftspersons worked for two years to complete the intricately carved statues, panels, and banisters—all made of exotic woods—that you continue to discover throughout your tour. There are eleven unique *kakelugnar* Swedish stoves made of porcelain tile. And at the first-floor stair landing is a grand stained-glass window based on a historic painting that depicts, of all things, the ransom of a Swedish community by a Danish king.

Rooms on three floors of the institute are dedicated to exhibits on con-temporary and historic Swedish artists and to the immigration experience. Per-haps the most unusual item on display is a pre-Viking glass beaker dating from the fifth century and believed to be among the earliest glass objects in the world. The institute also frequently shows films and has public programs related to Swedish culture. The building is open for tours Tuesday through Sunday, year-round, for a small fee. For more information call (612) 871–4907 or visit www.americanswedishinst.org.

On an obscure side street near the western shore of Lake Calhoun, one of Minneapolis's lovely urban lakes, is a singularly fascinating museum and library dedicated to the role electricity has played in our science and culture. Upon entering the 1920s English Tudor–style mansion that houses the **Bakken Library and Museum,** you are confronted immediately with several aquari-ums of electricity-producing fish. Such fish were used by the Romans as early as the first century in the treatment of arthritis. The afflicted patient was directed to go to the ocean shore and stand with one foot in the water and the other on top of one of these slithering fish, whose sensible response was to blast the offending foot with as much juice as it could muster.

The Bakken self-guided tour moves quickly from ancient times to displays of eighteenth-century devices and procedural drawings that illustrate the first widespread use of electricity for public entertainment and in medicine. Electric "showers," in which a simple static generator produced a mild current, or "fluid," which was allowed to flow through the body, were thought to have an invigorating influence on the subject's health. More powerful localized appli-cations via the "method of sparks" or, stronger still, the often painful "electric commotions" were used to cure anything from "hysteria" and other complaints thought to be peculiar to women to states of "suspended animation" resulting from drowning or heart failure.

In another room a series of nineteenth-century photographs reveals the results of an experiment in which the electrical stimulation of specific facial muscles was shown to produce in the same subject strained expressions cov-ering the full spectrum of human emotion. A number of early X-ray machines are displayed, as is a picture of Alexander Graham Bell using an early electric metal detector to find a bullet in the body of President Garfield. If you feel the need, you can even get a charge yourself and watch your hair stand on end by placing a hand on an eighteenth-century Ramsden generator. One of its new exhibits, *Frankenstein: Mary Shelley's Dream,* is a multimedia exploration of the history and science of Frankenstein. The exhibit includes artifact photos with links to information about the science, literature, and life experiences that inspired Mary Shelley to write *Frankenstein.*

The Bakken museum and 12,000-volume reference library were established in 1976 by Earl Bakken, the inventor of the first wearable cardiac pacemaker. The Bakken has switched from guided to self-guided tours. The museum is open Tuesday through Saturday from 10:00 A.M. to 5:00 P.M., and Thursday 10:00 A.M. to 8:00 P.M. The library is open Monday through Friday from 9:00 A.M. to 4:30 P.M. Admission is $7.00 for adults, $5.00 for students and seniors, free for children under three. For more information call (612) 926–3878 or log on to www.thebakken.org.

The invention of the telegraph by Samuel Morse in 1835 portended great things for human communication. With the telegraph, for the first time in the history of the planet, people could send messages halfway across the country in a matter of seconds. The only problem was that if the wires that carried these signals became damaged—as they frequently did in wild expanses of the largely unsettled North American continent—no message could be sent. So in 1895, after a series of experiments, Thomas Edison applied for a patent for his "wireless telegraph." With this device messages could be sent through the air via radio waves, and thus the age of radio was born.

From these forgotten beginnings the **Pavek Museum of Broadcasting** in suburban St. Louis Park traces the growth of radio and broadcasting in a most delightful manner. Founded by radio collector and enthusiast Joseph Pavek in 1988, the museum houses an impressive collection of radios, phonographs, tape recorders, and other equipment. Bing Crosby sounds remarkably good crooning on a recording made on one of the very first tape recorders. The museum also has a working ham-radio center and a 1960s-vintage recording studio, often used by schoolchildren on field trips to write and produce their own radio program.

The whole place takes you back to a simpler time, when families used to gather in living rooms—Mom and Dad in their favorite chairs, the kids lying on the floor with their heads propped on their hands—to listen to the radio. Nowhere is this innocence better illustrated than in the Minnesota Room's collection of paraphernalia from the state's radio past. Hidden in one of the display cases is a membership card to the Cowboy Bill Club (Cowboy Bill hosted a children's radio program in the 1930s and 1940s). Printed on the card are Cowboy Bill's Rules for Success:

1. Obey your parents.
2. Be cheerful.
3. Keep clean.
4. Save your money.

Ah, the good old days.

The Pavek Museum of Broadcasting, 3515 Raleigh Avenue, St. Louis Park, is open Tuesday through Saturday, year-round. Admission is inexpensive. Call (952) 926–8198 for group reservations, or check their Web site at www .pavekmuseum.org.

Are you someone who was convinced at one time or another that being a firefighter is life's highest calling? If so, you might enjoy a visit to the ***Firefighters Museum,*** in northeast Minneapolis near the northwest corner of Broadway and Central, where you can indulge in the fantasy once again. From a 1796-vintage hand-drawn water pump to the 1940s engine that roars in and out of the building, siren wailing, loaded with kids for a ride through the neighborhood, there are dozens of fire engines and plenty of firefighting memorabilia to spark your childhood recollections or generate some new ones. Modern trucks from the 1940s, 1950s, and 1960s dominate one part of the museum, whereas a second area is dedicated to horse- and hand-drawn pumps. There are big-billed firefighters' hard hats and rubberized coats to try on for photographs (bring your own camera), pictures of historic Twin Cities fires in progress, and models of various firehouses. The museum is open on Saturdays and charges a small fee. To find it, take Broadway to Jackson and go north 1 block to Twelfth, east 1 block to Van Buren, and then south for 1 block. If you get lost, listen for sirens or call (612) 623–3817.

If you escaped childhood without ever having dreamed of being a firefighter, then perhaps the ***Planes of Fame War Birds Air Museum*** would be to your liking. Occupying three hangars at Flying Cloud Airport in Eden Prairie, the air museum's high-quality exhibits and film-viewing area complement a collection of more than twenty-four World War II–vintage fighters, including a B-17 Flying Fortress bomber, all restored and maintained in flight-ready condition. Exhibits feature model planes, uniforms, and rifles from the war. A partially dismantled engine from a B-17 Flying Fortress reveals the engine's inner workings. Among the action-packed aerial-combat and training films is one starring a spunky Ronald Reagan, describing how to distinguish a Japanese Zero fighter from an American plane when the sun's in your eyes. For a hefty fee you can even go up for a ride in an open-cockpit Stearman Trainer. There is a modest admission charge at the museum, which is open afternoons daily during summer and is located at 14771 Pioneer Trail (County Road 1). Call (952) 941–2633 for more information.

There's no better way to soothe your shattered nerves after a ride in the Stearman Trainer (or any other high-tech stress inducer) than to stroll at a leisurely pace through the **Normandale Japanese Gardens** at Normandale Community College in Bloomington. Created by Tokyo designer Takao Watanabe, the garden's large waterfall and creek, three arch bridges, lagoon, and shrine exude serenity. A self-guided tour booklet is available for a small fee, and guided tours can be arranged for groups of ten or more. To find the garden, look for signs at the entrance to the college at 9700 France Avenue South, Bloomington, or call (952) 487–8200. The garden is always open, though the waterfall is turned off October through May. Sunsets are lovely.

Places to Stay in the Twin Cities Region

STILLWATER
(area code 651)

Country Inn,
2200 West Frontage Road;
430–2699

Lowell Inn,
102 North Second Street;
439–1100

Stillwater Inn,
1750 West Frontage Road;
430–1300

Note: Stillwater has twelve of the best bed-and-breakfast inns in Minnesota, all in historic mansions. For a list call the Stillwater Chamber of Commerce at 439–7700.

AFTON
(area code 651)

Afton House Inn,
3291 St. Croix Trail;
436–8883

Afton's Mulberry Pond on River Road,
3786 River Road;
436–8086

MARINE-ON-ST. CROIX
(area code 651)

Asa Parker House,
17500 St. Croix Trail North
(Hwy. 95);
433–5248

TAYLORS FALLS
(area code 651)

Pines Motel,
543 River Street;
465–3422

The Springs Country Inn,
361 Government Street;
465–6565

CHISAGO LAKES AREA
(area code 651)

Boathouse Bed & Breakfast,
30425 Vine Street,
Lindstrom;
257–9122

Country Bed & Breakfast,
17038 320th Street,
Shafer;
257–4773

Summit Inn Bed & Breakfast
208 Summit, Center City;
257–4987

Super 8 Motel,
11650 Lake Boulevard
(Hwy. 8), Chisago City;
257–8088

HASTINGS
(area code 651)

AmericInn,
2400 Vermillion Street;
437–8877

Country Inn & Suites,
300 Thirty-third Street;
437–8870

Super 8 Motel,
Highway 61 and
Twenty-fifth Street;
438–8888

ST. PAUL
(area code 651)

Chatsworth Bed & Breakfast,
984 Ashland Avenue;
227–4288

Covington Inn Bed & Breakfast,
100 Yacht Club Road;
292–1411

Embassy Suites,
175 East Tenth Street;
224–5400

Holiday Inn Express Hotel & Suites,
I–94 & Woodbury Drive,
Woodbury;
702–0200

Radisson Inn,
411 Minnesota Street;
291–8800

MINNEAPOLIS

Comfort Inn
Bloomington Airport,
1321 East Seventy-eighth
Street,
Bloomington ;
(952) 854–3400

Embassy Suites Airport,
7901 Thirty-fourth Avenue
South,
Bloomington;
(952) 854–1000

Hampton Inn Airport,
7745 Lyndale Avenue South,
Richfield;
(612) 861–1000

La Meridien Hotel,
601 First Avenue North;
(612) 677–1100

Places to Eat in the Twin Cities Region

STILLWATER
(area code 651)

Brines' Restaurant
(American),
219 South Main Street;
439–7556

The Daily Grind Espresso Cafe,
317 South Main Street;
430–3207

Gasthaus Bavarian Hunter
(German),
8390 Lofton Avenue;
439–7128

Lowell Inn
(full-course dining),
102 North Second Street;
439–1100

Pepito's (Mexican),
423 South Main Street;
351–5371

Savories (bakery,
lunch, dinner)
108 North Main Street;
430–0702

Tara Hideway,
15021 60th Street North;
439–9850

AFTON
(area code 651)

Afton House (American),
3291 St. Croix Trail;
436–8883

MARINE-ON-ST. CROIX
(area code 651)

Voyageur Cafe (American),
51 Judd Street;
433–2366

SELECTED WEB SITES IN THE TWIN CITIES

Hastings Area Chamber and
Tourism Bureau
www.hastingsmn.org

Minneapolis Convention and
Visitors Association
www.minneapolis.org

St. Paul Convention and
Visitors Bureau
www.stpaulcvb.org

Stillwater Area
Chamber of Commerce
www.ilovestillwater.com

SELECTED CHAMBERS OF COMMERCE

Chisago Lakes Area
Chamber of Commerce
(651) 257–1177

St. Paul Convention and
Visitors Bureau
(800) 627–6101

Minneapolis Convention
and Visitors Association
(612) 661–4700, (888) 676–6757

Stillwater Area
Chamber of Commerce
(651) 439–7700

Hastings Area Chamber of
Commerce
(888) 612–6122

Taylors Falls Chamber of Commerce
(651) 462–7550

TAYLORS FALLS
(area code 651)

Chisago House Restaurant
(American),
361 Bench Street;
465–5245

Coffee Talk,
479 Bench Street;
465–6700

Romayne's on Main
(American),
391 Bench Street;
465–3606

CHISAGO LAKES AREA
(area code 651)

Dinnerbel (American),
12565 Lake Boulevard,
Lindstrom;
257–9524

**Many Voices Bookseller
& Coffeehouse** (coffee),
12805 Lake Boulevard,
Lindstrom;
213–6604

Swedish Inn (American),
12690 Lake Boulevard,
Lindstrom;
257–4072

**Trapper's Inn Family
Restaurant**
(American),
Highway 8, Chisago City;
257–2512

HASTINGS
(area code 651)

Applebee's (eclectic),
2000 Vermillion Street;
438–8604

Emily's Bakery & Deli
(sandwiches),
1212 Vermillion Street—
Midtown Center;
437–3338

Levee Cafe (American),
100 Sibley Street;
437–7577

Perkins Family
Restaurant (American),
Vermillion Street
& Highway 55;
437–5028

Professor Java's (coffee),
202 East Second Street;
438–9962

ST. PAUL
(area code 651)

Boco Chica Restaurante
(Mexican),
11 Concord Street;
222–8499

Cecil's Deli & Restaurant
(American),
651 Cleveland Avenue
South;
698–0334

**Cosetta's Italian Market &
Pizzeria,**
211 West Seventh Street;
222–3476

Dixie's (Cajun),
695 Grand Avenue;
222–7345

Dunn Brother's (coffee),
1569 Grand Avenue;
698–0618

Grandview Grill
(American),
1818 Grand Avenue;
698–2346

Key's Restaurant
(American),
504 North Robert;
222–4083

MINNEAPOLIS
(area code 612)

Applebee's (eclectic),
3200 West Lake Street;
925–3403

Buca (Italian),
1204 Harmon Place;
288–0138

The Calhoun Grill
(American)
3220 West Lake Street;
455–1250

Key's Nicollet Mall Cafe
(American),
1007 Nicollet Mall;
339–6399

Old Spaghetti Factory
(Italian),
233 Park Avenue;
341–0949

Pizza Luce,
119 North Fourth Street;
333–7359

Roads to Take

Highway 95 from Stillwater
north to Taylors Falls follows
the St. Croix River

County Road 21 from Afton
south to Afton State Park
and north to I–94

Highway 8 from the
intersection with Highway 95
to Taylors Falls

County Road 16 north from
Taylors Falls to Almelund and
Wild River State Park

Bluffland

When driving into the southeastern corner of Minnesota, visitors will find a startling landscape not found anywhere else in the state. Along the Mississippi River, limestone bluffs tower above the valley floor, looking like sentinels that seem to guide the river on its journey south. Much of this land resembles parts of the Appalachians or Ozarks, and it has a more southern climate than any other area in Minnesota. The western edge of Bluffland is flat to mildly rolling farm country, and as you drive east to the Mississippi River, the landscape becomes much more rugged and dramatic.

Bluffland lies in the driftless area, a region of rocky uplands that covers 10,000 square miles in Minnesota, Wisconsin, Iowa, and Illinois. The last glaciers didn't cover this area, which left a landscape of rolling plains. Over time, rivers have carved spectacular valleys in this region, leaving behind gentle hills interrupted by these gashes. Since the underlying limestone is soluble, caves formed here but nowhere else in Minnesota. Because of this dramatic landscape, this region has become a favorite destination for weekend visitors who come to hike, bike, or just relax while staying in one of the scenic towns nestled among the hills.

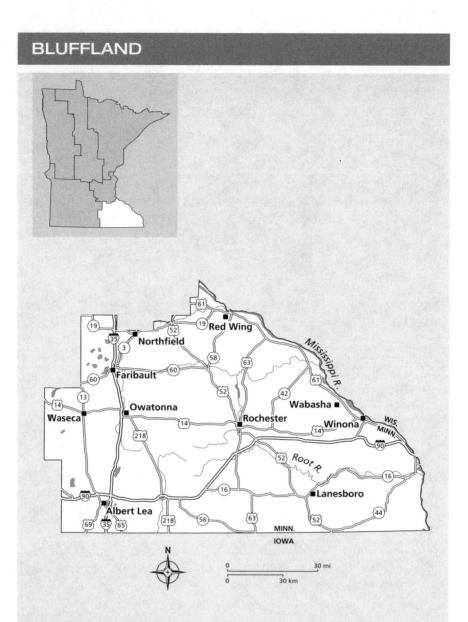

61
19
52
19 **Red Wing**
35 **Northfield**
3
58
63
Mississippi R.
60 **Faribault**
52
61
13
52
42
Wabasha ■
14
Owatonna
Waseca
14 **Rochester**
14
Winona
WIS
MINN
218
90
52 *Root R.*
16
16
90
56
63
52
44
Albert Lea
Lanesboro ■
69 35 65
218
MINN.
IOWA

N

0   30 mi
0   30 km

Goodhue County

When you enter the picturesque Mississippi River town of Red Wing, it's hard not to notice **Barn Bluff,** an oblong mountain that rises abruptly 300 feet above the heart of the business district like the back of some great subterranean elephant. Thousands of years ago this protrusion of ancient sandstone was an island surrounded by a much larger and glacial Mississippi River. Today Barn Bluff offers hikers the same grand views of the city and river environment as it did when Henry David Thoreau climbed to its peak in 1861.

Several hiking trails begin at the base of the mountain near the east end of Fifth Street. One trail winds through an old sandstone quarry that overlooks the river, while another passes near the remains of a large limestone kiln that was used in the late nineteenth century. A third trail ascends to the crest of the mountain and follows its ridge from one end to the other, offering great vistas of the town on one side and the wooded channels of the Mississippi on the other. Still another trail follows the southern side of Barn Bluff and allows hikers to peer into backyards all over town.

About the time of Thoreau's visit, **Red Wing** was well on its way to becoming the world's largest primary wheat market. This economic activity drew businessmen from all over the country, prompting local boosters in 1875 to build a monument to the town's prosperity in the form of a first-class hotel and restaurant. Thanks to an extensive and faithful restoration effort in 1979, the **St. James Hotel** today offers the same luxurious accommodations and excellent dining that it did more than a hundred years ago, when the *Minneapolis Mail* proclaimed the hotel was "second to none in the state, in arrangement, elegance of furniture and general appointment."

Graciously decorated and spacious guest rooms—many offering fine views of the river—are furnished with Victorian-era antiques and antique reproductions. There are two restaurants in the hotel; the **Port of Red Wing** in the lower level, where cozy candlelight meals are served surrounded by the

AUTHOR'S FAVORITES

Cannon Valley and Root River
bicycle trails

Towns along the Root River
(Lanesboro, Harmony, Preston,
and Fountain)

The drive on Highway 61
along the Mississippi River

building's original rough limestone walls, and *Jimmy's Pub* on the fifth floor. Rooms and meals at the St. James are moderately to expensively priced. For reservations contact the St. James Hotel, 406 Main Street, Red Wing, or call (651) 388–2846.

Although the St. James is certainly a fine place to stay, to keep with the theme of getting off the beaten path, you really should stay at one of the unique bed-and-breakfast inns located in or near town. At last count Red Wing had at least eight such establishments, most of which occupy restored homes in this historic river town. Accommodations range from an 1880 Queen Anne home with two guest rooms to a large home that housed three Red Wing Shoe Company presidents to a couple of inns located in the rolling countryside outside of town.

For dinner you may want to drive 3 miles across the Mississippi River to Bay City, Wisconsin, to the *Lavender Rose.* Now I know there's a separate *Wisconsin Off the Beaten Path* book, but dinner at this restaurant is worth the short side trip out of Minnesota. Located in what looks like a former machine shop and sporting a funky interior (with lots of lavender), the restaurant is known for excellent service and superb food. For reservations contact the Lavender Rose, W7171 135th Avenue, Bay City, Wisconsin; (715) 792–2464.

whygoatprairies?

As you drive through the magnificent Mississippi River Valley between Red Wing and Winona, the mighty river competes with the towering bluffs for your attention. From a distance, the vegetation that covers the sides of the bluffs looks unremarkable.

Known as goat prairies, the bluffs harbor several varieties of vegetation unique to this area of southeastern Minnesota. But the most important question remains. Why call them goat prairies? The name refers to the steep angle of the slopes because "only goats can graze it."

A second industry that drew national attention to Red Wing beginning in the late nineteenth century was the production of durable and attractive stoneware under the Red Wing label. Early in the 1880s three small stoneware manufacturing companies banded together to form the Red Wing Union and began nationwide distribution of their distinctive ceramic water jars, jugs, pitchers, crocks, and dinnerware, all of which were made from local clays. Until it was eclipsed by more economical glass production techniques in the 1940s, the Red Wing Union's pottery was in such demand that at one point the company was the largest stoneware manufacturer in the United States.

Today there are several sites in town that give visitors a glimpse into the Red Wing pottery tradition. *Pottery Place,* the large brick complex on Old

Main Street at the west end of town, was the center of stoneware production from the time of the building's construction in 1885. Now the complex is home to a series of factory-outlet retail stores, though photographs and displays offer some insight into the Red Wing Union and its operation. This building was also the site of the world's first tunnel kiln, and a small section of one of these kilns is on display to the south of the main entrance. In the **Pottery Salesroom,** located next door to Pottery Place, some of the original Red Wing pottery is sold, along with a large selection of glassware.

Red Wing Stoneware Co. is another point of interest for pottery buffs. Since 1987, when John Falconer converted a horse barn into a production plant and showroom, the popularity of traditional Red Wing stoneware has been on the rise once again. Visitors can meet Falconer at his new studio at 4909 Moundview Drive (2 blocks east of Highways 19 and 61) and see the Red Wing pottery revival in action. Incorporating the Red Wing Union's original glaze and color formulas, Falconer's exacting reproductions have attracted a widespread following. For more information contact Falconer Stoneware, 3572 Tyler Road, Red Wing, or call (651) 388–4610.

Besides pottery and stoneware, Red Wing is also home to the Red Wing Shoe Company. If you love shoes, or just enjoy seeing unique places, the **Red Wing Shoe Museum** is a fun place to visit. Exhibits include a display on how the company makes shoes, firsthand "shoe" tales, and a station for visitors to try their hands at assembling a boot. You won't find any footwear from the closets of Imelda Marcos, but you will see interesting exhibits on shoes of a more utilitarian function. The museum is located next to La Grange Park and in the Riverfront Center in downtown. For more information call the Red Wing Convention and Visitors Bureau at (800) 498–3444.

The drive west from Red Wing up and over the wooded bluffs and through a pastoral landscape of gentle hills dissected by an occasional river valley is a pleasant one. The same journey 500 million years ago, however, would have required a submarine, for at that time all of southern Minnesota was covered by what geologists call the Ordovician Sea—a warm, shallow ocean that stretched all the way south to what is now the Gulf of Mexico. Today, evidence of the primitive marine life that thrived in that body of water can be found all over southeastern Minnesota, wherever selected layers of limestone bedrock have been exposed to view.

One such site for collecting **Ordovician fossils** is located in a roadside cut along Goodhue County Road 8, less than a half mile north of County Road 9, and 7 miles west of the town of Goodhue. Park your car on the shoulder of the road, and with a good guidebook in hand, such as Constance Sansome's *Minnesota Underfoot* (Voyageur Press, Stillwater, Minnesota, 1983), start sifting through the gray-green rock fragments collected at the base of the exposed rock face on either side of the road. What you'll find without much effort will be fossilized remains of corals, sponges, and other long-extinct species of organisms. Some of these—such as clams or snails—will look familiar, whereas others will send your imagination reeling in unexpected directions, trying to recognize familiarity in their shapes.

In the nearby community of Zumbrota, there is preserved a historic landmark from a far more recent era. Just north of town, in the center of a city park on Highway 58, sits Minnesota's last **covered bridge.** From its construction in 1869 until 1932, the 120-foot wooden structure, which is listed on the National Register of Historic Places, carried traffic over the Zumbro River. The bridge originally was part of the stagecoach route from St. Paul to Dubuque, Iowa. Perhaps harried stagecoach drivers were the target of the sign above the bridge's entrance that reads: $10 FINE FOR DRIVING FASTER THAN A WALK ACROSS THIS BRIDGE.

Wabasha County

It was a hot, hazy day in **Lake City,** during the summer of 1922, when eighteen-year-old Ralph Samuelson walked down to Lake Pepin, strapped a couple of 9-foot-long wooden planks to his feet, and shouted the immortal words, "Hit it!" With that, the sport of waterskiing was born. Waterskiing has obviously grown by leaps and bounds since that fateful summer day, but its humble beginnings are still marked by Ralph's original pair of skis, mounted on the wall at the Lake City Chamber of Commerce (1515 North Lakeshore Drive).

Today Lake Pepin is still the center of excitement in Lake City, with countless sailboats, motorboats, and, yes, water-skiers dotting the surface on sunny summer days. A recently completed walkway provides strollers a good view of the lake. And should you work up an appetite on your stroll, **Skyline** at 1702 North Lakeshore Drive, (651) 345–5353, is an excellent place to stop. Located just off Highway 61 at the north end of town, the restaurant sits right on the shore of Lake Pepin and has an outdoor deck and an enclosed sunporch that overlook the waterfront. Should you arrive by boat, the dock out front provides ample parking.

Another favorite Lake City eatery is the **Chickadee Cottage Tea Room & Restaurant,** 317 North Lakeshore Drive (Highway 61). Modeled after a traditional English teahouse, Chickadee Cottage offers a delicious assortment of lighter fare for breakfast and lunch, including omelets, sandwiches, salads, and cheese plates. An afternoon tea, including scones, tea sandwiches, and various sweets, is served daily from 3:00 to 5:00 P.M. All-you-can-eat family breakfasts are offered Sundays from 8:00 A.M. to 1:00 P.M. Call (651) 345–5155.

What's in a Name?

In the case of the rivers that flow through Bluffland, many of the current names have come from the Indian or French and were loosely or inaccurately translated into English. Like many rivers in other parts of Minnesota, various tribes named them for the most prominent feature or characteristic.

Cannon River: A loose or inaccurate English translation of the French name *Riviere aux Canots* or "Canoe River." The French and Indians cached their canoes at the mouth of the river while hunting buffalo on the eastern edge of the prairie.

Zumbro River: Again a loose translation of French, in this case *Riviere des Embarras,* which meant an obstruction by logjams or driftwood, a common feature of the lower part of this river.

Whitewater River: From the Sioux name, *ska* for "white" and *mini* for "water."

Root River: Derived from a Sioux name for the river, possibly referring to tree roots exposed after floods. *Hokah* or *hutkam* was the Sioux word for "root," and the Houston County town of Hokah came from this word.

Mississippi River: This name originated in Minnesota, not the South as some believe. The Chippewa Indians called it *Mee-zee-see-pee,* or *Messipi,* and other tribes used *Mese-sebe, Missicipy,* or *Meschasipi.* Finally, *Mississippi* became the name, which means "Big River" or "Father of Waters." Enough said.

A beautiful B&B in Lake City offers a healthy dose of Victorian charm. The **Red Gables Inn** at 403 North High Street (651–345–2605, www.redgables inn.com) is located in the heart of Lake City, within walking distance of Lake Pepin. Also check out **St. Hubert House** at 29055 County Road 2, Old Frontenac (651–345–2668).

Driving east on Minnesota Highway 60 from Zumbrota through Wabasha County is a great way to appreciate the special geology of the bluff country. Tight, winding canyons with walls of crumbling limestone and sandstone alternate with straight stretches of road that offer sweeping views of the pastoral landscape. As the Mississippi River approaches, the valley widens, the bluffs become more pronounced, and hillsides are covered with hardwood forest.

About 7 miles from Wabasha, in the midst of all this splendor, is Dumfries— a blip on the map that you'll pass in the time it takes to sneeze. In fact about all that remains of this tiny Scottish milling community is the hundred-year-old **Dumfries Restaurant,** Highway 60 West, (651) 565–3747. This recently remodeled building served first as a post office and general store in the early part of this century and then as a saloon during the 1940s and 1950s, until the current owners added a restaurant with a reputation for fine steak and seafood.

A little farther east on Highway 60, just before you crest the last bluff and drop down to the Mississippi floodplain and the town of *Wabasha,* a sign will announce your arrival at the *Arrowhead Bluffs Exhibits.* A half-mile drive on a gravel road leads to the farmyard of Les and John Behrns, who have built a monument to thirty years of determined collecting. For a small fee visitors can study examples of every Winchester firearm ever made, from the company's beginning in 1866 to the present. As many as 435 rifles, shotguns, and pistols are on display, along with seventy big-game trophies bagged by the Behrnses on hunting expeditions all over North America. Miscellaneous antiques and Native American artifacts are exhibited as well. Arrowhead Bluffs Exhibits is open daily May through December and by appointment the rest of the year; call (651) 565–3829.

If you have the opportunity to stay overnight in Wabasha—or if you have time only for a meal—the historic *Anderson House* country inn is the place to stop. In continuous operation since its construction in 1856, this rambling, three-story brick structure is the oldest operating hotel in the state. Owners John and Jeanne Hall have garnered a national reputation for the inn's homey charm, for its very good Dutch-inspired cooking (the original Mrs. Anderson was from Holland), and for their renowned fondness for cats. The Anderson House may well be the only hotel in America where guests can "adopt" one of fifteen felines for the duration of their stay.

Other special amenities that have survived transition into the twenty-first century include quilt-wrapped hot brick footwarmers for warming a chilly bed on a cold winter's night and an overnight shoe-shine service for guests who leave their shoes outside their bedroom doors. Specialties on the menu include Grandma Anderson's chicken and dumplings and Pheasant Jubilee, all at moderate prices. Reservations can be made by contacting the Anderson House, 333 West Main Street, Wabasha 55981 or by calling (651) 565–4524. (The restaurant is open Friday through Sunday from November to April 1 and daily during the rest of the year. The hotel is closed each January for renovations.)

For many people the Mississippi River, flowing slowly southward a block from the entrance to the Anderson House, is an irresistible attraction. If you're such a person—someone fascinated with the incredibly rich history associated with the river, a lover of waterfowl, an angler, or a river rat in the Huck Finn tradition—stop in at *Great River Houseboats,* at the Wabasha Marina, 1009 East Main Street. This is one of the few places in the state where you can create your own Mississippi River adventure in comfort and style. Great River Houseboats has several 48-foot vessels to rent in two models (economy and deluxe), each of which sleeps up to ten people. The boats are appointed with a full kitchen, a living room, a head with shower, a barbecue grill, and ample deck space for sunning and fishing. No special experience is required to rent a boat; novice pilots are thoroughly oriented before being turned loose on the Big Muddy. Depending on group size and boat, prices are inexpensive to moderate. Reservations should be made well in advance by writing Great River Houseboats, 1009 East Main Street, Box 247, Wabasha 55981; by calling (651) 565–3376; or by logging on to www.greatriverhouseboats.com.

Capitalizing on the success of *Grumpy Old Men,* the 1993 hit movie starring Jack Lemmon and Walter Matthau, which was based in Wabasha (but filmed in Faribault), Wabasha now stages **Grumpy Old Men Days,** the highlight of which is an ice-fishing contest. For information regarding this event, which takes place in late February, contact Bonnie and Dave Koopman at The Bait Bucket (651–565–2326).

Wabasha is also home to a large bald eagle population, prompting volunteers to set up **Eagle Watch.** Every Sunday between 1:00 and 3:00 P.M., from November through March, volunteers from town set up telescopes and binoculars so that visitors can catch a glimpse of these majestic avians, once on the brink of extinction but now making a strong comeback in these parts. Call the Wabasha Chamber of Commerce at (651) 565–4158 for more information. You can also contact The **National Eagle Center,** 152 Main Street, Box 242, Wabasha 55981; call (651) 565–4989; or visit www.nationaleaglecenter.org.

Cruise 6 miles south of Wabasha just off Highway 61 and you will enter the magic kingdom of **L.A.R.K. Toys.** Opened in 1986 by Don and Sarah Kreofsky, L.A.R.K. Toys is a haven for lovers of the handmade wooden toys of yesteryear. The ever-expanding L.A.R.K. Toys compound currently includes an office building, a factory building, and a gift shop. In the near future it will also include a toy museum, a bookstore, and a gigantic carousel.

The highly entertaining gift shop offers an impressive collection of imported Christmas toys, tin toys, nesting dolls, handmade pull toys, books, and games. What's more, look carefully about this whimsical place and you may find trolls hidden in the rafters and large slingshots mounted here and there (used to propel the trolls on their nightly travels); there are even little mouseholes carved into

Eagle Watch

the baseboards. Gip, the Kreofskys' pet pig, keeps a watchful eye over this fanciful domain.

The Kreofskys' toy factory is also a delight to behold, for it is here that the hand-carved characters for the carousel are being made. Sure, we've all ridden a horse on a merry-go-round, but who among us has ever ridden a dinosaur? or a moose? or a fish? You'll have to wait until the Kreofskys' grand carousel is complete for these experiences, but meanwhile it's quite interesting to watch these characters take form.

L.A.R.K. Toys may not be the Fountain of Youth, but odds are you'll feel just a little bit younger by the end of your visit. Catalog and ordering information are available by writing L.A.R.K. Toys Inc., Kellogg 55945; by calling (507) 767–3387; or by logging on at www.larktoys.com.

Olmsted County

The city of Rochester repeatedly finds its way into the nation's headlines because of the Mayo Clinic—the world's first and largest private-practice medical facility and the city's largest employer. Perhaps it should be no surprise that most attractions in and around this city of 58,000 have something to do with the Mayo family, medicine, or both.

Free tours of the *Mayo Clinic* leave visitors with the distinct impression of having passed through the Grand Central Station of medicine: The modern, twelve-story marble-faced structure admits an average of 1,000 new patients *each day* from all over the world. Sculpture and murals by prominent artists are found throughout the building, including, on the exterior north wall, an inspiring figure reaching skyward with outstretched arms by Ivan Mestrovic and, in a nearby courtyard, a delightful statue by David Wynne of a boy flying through space holding fast with one hand to the dorsal fin of a dolphin. For tour information contact the Mayo Clinic, 200 First Street SW, Rochester 55905 or call (507) 284–9258.

After a tour of the Mayo Clinic, culinary adventurers may want to explore the *Broadstreet Cafe and Bar,* a moderately priced, other-side-of-the-tracks bistro serving outstanding continental and American cuisine in a charming old brick building at the corner of First Avenue NW and Third Street NW. The Redwood Room, downstairs, has an a la carte pizza and pasta menu and live music (507–281–2451).

A tour of downtown Rochester's main attractions should leave no doubts as to the influence of the Mayo family on the world of medicine. But a visit to *Mayowood*—the family's sprawling country estate, just west of town—reveals a flip side to the same coin that is just as interesting. This forty-room mansion,

TOP ANNUAL EVENTS IN BLUFFLAND

Grumpy Old Men Festival,
Wabasha, late February,
(800) 565–4158

**Sykkle Tur Bike Ride on the
Norsk Riviera,**
Fountain, mid-May,
(507) 268–4923

Steamboat Days,
Winona, late June to early July,
(800) 657–4972

Cedar River Days/ SPAM Jamboree,
Austin, early July,
(800) 444–5713

Fall Foliage Fest,
Harmony, late September,
(800) 247–6466

Three Rivers Rendezvous,
Rochester, late September,
(507) 282–9447

Swan Watch Weekend,
Winona, early November,
(800) 657–4972

built into a wooded hillside above the Zumbro River, is a testament to the great wealth and social influence that resulted from the Mayos' successes in the medical field.

Mayowood lies at the heart of what was once a 3,300-acre estate of rolling hardwood forest purchased by Dr. Charles H. Mayo at the turn of the twentieth century. The stone-and-poured-concrete mansion, built in 1910–11, was largely designed by its owner, who also had the Zumbro dammed as a power source for Mayowood and to form a private lake.

The Mayo family presence is almost palpable in the mansion today. Among the numerous personal effects and furnishings is a collection of signed photographs and framed letters from former guests at the estate, and in these the Mayos' considerable social influence can be gauged. Just consider these players on the world scene: Franklin Roosevelt, Dwight Eisenhower, Lyndon Johnson, the king and queen of Nepal, Emperor Haile Selassie of Ethiopia, and King Faisal of Saudi Arabia.

Mayowood can be rented for special events, and scheduled tours are offered Tuesday through Sunday for a modest fee by the Olmsted County Historical Center from April through October. For information and tour reservations, call (507) 282–9447 or write Olmsted County Historical Center, Box 6411, Rochester 55903.

Tucked away in a beautiful wooded valley west of Rochester, near the town of Byron, are a county park, nature center, and zoo unlike any other in the state. *Oxbow Park* is situated on 572 acres of an old farmstead around an oxbow bend of the Zumbro River. Ten kilometers of hiking and cross-country-skiing trails meander among the dense maples on the surrounding bluffs. The zoo, focusing on native Minnesota wildlife, doubles as a shelter for injured or orphaned animals, and the twenty-five species exhibited in tasteful displays include bison (buffalo), elk, wolves, a pair of playful otters, and an impressive group of owls, hawks, and eagles. Oxbow Park has picnic and camping facilities, too.

On weekends staff at the nature center offer hands-on educational programs covering a wide range of topics. Each March, for example, there's the A to Z of maple syrup production, whereas in the fall you can learn everything you'd ever want to know about how to tan deer hides by using the animal's brains. Special events are held on major holidays, too. The park, which is open daily, can be found 3 miles north of Byron and Route 14 on County Road 105 (the route from Byron is well marked). Admission is free. For more information write to Oxbow Park, Route 1, Box 170, Byron 55920 or call (507) 775–2451.

Dodge County

There is probably no town in Minnesota where the late nineteenth century is as alive and healthy as it is in *Mantorville,* the Dodge County seat. This unpretentious little community of 750 has been named to the National Register of Historic Places in toto. The reason? Virtually every commercial building to be found and many residential ones as well have been preserved and maintained in the spirit of the town's past.

A good place to begin a walking tour of Mantorville is the *Dodge County Courthouse.* Like many buildings in town, the courthouse, circa 1865, was constructed of Mantorville limestone—the industry that is largely responsible for having kept the community afloat since its founding in 1854. But unlike those of any other structure, the courthouse's walls are a full 40 inches thick. Perhaps this ample use of Mantorville's greatest natural and economic resource accounts for the building's survival as the oldest working courthouse in the state and the only remaining one that was built in the Greek Revival style.

Mantorville's other most famous landmark is the *Hubbell House.* This fine restaurant, which was also built of native limestone, has been in continuous operation since its establishment in 1854. The original Hubbell House served as a hotel for travelers who were passing from the Mississippi River to St. Peter. The guest lists reads like an eclectic who's who of American society: Dwight D. Eisenhower and Ulysses S. Grant represent past presidents; Senator Alexander Ramsey, two Drs. Mayo from Rochester, and Bishop H.P. Whipple hold up Minnesota's historical tradition; and from the sports and entertainment world hail Mickey Mantle, Roy Rogers, and the Ringling Brothers, among others. The guest register is prominently displayed, along with many photographs and documents of historical interest. What's more, the American-style food is good and moderately priced. For reservations call (507) 635–2331 or visit www.hubbell-house.com.

Winona County

The county seat of **Winona** is a classic Mississippi River town—rich with history and graced with natural beauty—that has grown into a city. From the lookout at **Garvin Heights Park**, perched atop the limestone bluff 500 feet immediately above the city, many of Winona's outstanding architectural attractions are visible against the backdrop of the twisting channels of the river and the Wisconsin shoreline beyond.

Among the most noteworthy buildings in Winona are two banks: the **Merchant's National Bank** and the **Winona National Savings Bank.** The ornately detailed, somewhat boxlike Merchant's Bank, built on the corner of Third Street and Lafayette in 1911 by Purcell, Feick, and Elmslie, is considered one of the state's greatest examples of the Prairie School tradition. The National Savings Bank, with its huge pair of granite pillars looming skyward before the entry, is a fine example of the Egyptian Revival style. It was built by George Maher in 1914 at Fourth Street West and Main and, like the Merchant's Bank, boasts extremely beautiful stained-glass windows and skylights. The National Savings Bank also has an extensive collection of mounted African game animals that were hunted by a bank manager in the 1920s.

Although several interesting museums in town document Winona's booming development as a riverboat and lumbering community in the latter part of the nineteenth century, perhaps the most unusual among them is the **Polish Museum,** located in a former lumber warehouse at 102 Liberty Street. The museum claims to house the country's largest collection of objects from the Kashubian region of northwestern Poland—a contention supported by the fact that historically about one-third of the town's residents were from that part of the country. Poles who settled in Winona were largely members of the working class, and items in the museum document their lifestyle through examples of clothing, household objects, and photographs of laborers, fishermen, and housewives going about their daily tasks. A Winona Wagon Works wagon recalls the westward treks once made by settlers arriving by riverboat. Also, the museum's close association with St. Stanislaus Catholic Church is revealed in the many religious articles that are on display. The museum is open several days each week free of charge (donations accepted) from May through October

Fun Facts about Winona

Winona is the only place in Minnesota where you face north when looking at Wisconsin, a neat trick since the Mississippi River flows north to south. A jog that causes the river to flow briefly from west to east creates this geographic anomaly.

Actress Winona Ryder was born Winona Laura Horowitz on October 29, 1971, in Winona.

The dentist who invented the formula for concentrated grape juice lived in Winona from 1858 to 1868. His name? Dr. Thomas Welch.

William Windom of Winona is the only person from Minnesota to have appeared on U.S. currency. Windom was a congressman, senator, twice Secretary of the Treasury, and leading contender for the Republican nomination for president in 1880. He appeared briefly on two-dollar bills.

and is a site of great festivity each April for the Polish Heritage Days and in October for the Polish Apple Festival celebration.

One of Winona's less well-known claims to fame is that of being the Stained Glass Capital of the United States. The nation's two largest art-glass companies, along with another smaller studio, are located in this town of 30,000. The second largest, *Conway Universal Studios,* offers informal tours of its operation at 503 Center Street. In this nondescript ex-grocery store you can see artists designing windows for churches and other institutions and workers scoring and breaking glass to fit the designs and then piecing the rich colors together with sections of lead channels soldered at each joint. Universal also works with the much-thicker slab glass and does a limited amount of glass etching using sandblasting equipment. Viewing the entire production process takes forty minutes to an hour. Visitors should call (507) 452–9209 to arrange for tours.

A visit to the *Bunnell House,* which commands a good view of the river 5 miles south of Winona on Highway 61, in the little town of Homer, provides some rare insights into the lives of several of the area's earliest pioneers. This Gothic Revival–style, three-story structure—whose white-pine, board-and-batten exterior has never been painted—was built in the late 1850s by Willard Bradley Bunnell and his family, the first permanent white settlers of Winona County. The house is well appointed with period furniture, suggesting a simple but comfortable lifestyle for the Bunnells and their children. But more interesting still are the lessons to be learned about its original inhabitants.

Willard was a Great Lakes steamboat captain and fur trader who apparently was on good terms with Dakota chief Wapasha, who gave him permission to build his home in Homer. Willard's wife, Matilda, was described by one contemporary as a model pioneer woman who spoke French, English, Ojibway, Winnebago, and Dakota, as well as several other Indian dialects. She was also a capable markswoman and canoeist, while remaining "lady-like and modestly feminine."

The Bunnell House is open for tours Memorial Day through Labor Day (call 507–454–2723 for hours). A modest fee is charged.

The Winona Historical Society, which operates the Bunnell House, offers yet another perspective on Victorian life in the Mississippi River valley via a **Victorian Fair** held in late September or early October. Food complements period music, craft demonstrations, fortune-telling, juggling, clowns, puppets, river cruises, and carriage rides. The Victorian Express, a 1907 steam engine–powered train with deluxe and luxury passenger cars, has been pressed into service for this event as well. Full- or half-day rides aboard the train can include meal service and are moderately to expensively priced. For more information call (507) 454–2723.

Another historic site of special interest is found 10 miles south of Winona, along a tributary of Big Trout Creek on County Road 7 at the tiny town of Pickwick. Here in a lovely, narrow valley dominated by steep limestone bluffs is the **Pickwick Mill,** which, when built in 1854, was one of the first industrial sites in Minnesota. The mill is an imposing, seven-story native limestone building that was built with such fortitude that it has withstood a tornado and a major flood. These facts are even more remarkable considering that there isn't a single nail to be found in the structure's beams, rafters, and floor columns—they are held in

The Victorian Express

place by weight alone. Flour from the mill helped feed troops of the Union army during the Civil War; in the years that followed, Pickwick flour was also shipped to destinations worldwide. The mill is open weekends only. For information contact Pickwick Mill Incorporated, Rural Route 4, Box 219, Winona 55987, or call (507) 452–9658 or (507) 457–0499; or log on at www.pickwickmill.org.

Fillmore County

It seems impossible, but of the 10,000-plus lakes located in Minnesota, Fillmore County contains exactly . . . none. That doesn't mean, however, that there's no fishing in this part of the state. In fact the area's cold-water streams support native trout populations that attract anglers from throughout the region. A good way to find your way to the area's hot fishing spots is to call *Root River Outfitters* at (507) 467–3400 or you can call Bill Haugen at *Magic Ring Trout Flies* at (507) 864–2867, *The Fly Guys* at (507) 452–1986, or visit www.mwfly .com and go to the guides section.

The Root River, which flows west to east through the heart of Fillmore County, is one of the region's waterways deserving special note. The valley that it has carved is deep—up to 300 feet in some places—and forested with remnants of the Big Woods that once blanketed much of the southeastern part of the state. Wild turkey, eagles, osprey, and deer abound. And the towns that the river passes along the way—Chatfield, Lanesboro, Rushford—are charming and steeped in history.

Depending on the time of year and personal predilection, there are several ways to take in the splendors of this river valley. Minnesota Highway 16 follows the river from *Lanesboro* nearby to its confluence with the Mississippi River and is a lovely drive any time of year. In warmer months the Department of Natural Resources–designated *Root River Canoe Route,* which begins just downstream of Chatfield and runs for 90 miles to the Mississippi, is excellent for swimming and canoeing.

Bicyclists and hikers can follow the 35-mile *Root River State Trail*—an old railroad grade that has been converted to a multiple-use recreational trail—along its gentle downhill course from Fountain (9 miles west of Lanesboro on County Road 8) to Rushford. The same trail is groomed for cross-country skiers in winter.

Regardless of your mode of travel, picturesque Lanesboro is a great place to begin or end any adventure in the valley. The *Lanesboro Trail Center,* in the lower level of the *Lanesboro Historical Museum* at 105 Parkway South, has maps and information about local canoe and bicycle rentals. History buffs can acquaint themselves with the town's past by perusing the two floors of exhibits upstairs.

Stores in well-preserved nineteenth-century brick buildings on Parkway and Coffee Mill Streets include the studio of local wood-carver *John Thompson* (100 Parkway South). The *Scenic Valley Winery,* located at 103 Coffee Street in an old creamery, has a showroom downstairs where bottles of Minnesota-grown raspberry, rhubarb, apple, and wild plum wines are sold, along with more exotic onion and green-pepper cooking wines. Visitors, who are welcome to sample the winery's wares, will probably find members of the Brehm family hard at work with their handpresses. Call ahead (507–467–2958) to arrange for tours if your group is large.

With three moderately priced bed-and-breakfasts in town, Lanesboro isn't lacking in interesting places to stay, either. The flavor of a small late-nineteenth-century hotel has been lovingly re-created at *Mrs. B's Historic Lanesboro Inn* (507–467–2154), though the building, circa 1872, was originally used by an undertaker and furniture maker. Five-course dinners prepared from locally grown ingredients are served at Mrs. B's Wednesday through Sunday evenings. The *Scanlan House* (507–467–2158), *Historic Lodge Inn* (507–886–2409), and *Carrolton Country Inn* (507–467–2257) are the other choices for an overnight stay. And for dinnertime you may want to make a reservation at the restored *Victorian House Restaurant* (507–467–3457), where authentic French gourmet cuisine is served nightly by chef Jean Claude Venant and his wife, Sonja.

There are two destinations just outside Lanesboro that outdoorsmen and women will find interesting. The *Lanesboro State Fish Hatchery,* built around a freshwater spring at the site of an old mill just south of town on Highway 16, produces two million trout annually—nearly half the trout stocked in Minnesota waters. An educational slide show and self-guided tours are available free of charge.

Three miles north of Lanesboro on Minnesota Highway 250, signs point the way to the *Eagle Bluff Environmental Learning Center.* This small, nonprofit environmental education center sits in the middle of 900 acres of state forest on top of a spectacularly steep bluff overlooking the Root River. Excellent skiing and hiking trails radiate from the main lodge, which also serves as a great site for observing golden and bald eagles (up to twenty of the latter have been spotted in a single autumn day), wild turkey, and osprey. A tunnel, dug decades ago beneath the bluff to power a now-defunct hydro plant, has become home for the largest known wintering population of pipstrel bats. More accessible to visitors is a bat condominium, located at the center's main facility, which houses

Karst Topography

While the lack of recent glaciation in the driftless region of southeastern Minnesota resulted in a scenic landscape of gently rolling highlands carved up by deep ravines, another less obvious geologic feature exists. A good example of Karst topography runs through Fillmore County, and a short drive on Minnesota Highway 80 from Fountain to Wykoff provides good views of this unique geology. In fact, Fountain has claimed the title of "Sink Hole Capital of the U.S.A."

Along this route, fields of corn and soybeans are pitted with small, round tree islands. These small circles are steep, rocky holes and from a distance look just like unplowed parts of a field. They range from 30 to 150 feet in diameter and may be up to 30 feet deep. While generally dry, they will fill with water during heavy rainstorms but will drain in a few hours or days.

Karst topography exists in other parts of the world, but in Minnesota only in a few southeastern counties. Fillmore County has the most sinks, with an estimated 5,750 dotting the landscape. The Karst sinks resemble potholes in some respects but are formed much differently. Sinks form when rain causes limestone to dissolve; potholes form in solid rock at the base of waterfalls or where sand and gravel are spun around in a stream.

up to 3,000 of the fascinating nocturnal creatures. Also, tours are given of the country's largest shiitake mushroom–growing operation—the center's main demonstration project and source of income; the delicious mushrooms are sold here, too. The center is open year-round. For program information write Eagle Bluff Environmental Learning Center, Route 2, Box 156A, Lanesboro 55949, or call (507) 467–2437 or (888) 800–9558; or visit www.eagle-bluff.org.

Upstream from Lanesboro a few miles along the banks of the Root River is the town of ***Preston,*** where many years ago a group of desperate prisoners tried to escape the Fillmore County Jail by tunneling out with their spoons. Although their laborious plan failed, today you would never be driven to such desperation—you wouldn't even *want* to escape from the place—because the old Fillmore County Jail has been transformed into the ***Jail House Inn,*** a charming and most unusual B&B. Through much sweat and finance, the building has been restored to its original Victorian architectural style and graciously appointed, with breathtaking results.

There are twelve beautiful guest rooms, some with fireplaces, some with whirlpool tubs, all decorated with exquisite taste. From the hand-tiled bathrooms to the ornate wallpapers to the authentic antique furnishings, each room has its own distinct flavor. Some are named for their original function (the Sheriff's Quarters, the Drunk Tank, to name two), whereas others are named after their decor (the Oriental Room, the Amish Room, etc.). Perhaps most interesting of all is the Cell Block, which contains two queen-size beds, a shower, a bath, and the original iron jail bars.

Breakfast, every bit as tasty as the scrumptious accoutrements would lead you to expect, is served in a bright and sunny modern dining room. The entire premises can be rented, space permitting, for company retreats and other group lock-ups. Call innkeepers Marc and Jeanne Sather at (507) 765–2181; or write to Jail House Inn, 109 Houston 3 NW, Preston 55965; or visit www.jail houseinn.com.

Those seeking a more traditional incarceration experience may want to consider doing time at the **_Historic Wykoff Jail Haus._** Located just 10 miles west of Preston, the Jail Haus was, until recently, an abandoned one-room jail scheduled for demolition. A group of concerned citizens realized that this would be a waste of a charming brick structure, so they decided to refurbish it and turn it into a bed-and-breakfast.

Touted as the smallest B&B in Minnesota, the Jail Haus accommodates just one couple per night, but guests have free rein over the entire structure. This consists of a combination sitting-sleeping room, a modern bathroom, and a "cell room," complete with the original iron bars and narrow bunk beds. The bunk beds have been fitted with cushy new mattresses, which, had they been in place one hundred years ago, might have made the area's more notorious hombres—folks such as Jesse James—a lot less ornery. Breakfast is served up the block at the **_Gateway Inn_** restaurant. For reservations or more information, call the Bank Gift Haus at (507) 352–4205, or write to the Jail Haus, P.O. Box 205, Wykoff 55990.

Harmony, a sleepy little town a few miles north of the Iowa border, is unquestionably in the heart of farm country, and an unusual opportunity to become immersed in the pastoral life is made possible through a bed-and-breakfast network known as **_Michel Farms Vacations_**. Vernon Michel, himself an ex-farmer, works with a dozen of the area's grangers to arrange getaways that many travelers find refreshingly different. Some farmsteads are historic and furnished with antiques, others are clean and modern, but all offer a taste of farm life and afford a glimpse into the lifestyle of the Amish living nearby in Minnesota's largest

harmony

The Bluffland town of Harmony got its name accidentally. The village started as a railroad stop, and during a heated discussion of what to name the new town, one resident who had grown tired of the arguing stood and exclaimed, "Let us have harmony in here!" The surprised group stopped fighting, thought about the statement, and decided that Harmony would make a good name.

Amish colony. Prices are modest. Write Michel Farm Vacations, 45 Main Avenue North, P.O. Box 156, Harmony 55939, or call (507) 886–5392.

A few miles south of Harmony is a hole in the ground that has been swallowing up visitors for decades. The **Niagara Cave** used to rate right up there with Wall Drug and Reptile Gardens as one of the most heavily advertised tourist attractions in the country, as a result of an extensive billboard and bumper-sticker campaign (the attraction used to have three kids working full-time on bumper-sticker detail). But highway-beautification laws in the 1960s changed all that, and now Niagara Cave draws a relatively modest stream of visitors who seek it out because they know what they're looking for.

The hour-long tour begins in the basement of the entrance building and quickly descends to a series of well-lit, horizontal passages that were cut into the ancient limestone bedrock by seeping underground streams. One of these waterways still courses through sections of the cave and in one place forms an impressive 60-foot waterfall that visitors can view from a suspended platform projecting past the brink of the falls.

In the cave, too, are many other interesting formations—deposits of colorful minerals, numerous fossils, impressive stalactites, and unusual eroded limestone shapes, some of which have been given cute names and labeled with placards by the cave's managers. There is also a damp little "wedding chapel" that, believe it or not, has been the site of more than 200 weddings. The entire round-trip hike is a mile in length and represents only half of the known extent of the cave. At its deepest point, more than 200 feet below the surface, the stream briefly reemerges into view in a room that is adorned with a fine collection of still-growing stalactites.

A modest fee is charged for the guided tour, which is offered on weekends during April and October and daily from May through September. The cave is closed November through April except by special arrangement (call 507–886–6606 or (800) 837–6606). Niagara Cave can be found just south of Harmony and west of Highway 139 on Niagara Cave Road (www.niagaracave.com).

Southeast of Spring Valley is a second cave system open to public tours. The **Mystery Cave** has known passages that total 12 miles in length. Tours highlighting the natural history of the cave are staffed by naturalists at nearby **Forestville State Park,** which now owns and manages the cave system.

One tour begins along the banks of the Root River at a spot where a portion of the river disappears underground—a common occurrence in this region of the state. Most of this cave is in the 400-million-year-old Dubuque limestone layer, a formation of huge blocks that results in square-shaped passages and large rooms. A second tour, starting at the Minnesota Caverns entrance, is mostly in the 500-million-year-old Galena limestone layer, which is characterized by high, narrow, irregularly shaped passages. In the Mystery Cave system are two brilliant turquoise lakes, as well as dramatic and colorful collections of stalactites, stalagmites, and flowstones (all of which are formed by water-deposited calcite). The Mystery Cave is maintained in its natural state (neither placards naming formations after familiar shapes nor wedding chapels are to be found), and the inexpensive tours, which begin at the state park, have a strong natural-history focus.

Thomas Meighen's Farm Village, also part of Forestville State Park, offers an immersion experience of a different sort. Park your car and cross the bridge to the farm village and you will be magically transported to the year 1899. The "locals" (costumed interpreters portraying Forestville residents) are likely to strike up a conversation about the politics of the day or perhaps the bright future of the railroad industry. They will then lead you on an informal tour of the Meighen Farm Village, which includes a general store, a barn, a gristmill, an herb garden, and a homestead, complete with office, parlor, and kitchen. Not only can you talk with the laborers as they go about their daily chores, you may even be asked to help with a little cooking, grinding, or gardening. If you're lucky, they may even offer you the going wage (about 25 cents a day).

The original community of Forestville died out because the railroad went to Wykoff instead. **Historic Forestville,** on the other hand, is alive and well and lots of fun. Admission is free, but a state park vehicle permit is required. For more information on cave tours and park programs, write Forestville State Park, Route 2, Box 128, Preston 55965, or call (507) 765–2785 for Historic Forestville, (507) 352–5111 for the main park, (507) 937–3251 for Mystery Cave, or, toll-free from within Minnesota, (800) 652–9747 (ask for Department of Natural Resources) or visit www.dnr.state.mn.us and click on State Parks.

For several decades around the turn of the twentieth century, farms in southern Minnesota were worked by teams of farmers using gigantic steam-powered engines. This tradition is proudly celebrated today in the little town of Mabel.

Since 1960 **Mabel** has been the annual site of the **Steam Engine Days** festival, which each year draws some 35,000 people to town the first weekend after Labor Day. Because of the widespread interest in this event, in 1988 a **Steam Engine Museum** was established on the Steam Engine Days festival grounds. From May to September visitors can see various models of these huge iron workhorses, as well as classic and antique tractors, early gasoline engines, and several different evolutions of the threshing machine. Call (507) 493–5350 for museum times and for information on the annual Steam Engine Days celebration.

Views—and Memories—from a Train

In the mid-1960s, my parents decided that my brother and I should go on a train ride just in case passenger service ever stopped. To make sure we got a decent ride yet still ended up close enough for my dad to pick us up, mom rode with us on the Empire Builder the 125 miles from St. Paul to Winona. Riding in the glass-covered Vistadome car, with the bluffs of the Mississippi River Valley towering above us on one side and the Great River just feet away on the other side, remains as one of my most vivid memories of the ride.

Since then I've taken the Empire Builder to Idaho and Montana for ski vacations. I've been stranded because of a snowstorm in Glacier Park that made rail travel through the mountains impossible, and I was delayed when extreme cold caused equipment to quit working. And though I have seen some awesome scenery while riding the train from the mountains of Glacier to the amazing open spaces and solitude of the northern prairies, that first ride along the Mississippi remains as a fond memory of one of my first "long" trips.

Houston County

In the heart of Houston County, 3 miles west of the county seat of Caledonia, is a lovely pocket of wilderness encompassing a series of steep wooded ravines that dissect the valley of Beaver Creek, a tributary of the Root River. **Beaver Creek Valley State Park,** as the area is known, has fine hiking trails, trout fishing, camping, and weekend interpretive programs in the summer (for information on park programs, write Beaver Creek Valley State Park, Route 2, Box 57, Caledonia 55921, or call 507–724–2107). The park also has within its boundaries a unique anachronism: the only unadulterated, fully functional water-powered gristmill in the state.

Though it's within the boundaries of the park, **Schech's Mill** is actually situated on the working farm of Ivan Krugmire, who still uses the original machinery to custom-grind feed for his livestock. The facility has been operating in this lovely little valley since the mill's completion, in 1876, by Bavarian master miller Michael J. Schech.

When visitors step inside the building's 2-foot-thick native limestone walls, Ivan briefly explains the history of the mill and sends visitors on a self-guided tour of the mill's upper two levels. Then everyone gathers around the millstones on the main floor, and Ivan sets the turbines in motion to demonstrate the New Process milling technique.

As the floodgates are opened and the heavy grindstones start to spin, the entire interior of the solidly constructed building—from the maple flooring to the heavy fir timbers far below—is sent into a shudder. Thick leather belts that run through the floor to connect wheels, axles, and wooden gears on different levels of the mill whir into motion. And the kernels of dried corn that trickle into a hole in the center of the 22-inch Diamond Buhr millstone are ground into a coarse powder. Tours are given for a small fee on weekends from April through October; call (507) 896–3481 for more information.

Rice County

The exterior limestone wall of the building housing the ***Northfield Historical Society***—a building that originally served this Cannon River town as the First National Bank—has the kind of rough and weathered look that you'd expect of a structure that's more than a century old. But closer inspection reveals some telling pockmarks that, to the residents of ***Northfield,*** carry a special signifi-cance, for it was here, on an autumn day in 1876, that one of the most famous bank robberies in Minnesota history was thwarted by a group of uncommonly brave citizens.

A visit inside the museum reveals the whole story. With its teller windows, vault, and account books open on the tables, the scene looks just as it did on that fateful September Thursday when three members of the notorious James-Younger gang strolled through the door to make an unauthorized withdrawal. Five more robbers, all wearing the gang's characteristic knee-length linen "dusters" to conceal their weapons, were stationed in the street outside.

Although the gang was accustomed to carrying out an operation like the Northfield raid without encountering significant resistance, on this occasion it was in for a surprise. Two citizens on the street who detected what was afoot gave out a call to arms, while inside the bank the acting cashier, Joseph Lee Heywood, refused to open the vault (which was actually unlocked). After a second bank employee escaped out the back door, taking a bullet in his shoul-der as he went, the robbers decided to abort the raid. One of them paused long enough while exiting the bank to end Heywood's life with a shot to the head. Meanwhile, outside, a street battle was blazing.

In the end two townsfolk were killed in the fight, as were two of the out-laws. Several days later four of the remaining six bandits, who had fled west-ward, were captured or killed, leaving only Jesse and Frank James as fugitives.

Visitors to Northfield the first weekend after Labor Day can witness a reen-actment of this event in the annual ***Defeat of Jesse James Days*** celebration. During the rest of the year, exhibits and a videotape at the historical society tell the tale. The museum, open daily, is at the corner of Division and Fourth Streets; call (507) 645–9268 for hours, or visit www.northfieldhistory.org.

Though Northfield has calmed down considerably since the James-Younger boys were driven from town, there are still many interesting attractions for curious and adventuresome visitors. But first there's the question of lodgings, a question easily resolved at the ***Archer House.***

When this grand, four-story, French Second Empire–style hotel was built in 1877, the local press noted, "There is unequivocal indication of taste in every room"—a statement that couldn't be truer today. Owner Dallas Haas's loving renovation and redecoration in 1984 show unusual attention to details, as in the dried-flower bouquets, occasional antique household items, antique furniture reproductions, and strategically placed stuffed animals that highlight the distinctive shape and personality of each room. Even the smallest and least expensive rooms (prices are moderate to expensive) are amply comfortable, steeped in charm, and in many cases possess fine views of the walkways bordering Northfield's lovely Cannon River waterfront. Reservations can be made by writing the Archer House, 212 Division Street, Northfield 55057 or by calling (507) 645–5661 or, toll-free within Minnesota, (800) 247–2235.

Not far from Northfield are the studio and showroom of a soft-spoken, Minnesota-born potter of wide renown, ***Charles Halling.*** Wheel-thrown and hand-built pottery made by Charles has received regional and national acclaim; one of his dinnerware sets is even in the Minnesota governor's residence. Best of all, prices for Halling's gracefully simple porcelain and stoneware designs start at less than $20. The studio is found at 11967 Gates Avenue, Northfield 55057 (507–645–6256).

If, for whatever reason, you find yourself beating a hasty retreat from Northfield into the sunset, you may want to do what the fleeing James-Younger gang did—stop in at the ***Millersburg Store.*** What was at that time a general

Archer House

A New/Old Era of Travel

The powerful tow boats, large cabin cruisers, and fast fishing boats that ply the Mississippi River today are far different from the simple boats used by the Indians and early explorers and settlers. For many years the bark canoe served as the main mode of transportation on the big river and its tributaries. Portable and easy to build, Indians, explorers, and trappers used canoes for hauling supplies as well as for transportation.

As more people started arriving in the region, the need to haul larger loads not only down the river but back up led to the development of the keelboat. First used on the upper Mississippi by the French in 1751, keelboats could haul large loads of cargo, and the flat bottoms made them useful for navigating in even shallow water. Although crews could move keelboats upstream, it was hard work done by poling or tying ropes to tree stumps on shore and pulling the boats along. Despite the manual labor involved, keelboats could go eight to twelve miles upstream per day.

In 1823 the first steamboat to visit Minnesota docked at Fort Snelling and started a new era of river travel. Soon thereafter, as the lumber industry began along the Upper Mississippi in the mid-1800s, a boat called a flatboat or broadhorn became a popular vessel. Made of lumber and logs, the 60-foot-long by 20-foot-wide boats that evolved from simple rafts floated downriver with lumber and other products from the north woods. After reaching their destination, the boats were torn apart and sold piece by piece along with the cargo.

The only way the often rough crews could return upriver was to catch a ride on a steamboat. It must have been a funny sight to see these hardworking (and hard-drinking) river men riding a fancy steamboat with the more refined passengers. Although romanticized in stories, steamboats faced many hazards including snags, boiler explosions, and collisions with other boats, log rafts, ice, and floating trees. By 1915 the banner days of the fancy river steamboats had ended, with the surviving ones tied up at river towns as tourist attractions.

store down the block from a hotel used by several members of the gang the night before the bank raid is now a lively saloon and restaurant run by Rose Hanzel. A few historical pictures on the walls recall the store's earlier incarnation, but the main attractions are the outlaw-size hamburgers, criminally delicious ice-cream drinks, and the sprawling beer garden out back, which is replete with a horseshoe pit. The store is located in the heart of tiny Millersburg, 2 miles west of I–35 on Rice County Road 1.

In 1826, knowing a good thing when he saw it, a French-Canadian fur trader named Alexander Faribault set up a trading post for the American Fur Company below a rampart of high bluffs where the waters of the Straight River joined the larger-flowing Cannon. Business with the neighboring Dakota Indians was good, and Faribault eventually decided to settle at this picturesque spot permanently, building in 1853 the *Alexander Faribault House,* a Greek Revival design that stands today as the first frame house built in Rice County. Two years later the town of Faribault was named after its founder. Public tours of the completely restored Alexander Faribault House, located at 12 First Avenue NE, are given for a modest fee May 1 through October 1. Call the Rice County Historical Society at (507) 332–2121 for times and prices of tours.

Soon to follow Faribault's example was a German cabinetmaker named Carl H. Klemer, who in 1865 established a woolen mill on the banks of the Cannon River. Though in Klemer's time woolen mills were common enough in river communities like Faribault—his was one of 800 in the country—today the *Faribo Mill* exists as only one of three such operations nationwide and produces more than half of all wool blankets made in the United States.

Tours of the old mill are offered on weekdays (for information write Faribo Woolen Mill, 1819 Second Avenue NW, Faribault 55021, call 800–448–9665, or visit www.faribowool.com) and allow visitors to witness the entire manufacturing process—from the cleaning of raw wool stock from all over the world to the dyeing of fibers in huge basement vats to the now-mechanized weaving process in a large room full of clattering electronic looms. The Faribo Woolens Factory Store (on Second Avenue just across the river), which offers blankets at discounted prices, is open every day except holidays.

In the heart of Faribault's downtown Heritage Preservation District, which includes two fine examples of Art Deco–influenced architecture in the *Rice County Courthouse* and the *Thomas Scott Buckham Memorial Library,* are several other destinations worthy of a visit. Wood-carver *Ivan Whillock's studio* is located at 122 Northeast First Avenue, just a couple of doors away from the Alexander Faribault House. Since 1962, when Ivan established his studio in Faribault, he has been upholding the Classical Spanish style of craftsmanship by working exclusively with chisels, gouges, and other hand tools to produce a variety of religious images for churches throughout the region. He also creates secular pieces, such as landscapes and wildlife scenes that reveal the visual perspectives gained by the artist during his early work as a painter.

The *Cathedral of our Merciful Saviour,* at 515 Northwest Second Avenue, holds special interest from an architectural and historical perspective. Hailed by architectural historians as one of the most impressive English Gothic–style churches in Minnesota, it was completed in 1869 as the first cathedral in the American Episcopal Church. Moreover, the structure's high vaulted ceilings were home to one of the most important religious figures in Minnesota history—the Reverend Henry Benjamin Whipple, the state's first bishop. Whipple, whose crypt is in the basement of the cathedral, was a great advocate of Indian rights. As a result of his intercession with President Lincoln on behalf of some 300 Dakota who were held responsible for deaths in the great Dakota conflict in 1862, 262 of the Indians were spared.

Another highlight of a visit to the cathedral (tours can be arranged by calling 507–334–7732) is the lever-operated bell chimes, circa 1903, in the bell tower. Visitors are given an opportunity to try their hands ringing out a tune for the benefit of the long-suffering residents who live close by.

Steele County

Legend says that during the worst winter in memory, Owatonna, the daughter of the Indian Chief Wabena, became gravely ill. Desperate to save her, he moved his village from the Minnesota River area to a place where the endless prairie started changing into the hardwood forest of southeastern Minnesota. They ended up finding a place where a spring known as a *minnewaucan* ("curing water") flowed from the earth. Owatonna recovered after drinking the water, and today the town of the same name occupies this place.

Except for the likes of Jesse James, most people aren't inclined to go far out of their way to investigate a bank that holds none of their money. The *Wells*

West Hills Museum

The topic of orphans and neglected children is a subject that most people try to avoid. It's a subject sure to evoke strong feelings and opinions among others and has become news again as some politicians have talked about reviving orphanages as a way to take care of neglected children. For anyone interested in an honest and detailed look at the history of orphanages, the **West Hills Museum** in Owatonna is a must to visit.

Created in 1886, the Minnesota State Public School for Dependent and Neglected Children provided education and housing for 20,000 children over sixty years. Besides a school, hospital, gymnasium, and assorted other buildings, the orphanage had its own power plant, greenhouse, ice house, cemetery, and farm. It eventually expanded to 329 acres, 42 for the buildings and 287 for crops, and became virtually self-sufficient.

Today the main building, which made the National Register of Historic Places in 1975, also houses the Owatonna city administrative offices. The museum provides a compelling look at how the state cared for dependent children through displays of pictures, artifacts, personal stories, and movies. The address is West Hills Museum, 540 West Hills Drive, Owatonna. For more information call the Owatonna Visitors and Convention Bureau at (800) 423– 6466 or (507) 451–7970.

Fargo Bank at 101 Cedar Street North in Owatonna, however, is one such institution that cries out to be visited. Completed in 1908 as the National Farmers Bank, this nationally acclaimed architectural treasure represents the most celebrated work of one of America's outstanding architects, Louis H. Sullivan. The cubelike shape of the building's exterior, adorned with huge arched windows of stained glass by Louis Millet, quickly earned the building widespread recognition as, according to one historian, "a jewel box set down in a prairie town."

Entering the bank through the low-hung entry, one is suddenly overwhelmed by the beauty of the interior. The arched shapes of the resplendent windows are repeated in lovely pastoral murals on two walls, whose earth tones blend harmoniously with the surrounding terra-cotta and cast-iron ornamentation that was built by the country's best craftsmen of the time. Though the building has undergone several renovations since its completion, these have been undertaken with a dedication to preserving the spirit and many of the details of Sullivan's original masterpiece. Brochures explaining the history of the bank are available, as are brief tours by bank personnel.

Another interesting historic site in Owatonna can be seen on the grounds of the Owatonna Tool Company, located at 655 Eisenhower Drive. Resting on a short stretch of tracks next to the old Owatonna Railroad Depot sits *Engine 201,* a steam locomotive that happens to have been the first engine ever driven by railroad legend Casey Jones. Tours of the engine for groups of five or more can be arranged by calling (507) 455–7000. Also, a booklet describing the history of the engine and the story of Casey Jones is available.

Waseca County

Before it was extensively developed for agricultural purposes, the heart of Waseca County used to represent the dividing line between the Big Woods to the east and the prairies that stretched for hundreds of miles westward. Today at this historic ecological junction is an institution that enables visitors to contemplate the changes that have taken place since the plows of the first white settlers left their marks.

Farmamerica is an interpretive center that chronicles the evolution of the Minnesota farm from the late 1850s until the present. Visitors make this historic journey by exploring three different farmsteads: an 1850s settlement farm, a 1920s dairy farm, and a contemporary farm operation. There are also a prairie restoration area, a historic one-room schoolhouse, a blacksmith shop, and a church. From June to October, when Farmamerica is open each weekend for a small fee, interpretive volunteers occupy each farm site and illustrate historic farming activities. Festivals are held the second Sunday each month.

Farmamerica is located 4 miles west of the town of Waseca on County Road 2. For more information contact Farmamerica, Box 11, Waseca 56093; call (507) 835–2052; or visit www.farmamerica.org.

Freeborn County

Ever since humans first occupied the prairies of southern Minnesota, Albert Lea Lake, just east of the city of Albert Lea, has been a busy place. Following the retreat of the last glacier some 10,000 years ago, the shores of the lake were frequented by hunters surviving on large game animals. In the ensuing millennia the area's rich natural resources continued to support groups of nomadic small-game hunters and fishermen as well as more sedentary, village-dwelling prehistoric farmers.

Those who would like to learn more about how these early Native Americans adapted to southern Minnesota's changing environment over the centuries would do well to visit *Big Island State Park,* just east of Albert Lea at exit 11 on I–35. Within this beautiful 1,600-acre sanctuary, three natural communities characteristic of the region during late prehistoric times—oak savanna, wetlands, and northern hardwood forests—can be explored firsthand. Also, the close proximity of these different natural environments creates a lush habitat

Saving the Wetlands

When the first settlers arrived in southeastern Minnesota, they must have felt as if they had landed in paradise. Clear streams flowed through heavily forested hills, and fertile soil covered the valley floors. They soon set to work planting crops, cutting trees for lumber, and grazing cattle on the steep hillsides. But exploitation of the land eventually led to serious erosion of the rich topsoil that fouled streams and forced people to leave the area.

To look at the neat farms, prosperous towns, and heavily forested hills of southeastern Minnesota today, it doesn't seem possible that much of this region lay in ruin in the early 1900s. Minnesotans owe a debt of gratitude to Richard J. Dorer, who through his work for the Minnesota Department of Conservation and Bureau of Game surely saved this spectacular area. He appealed to and worked with many groups, from hunters and anglers to garden clubs and the Izaak Walton League.

He shared his love of the land with others through his poetry and children's books, and he initiated the "Save the Wetlands" movement, a Minnesota program now spreading throughout the world. Today the Richard J. Dorer Memorial Forest covers a large section of southeastern Minnesota and has become a rich habitat for wild turkey and trout and supports a booming tourism industry.

for wildlife. Deer, several species of birds of prey, waterfowl, and white pelicans are plentiful, especially during fall migration.

Prehistory buffs will want to spend some time at the park's Owen Johnson Interpretive Center, where exhibits from a collection of 30,000 local prehistoric stone artifacts (one of the state's largest private collections) provide insight into past cultures. From the big-game hunters' exquisitely crafted large spear points to the hand-carved fishhooks of a later time, one can gain real respect for the ingenuity and craftsmanship of those whose technology depended on stone, clay, wood, and bone. Some of the stone knives on display reputedly hold an edge to leather better than any modern metallic blade. For more information about the park, write Big Island State Park, Route 3, Box 33, Albert Lea 56007 or call (507) 373–3403 or, toll-free within Minnesota, (800) 652–9747 (ask for DNR).

Each autumn Bancroft-Bay Park in Albert Lea is the site of the ***Big Island Rendezvous,*** a gathering of groups dedicated to celebrating the lifestyle of the fur trade. Highlights of this event, which is held in early October, include a black-powder shoot, tomahawk- and knife-throwing contests, dancing and crafts displays, and a tepee village and trading post. For more information call the Albert Lea Chamber of Commerce at (507) 373–3938.

gimmetheskinny

What must be one of the skinniest attractions in the world runs through Bluffland. The *Upper Mississippi River National Wildlife and Fish Refuge* begins above Wabasha, Minnesota, and runs to Rock Island, Illinois. It measures more than 260 miles in length and up to 3 miles at its widest point.

Covering more than 200,000 acres, it provides habitat for 292 species of birds, 57 species of mammals, 45 species of amphibians and reptiles, and 118 species of fish. Although it's not preserved as a national park, the countless backwater channels, islands, and peninsulas provide the perfect habitat for animals, and one in which humans can easily get lost.

Places to Stay in the Bluffland

RED WING
(area code 651)

AmericInn,
1819 Old West Main;
385–9060

Best Western Quiet House & Suites,
Highway 61 and Withers Harbor Drive;
388–1577

Candlelight Inn Bed & Breakfast,
818 West Third Street;
388–8034

Days Inn,
Highway 61 & 63;
388–3568

Red Wing Blackbird Bed & Breakfast,
722 West Fifth Street;
388–2292

St. James Hotel,
406 Main Street;
388–2846

Super 8 Motel,
232 Withers Harbor Drive;
388–0491

Special Note: Besides the two listed, Red Wing has six more beautiful bed-and-breakfast inns, all in historic mansions. For a list call the Red Wing Convention and Visitors Bureau at (800) 498–3444.

LAKE CITY
(area code 651)

AmericInn,
1615 Lakeshore Drive;
345–5611

Lake City Country Inn,
1401 North Lakeshore Drive;
345–5351

Red Gables Inn,
403 North High Street;
345–2605

WABASHA
(area code 651)

Anderson House Hotel,
333 West Main Street;
(800) 535–5467

Bridgewaters Bed & Breakfast,
136 Bridge Street;
565–4208

Coffee Mill Inn and Suites,
Highway 60 West;
565–4561

Eagles on the River Bed & Breakfast,
1000 Marina Drive;
(800) 684–6813

Wabasha Motel,
1110 Hiawatha Drive East;
565–9932

ROCHESTER
(area code 507)

AmericInn Hotel & Suites,
5708 Highway 52 Northwest;
(800) 634–3444

Comfort Inn,
1625 South Broadway;
281–2211

Country Inn & Suites,
4323 Highway 52 North;
285–3335

Hampton Inn,
1755 South Broadway;
287–9050

Springhill Suites by Marriott,
1125 Second Street Southwest;
281–5455

Super 8 South #1,
1230 South Broadway;
288–8288

Note: Rochester has 56 hotels and motels with a variety of rates and amenities. Contact the convention and visitors bureau listed on page 63 for a complete list.

WINONA
(area code 507)

Americinn,
60 Riverview Drive;
457–0249

Best Western Riverport Inn & Suites,
900 Bruski Drive;
452–0606

Carriage House Bed & Breakfast,
420 Main Street;
452–8256

Nichols Inn & Suites,
1025 Sugar Loaf Road;
454–6066

Quality Inn,
956 Mankato Avenue;
454–4390

Windom Park Bed & Breakfast,
369 West Broadway;
457–9515

HARMONY/LANESBORO
(area code 507)

Cottage House Inn,
209 Parkway Avenue North, Lanesboro;
467–2577

Country Lodge Motel,
Highway 52 North, Harmony;
886–2515,
(800) 870–1710

Green Gables Inn,
300 Sheridan Street West, Lanesboro;
467–2936

SELECTED CHAMBERS OF COMMERCE

Albert Lea Convention &
Visitors Bureau
(800) 345–8414

Austin Convention & Visitors Bureau
(800) 444–5713

Faribault Area Chamber of Commerce
(800) 658–2354

Harmony Tourism Center
(800) 247–6466

Historic Bluff Country
(800) 428–2030

LaCrescent Chamber of Commerce
(800) 926–9480

Lake City Area
Chamber of Commerce
(877) 525–3248

Lanesboro Office of Tourism
(800) 944–2670

Northfield Area
Chamber of Commerce
(800) 658–2548

Owatonna Convention &
Visitors Bureau
(800) 423–6466

Red Wing Convention &
Visitors Bureau
(800) 498–3444

Rochester Convention &
Visitors Bureau
(800) 634–8277

Wabasha Chamber of Commerce
(800) 565–4158

Waseca Area Chamber of Commerce
(507) 835–3260

Winona Convention & Visitors Bureau
(800) 657–4972

**Historic Scanlon House
Bed & Breakfast,**
708 Parkway Avenue South,
Lanesboro;
467–2158, (800) 944–2158

**Selvig House Bed &
Breakfast,**
140 Center Street East,
Harmony;
886–2200

Note: The Harmony/Lanesboro area has many bed-and-breakfast inns, all in historic mansions. For a list call the tourist offices in Harmony (800) 247–6466 or Lanesboro (800) 944–2670.

LaCRESCENT
(area code 507)

Ranch Motel,
Highway 14/16 & 61;
895–4422

FARIBAULT
(area code 507)

AmericInn,
1801 Lavender Drive;
334–9464

Best Western
Galaxie Motor Lodge,
1401 Highway 60 West;
334–5508

**Cherub Hill Bed
& Breakfast,**
105 First Avenue
Northwest;
334–2024

Super 8 Motel,
2509 Lyndale Avenue North;
334–1634

NORTHFIELD
(area code 507)

**Another Time Bed &
Breakfast,**
305 Railway Street South;
645–6367

Archer House
212 Division Stree;
645–5661

Country Inn,
300 Highway 3 South;
645–2286

**The Magic Door Bed &
Breakfast,**
818 Division Street South;
664–9096

Super 8 Motel,
1420 Riverview Drive;
663–0371

OWATONNA
(area code 507)

AmericInn,
245 Florence Avenue;
455–1142

Country Inn & Suites,
130 Allan Avenue
Southwest; 455–9295

Holiday Inn Hotel & Suites,
2365 Forty-third Street
Northwest;
446–8900

**Northrup-Oftedahl House
Bed & Breakfast,**
358 Main Street;
451–4040

Super 8 Motel,
Highway 14 & I–35;
451–0380

WASECA
(area code 507)

American Motel,
1313 North Highway
13 Service Road;
835–4300

Waseca Inn & Suites,
2201 North State Street;
835–0222

ALBERT LEA
(area code 507)

AmericInn Motel,
811 East Plaza Street;
373–4324

Comfort Inn,
810 Happy Trails Lane;
377–1100

**Fountain View Inn Bed
& Breakfast on the Lake,**
310 North Washington;
373–2899

Super 8 Motel,
2019 East Main Street;
377–0591

**Victorian Rose Inn Bed
& Breakfast,**
609 West Fountain Street;
373–7602

Places to Eat in the Bluffland

RED WING
(area code 651)

Fiesta Mexicana,
Highway 61 and Old Main
Street;
385–8939

Golden China Restaurant,
3038 North Service Drive;
388–8020

**Lily's Coffee House
& Flowers,**
419 West Third Street;
388–8797

Marie's Casual Dining
(American),
2107 Plum Street;
388–1896

Pizza Hut,
3048 North Service Drive;
388–1568

Pottery Espresso & Deli,
240 Harrison Street;
388–7655

Staghead Restaurant
(American),
219 Bush Street;
377–6581

**Tale of Two Sisters Tea
Room,**
204 West Seventh Street;
388–2250

LAKE CITY
(area code 651)

Cheung's,
220 South Washington
Street;
345–3818

**Gallagher's Restaurant
and Ice Cream** (American),
113 Lakeshore Drive;
345–5535

Papa Tronnio's Pizza,
211 Lyon Avenue;
345–3540

Rhythm & Brew,
220 East Chestnut;
345–5331

Rouletti's (Italian),
214 South Lakeshore Drive;
345–5333

WABASHA
(area code 651)

Anderson House
(American),
333 West Main Street;
(800) 535–5467

Dairy Queen,
1000 Shields Avenue;
565–2100

Eagle Nest Coffee House,
330 Second Street West;
565–2077

Eagle Valley Restaurant
(American),
Highway 61;
565–2040

River Town Cafe, (American)
119 Pembroke Avenue;
565–2202

ROCHESTER
(area code 507)

Applebee's (eclectic),
320 Apache Mall;
252–0155

Billotti's Italian Village,
304 First Avenue
Southwest;
282–8668

Cafe Fez (Indian),
420 Second Street
Southwest;
281–5888

Cheap Charlie's (American),
11 Fifth Street Northwest;
289–9591

China Dynasty,
701 Broadway Avenue
South;
289–2333

Fiesta Mexicana,
1645 North Broadway
Avenue;
288–1116

**Jaspers Alsatian Bistro
and Wine Bar**
14 Historic Third Street
Southwest;
280–6446

Pizza Hut,
2001 West Highway 52;
287–6396

WINONA
(area code 507)

Acoustic Cafe
(American, coffee),
Second and Lafayette;
453–0394

**The Blue Heron
Coffeehouse,**
451 Hufff Street;
452–7020

Chula Vista (Mexican),
1415 West Service Drive;
452–8202

Golden China,
411 Cottonwood Drive;
454–4261

Lakeview Drive Inn
(American),
610 East Sarnia;
454–3723

Pickwick Inn Restaurant
(American),
RR4 Box 150,
Pickwick 55987;
454–7750

Rocco's Pub & Pizza,
5242 West Sixth Street;
454–5911

**Wellington's Backwater
Brewing Co.,**
Westgate Shopping Center;
452–2103

HARMONY/LANESBORO
(area code 507)

Apple Dumpling Cafe,
downtown, Lanesboro;
467–0101

Country Bread Basket
(American),
Highway 52 and Fourth
Avenue,
Harmony;
886–6277

Das Wurst Haus,
downtown, Lanesboro;
467–2902

**Harmony House
Restaurant** (American),
57 Main Avenue North,
Harmony;
886–4612

Intrepid Traveler (eclectic),
121 Main Avenue North,
Harmony;
886–3479

Mrs. B's Inn & Restaurant
(American),
101 Parkway Avenue North,
Lanesboro;
467–2154

Old Barn Restaurant
(American),
downtown, Lanesboro;
467–2512

The Trail Inn (pizza),
downtown, Lanesboro;
467–2200

Village Square of Harmony,
51 Main Avenue North,
Harmony;
886–4406

LaCRESCENT
(area code 507)

Apple on Main Tea Room
(coffee, sandwiches),
329 Main Street;
895–1995

Corky's Pizza & Ice Cream,
25 South Walnut Street;
895–6996

FARIBAULT
(area code 507)

A & W Family Restaurant
(American),
404 Wilson Avenue;
334–9379

**El Tequila Mexican
Restaurant,**
951 Faribault Road;
332–7490

Godfather's Pizza,
328 Fourth Street Northwest;
334–1672

Javalive,
313 North Central Avenue;
333–2979

**Long Cheng Chinese
Restaurant,**
318 Central Avenue;
334–3002

Perkins Family Restaurant
(American),
333 Western Avenue;
332–7997

Taco John's (Mexican),
1431 Fourth Street
Northwest; 334–3287

Wimpy's Restaurant
(American),
520 Central Avenue North;
334–4996

NORTHFIELD
(area code 507)

**Bagel Brothers
Bakery & Coffeehouse,**
306 Division Street;
645–2288

Basil's Pizza,
301 Water Street South;
663–1248

**Diamond Dave's
Mexican Restaurante,**
620 Water Street South;
663–1056

**Hogan Brothers Acoustic
Cafe** (American),
415 Division Street;
645–6653

**Mandarin Garden
Restaurant,**
107 East Fourth Street;
645–7101

Quality Bakery & Cafe,
410 Division Street;
645–8392

Ranch House Restaurant
(American),
1401 Riverview Drive;
645–8298

OWATONNA
(area code 507)

A Taste of the Big Apple
(delicatessen),
104 West Broadway Street;
455–3633

Applebee's (eclectic),
690 West Bridge Street;
451–0006

China Buffet,
114 West Broadway Street;
444–0871

Dairy Queen (ice cream),
670 West Bridge Street;
451–8398

SELECTED WEB SITES IN THE BLUFFLAND

**Albert Lea Convention &
Visitors Bureau**
www.albertleatourism.org

Faribault Area Chamber of Commerce
www.faribaultmn.org

Harmony Tourist Information
www.harmony.mn.us

Historic Bluff Country
www.bluffcountry.com

**Lake City Area Chamber of
Commerce**
www.lakecity.org

Lanesboro Office of Tourism
www.lanesboro.com

LaCrescent Chamber of Commerce
www.lacresent.com

**Northfield Area
Chamber of Commerce**
www.northfieldchamber.com

**Owatonna Convention &
Visitors Bureau**
www.owatonna.org

**Red Wing Convention &
Visitors Bureau**
www.redwing.org

**Rochester Convention &
Visitors Bureau**
www.rochestercvb.org

**Wabasha-Kellogg
Chamber of Commerce**
wwww.wabashamn.org

Waseca Area Chamber of Commerce
www.wasecamn.info

Winona Convention & Visitors Bureau
visitwinona.com

**Grace's Mexican
& American Restaurant,**
1170 North County
Road 45;
451–1908

Perkins Family Restaurant
(American),
1200 I–35 North;
451–6831

WASECA
(area code 507)

Busy Bee Cafe (American),
214 North State Street;
835–9908

Daily Grind Espresso,
101 State Street South;
835–9186

David's Old Towne Eatery,
200 South State Street;
835–7267

Godfather's Pizza,
North Highway 13;
835–8135

New China Buffet,
105 Seventeenth Avenue
Northeast;
835–2699

**Yellow Mushroom/
Bridgeman's**
(American, ice cream),
South Highway 13;
835–5000

ALBERT LEA
(area code 507)

Abrego's Cafe
(Mexican, American),
120 South Washington;
373–5469

Bagels and Beans,
152 Bridge Avenue;
377–7517

China Restaurant
(Chinese, Vietnamese),
805 East Main Street;
377–8888

Elbow Room (American),
310 Eighth Street;
373–1836

Jake's Pizza,
126 West Clark;
373–7350

Trumble's (American),
1811 East Main;
373–2638

Roads to Take

Amish Buggy ByWay,
Highway 52 between
Highway 16 and 44*

Apple Blossom Drive Scenic
Drive ByWay,
17 miles from LaCrescent
along county roads*

Bluff Country Drive Scenic
ByWay, 88 miles from
Dexter to LaCrescent on
Highway 16*

Shooting Star Scenic ByWay,
32 miles,
designated wildflower route*

Highway 61 from Winona to
LaCrescent

*Call Historic Bluff Country at
(800) 428–2030 for a guide
to these drives.

Prairieland

In a state known for thousands of lakes, countless miles of streams and rivers, and thousands of acres of wetlands, this region of Minnesota presents to travelers an anomalous landscape. Resembling the great open spaces of the Dakotas more than the forested hills of eastern Minnesota, it doesn't seem as if Prairieland belongs to the state. Prairieland covers southwestern and west-central Minnesota and contains the headwaters of the Minnesota River and some of the most intensively farmed land in the state.

Visitors to this region will find panoramic views of fields of row crops stretching to all four horizons. Broken only by the occasional farm with its silos or island of trees, this vast landscape exists in an area where nature can be both cruel and kind. While enough rain usually falls to ensure a good crop, Prairieland is drier than eastern Minnesota, which can make for stressful times for the stoic farmers of the region.

Although now a land of agricultural bounty, we can only imagine what this region looked like to the Indians and first white settlers. Historical records show us a scenic land of dry prairies, wetlands, and shallow lakes, all set among rolling hills. Bison, elk, and antelope lived on the fertile grasslands, while the marshes and creeks supported populations of waterfowl

PRAIRIELAND

N

0   40 mi

0   40 km

27 75

28

7

59

12 71

7 12

29

Milan 40 Willmar 4 15

75 23 Litchfield 12

Montevideo

212 7 7

Granite Falls

59 212

23 4 5

Marshall 19 19

71 169

14 14 New Ulm St. Peter

Minnesota R.

Currie 60

30 Mankato

Pipestone 59 22

23

75 Windom 169

60 71 4 15

90 90

Worthington

MINN.

IOWA

S.D.

MINN.

that at times darkened the sky. Unfortunately the conversion to intensive farming led to the draining of wetlands and straightening of countless creeks, which forever altered the landscape.

Meeker County

When the first railroad train steamed across the Meeker County line on its way westward from the bustling Twin Cities in 1869, the first town it encountered was *Dassel,* east of Litchfield on U.S. Highway 12. The train screeched to a stop at a small wooden station, disgorged a few passengers and some freight, and then slowly chugged its way back up to speed, leaving a cloud of black smoke and ash in its wake.

In those bygone days—when huge steam-powered machines were transforming American life and half the North American continent seemed to many to be crying out for settlement—the railroad and accompanying telegraph service were the primary lifelines connecting little towns like Dassel with the rest of the civilized world. Today in this community of 1,000, there is a museum dedicated to the role that the iron horse has played in the history of many a Minnesota small town.

Originally, Dassel's *Old Depot Museum* stood in nearby Cokato. In 1985 the building was moved 6 miles west to its present site on the north side of US 12 in "downtown" Dassel. Parked out front of the well-maintained wooden structure is a 1922-vintage wooden caboose that's been restored with such details as a coal-fired stove, a spring-mounted kerosene wall lamp, a real icebox, and a primitive "flush" toilet that could be operated in good conscience only when the train was at least a mile from the nearest town.

Inside the depot is a gallery of paintings and prints by Currier and Ives, Norman Rockwell, and others that capture the incomparable mystique of traveling by train to exotic locations. Another room contains collections of such railroad

AUTHOR'S FAVORITES

Blue Mounds State Park,
Luverne,
(507) 283–4892

Camden State Park,
Lynd,
(507) 865–4530

Lower Sioux Interpretive Center,
Redwood Falls,
(507) 697–6321

Pipestone National Monument,
Pipestone,
(507) 825–5464

artifacts and memorabilia as railroad lanterns, signs, buttons, playing cards, uniforms, and dining-car china. There are also two delightful vehicles formerly used by track and telegraph-line workers: a velocipede (an odd-looking, three-wheeled-bicycle–like contraption that reached speeds of 20 miles per hour by means of a two-handled push-pull stick) and another one-person scooter, with bicycle handlebars, that was actually pedaled along the tracks. The museum is open daily Memorial Day through September; a small fee is charged.

A few miles farther down the line, in the even-smaller hamlet of Darwin (population 282 by last count), there stands what is indisputably Minnesota's greatest monument to the archetypal human urge to collect: the *World's Largest Ball of Twine.*

The ball of twine is only one of many achievements realized by Francis A. Johnson, who passed away recently at the end of a long life of collection. During odd moments in his career as a farmer, he claimed to have squirreled away some 5,000 pencils, 200 feed caps, and untold numbers of wooden ice-cream containers and paddle locks. Still, it was The Ball that elevated him to such heights of notoriety as being listed in the *Guinness Book of World Records* (which officially lists The Ball's weight as a staggering 10,000 pounds), *Ripley's Believe It or Not,* and Charles Kuralt's *On the Road.* Drive into Darwin on Meeker County Road 11 and see The Ball for yourself—it is slowly rotting beneath the water tower.

Birdwing Spa is hidden in the heart of the farm country south of Litchfield—the next town west of Darwin on US 12—though it's a destination that one would be much more likely to discover in the countryside of France or Germany. To find Birdwing you must zigzag around the edges of several large cornfields and kick up a couple of miles of dust on an unmarked gravel road that looks as if it's heading nowhere. Then suddenly a pair of commanding wrought-iron gates appear amid a thick stand of hardwoods, and you know at once that you've arrived someplace special.

Occupying the grounds of a lush country estate and hobby farm that was built in 1976, Birdwing is Minnesota's only full-service holistic health spa. Since 1985, when Elizabeth and Richard Carlson welcomed their first guests, people have been coming to Birdwing from all over the country to be pampered for two days, five days, a week, or more in a tradition that reflects Elizabeth's Austrian upbringing. Guests stay in nine graciously appointed rooms in a large English Tudor–style mansion. There are exercise and aerobics classes led daily by trained instructors, opportunities for hiking and skiing in Birdwing's 300 acres of lakeside forests, yoga and massage sessions, a sauna and hot tub, a fully equipped beauty room, and low-calorie gourmet meals. Rates at Birdwing are expensive, though they include all meals and services and are modest in comparison with those of most other spas. For more information write Birdwing Spa, 21398 575th Avenue, Litchfield 55355; or call (320) 693–6064; or visit www.birdwingspa.com.

On the way to Birdwing, there's one farm that warrants closer inspection. Prefabricated metal sheds and modern field equipment are nowhere in sight, and without them the neat red-and-white barn and outbuildings, old cement silo, and turn-of-the-twentieth-century farmhouse create the image of a farm perhaps from an earlier time. That's exactly the effect that Don and Sonja Nelson had in mind when they began offering *Experience Agriculture* tours of their farmstead in 1987.

Don, whose farming career has included work as an agriculture teacher, saw the need to educate the public about the importance of agriculture and the dying institution of the family farm. Accordingly, he and his family restored their farmyard to its original appearance. The Nelsons only conduct farm tours for groups such as school field trips and family reunions. But for six weeks in September and October, they have a pumpkin festival that is open to the public.

Visitors are welcomed into the haymow, where they can make themselves comfortable on a bale of hay beside a collection of antique farm implements that hangs on the walls and listen to Dan introduce the state of the farm, circa 1900. Visitors are then free to wander through the active henhouse, the pungent silo, and the livestock pens, while interpretive staff explain how domestication and agricultural practices have evolved over the years. Kids get a special thrill out of romping in the hayloft, where Don has left several heavy ropes hanging from the rafters for swinging. A modest fee is charged to visitors, and the place is open to the public by arrangement. Organized tours are welcome,

TOP ANNUAL EVENTS IN PRAIRIELAND

Ole & Lena Days,
Granite Falls, early February,
(320) 564–4039

Buffalo Days,
Luverne, early June,
(507) 283–4061

Aebleskiver Days,
Tyler, late June,
(507) 247–3905

Song of Hiawatha Pageant,
Pipestone, late July and early August,
(507) 825–4126

Oktoberfest,
New Ulm, first two weekends in October,
(888) 463–9856

Norsefest,
Madison, early November,
(320) 598–7301

too. For directions, write the Nelsons at Route 1, Box 382, Litchfield 55355; call (320) 693–7750; or log on to www.nelsonfarm.com.

In 1956 Minnesota's last surviving Civil War veteran died in Duluth at the venerable age of 106. Since his death, anyone wishing to visit the state's most enduring memorial to the War of the Rebellion has had to travel to *Litchfield,* where the *Grand Army of the Republic Hall and Museum* has proudly stood since its construction in 1885. Facing a large park in the center of town, the building's distinctive brick facade—replete with a large, castlelike half-tower in the center and small turrets on the corners—creates an unmistakably military aura. It is the only building erected by the GAR veterans' organization that is still in use in Minnesota and just one of thirteen in the country.

When visitors pass through the small entrance beneath a recessed portrait of Abraham Lincoln, they enter the original library, which now also serves as an exhibit space for a small, but very interesting collection of items left behind by local veterans of the American Civil War. Most of the men who built the Litchfield GAR hall first came to Minnesota after the fighting was over to take advantage of the land grants allotted to Union soldiers in lieu of pay. Thus the stories generated by the museum's artifacts reflect the experiences of such famous fighting units as the First Minnesota Volunteer Infantry, whose members led a decisive and near-suicidal charge at Gettysburg, as well as men from other parts of the country.

One exhibit case displays a leather belt whose buckle reads "CSA," that is, Confederate States of America. According to museum staff the belt was exchanged for one bearing the Union army's insignia when a pair of soldiers who had been friends in Ohio before the war confronted each other as "enemies" during a battle. On another shelf rests a photograph of a Minnesota volunteer who died of starvation in Georgia's infamous Andersonville prison camp. Elsewhere in the building a framed drawing of the camp depicts the desolate site at which 11,000 Yanks died of starvation and disease in the one-year period that the facility was in operation. Also on display are rifles and muskets, a pair of prized boots (many soldiers were reduced to wrapping their feet in rags), articles of clothing, and various personal effects.

The walls of the interior meeting room are hung with portraits of many GAR members, paintings of battle scenes, and original furnishings. In large letters just below the ceiling are rendered two proclamations: IN MEMORY OF OUR LOYAL DEAD and WE ARE THE BOYS OF '61.

Adjacent to the rear of the hall is the *Meeker County Historical Society Museum,* which features items of local history. Both buildings, located at 308 North Marshall Avenue, Litchfield, are open Tuesday through Sunday for a small fee throughout summer. Call (320) 693–8911 for more information.

Though you might not guess it today, in the early years of Meeker County's history, the little town of **Forest City,** 6 miles northeast of Litchfield on Minnesota Highway 24, was a community of some consequence. By the early 1860s enough bustling activity had been generated by a sawmill and flour mill located on the banks of the north fork of the Crow River that for a time the town was designated the Meeker County seat (an honor that was later permanently bestowed upon Litchfield). This explains why so many of the area's settlers simultaneously sought protection at Forest City during the panic that swept the countryside immediately following the outbreak of the Dakota conflict in late August of 1862.

On September 3, the settlers, using logs and lumber from the sawmill, hastily erected a 120-square-foot stockade around a two-story log cabin and barn, which now houses antique farm tools, circa 1860–1880. Today a reconstructed **Forest City Stockade** stands near the site of the original, looking much the same as the first one did more than a century ago.

Strolling about inside the enclosure's 10-foot-high walls, one feels a little claustrophobic, considering that this cozy space was shared for ten days by 240 men, women, and children. It was largely the women and children, however, who bore the brunt of this confinement, as many of the men ventured out to work their fields during the daylight hours despite the fact that the stockade was attacked the first night. Throughout the event there were no casualties—even a thirteen-year-old girl whose frightened family left her behind in the fields to find her own way to Forest City arrived safely at the stockade by nightfall.

The stockade, located just east of Highway 24 on the south edge of town, is open daily from mid-June through August. An annual Furtrade Rendezvous is held at the site the third weekend in August, featuring black-powder shooting, craft demonstrations, and plenty of characters camped out in 1860s regalia.

Kandiyohi County

If it's a hot summer afternoon, one of the first things you'll notice upon your arrival at **Spicer Castle**—a grand turn-of-the-twentieth-century bed-and-breakfast estate near the town of **Spicer,** northeast of Willmar—is the breeze off the lake. Wander among the original furnishings of the spacious living and dining rooms, then settle into a wicker chair on one of the surrounding porches with a glass of iced tea. You'll continue to feel the cool air pushed up the high, steep shoreline of Green Lake, carrying with it the sound of lapping waves.

This is one of the effects that John Mason Spicer had in mind in 1893 when he began building the six-bedroom English Tudor–style home, which was originally called Medayto Cottage. The other consideration that steered this pioneer farmer, statesman, and developer of Kandiyohi County to this site is—as you'll discover yourself, if conditions are right—the lovely vantage point offered by Green Lake's south-shore bluff for observing the setting sun. When seen from the lake, the prominence of the stately "cottage," with its crenellated tower that protrudes above the roofline, prompted the nickname Spicer Castle, first used by fishermen in the 1930s.

In addition to the six comfortably appointed guest rooms in the main house are a log cabin and a cottage, originally John Spicer's office, on the grounds nearby. Rates at Spicer Castle are moderate to expensive. For more information and reservations, contact Spicer Castle by calling toll-free, (800) 821–6675 or by logging on to www.spicercastle.com.

Chippewa County

A walk down the main street of the little Minnesota River town of **Milan,** population 417, is enough to convince a visitor that this Norwegian-American community maintains an exceptionally strong tie with the old country and its traditions. Several wall murals depict Norwegian themes and locales, and the trim on many storefronts displays the work of Milan's two gold-medal–winning rosemalers (only four artists in the state have achieved this national recognition for their delicate and highly stylized painting on backgrounds of painted wood).

Drop in to the **Arv Hus Museum and Gift Shop** on Second Street to get a feel for the range of talents that the citizens of Milan have to offer. A gift shop of Norwegian craft items features samples of *hardanger* (embroidery), wheat weavings, pottery, and rosemaling.

In the back of the store there's a museum dedicated to the life's work of a local inventor, William Thompson, who in 1925 created a toaster-size device called the radio booster that enabled rural listeners to pick up a dozen stations instead of only two or three. Thompson was also a pioneer in portable-radio technology. Wrapping 100 feet of wire back and forth over the roof of his Model T enabled him to boast of owning the region's first car radio. In the 1930s he built the country's first portable broadcast truck.

A block away from the Arv Hus Museum, at **Karen Jenson's studio** (104 Lincoln, Milan), visitors are welcome to stop by and see works in progress by one of Milan's top rosemalers. More locally generated artistry is also on display 1 block behind Jenson's home, at the **Kviteseid Lutheran Church.** A beautiful baptismal font with a rich green-and-red floral design was produced by Karen's brush, as were four playful murals in the church's downstairs bathrooms. The altar and pulpit paraments are handmade *hardanger* designs by another of Milan's artists.

Milan's folk traditions have developed such a following that a new folk school, *Milan Village Arts School,* now offers weekend workshops and classes for those interested in developing old-world skills in weaving, silversmithing, painting, carving, and, of course, rosemaling. For information on classes call (320) 734–4807.

For more information on Milan and the surrounding area log on to www .milanmn.com. Its Web site is excellent and has a wealth of information and links.

For Native Americans and European explorers alike, the earliest highway through this part of the state was the Minnesota River. Enough water flowed down the river to make for an easy passage throughout the summer, and the heavily forested banks offered shelter from the surrounding open prairie. Thus, when the area's first missionaries set out to begin their work, they had good reason to choose a place like the *Lac Qui Parle Mission,* found today in a wooded grove south of Milan.

Lac Qui Parle was a thriving mission outpost from 1835 to 1854, serving a nearby Dakota village of 400. Of the half-dozen buildings that were once clustered at this site, only a rebuilt church stands today. The towering cottonwoods

Salt on the Prairie

If you're the type of person who likes to dazzle or confuse your friends with your knowledge of the obscure and unique, here's one for you. Among Minnesota's 10,000-plus lakes, do any of them contain salt water?

One does and it's appropriately named Salt Lake. This briny body of water, which is one-third as salty as an ocean, sits on the border of Minnesota and South Dakota west of the small town of Madison. An anomaly in a state known for freshwater but not salt water, Salt Lake attracts many species of birds and has a variety of unusual plants that have adapted to the saline environment.

Brine-water lakes are more common in the western United States, including North and South Dakota, and it's rare to find a saline lake as far east as Minnesota. Salt Lake is popular with bird-watchers who come to see the prairie and salt-water birds not found elsewhere in the state.

To reach the lake follow Highway 40 west from Madison for 11.5 miles, turn south at the Salt Lake sign, go 3 miles south and finally west for 1 mile. And while you're in the area, take some time to visit some of the native virgin prairie sites in Lac Qui Parle County. Although you won't find heavy surf at Salt Lake, you will have the satisfaction of visiting a unique attraction in Minnesota and one that is most definitely off the beaten path. For more information on Salt Lake and native prairie reserves in western Minnesota, go to www.prairiewaters.com.

Just Go Get It!

One of the more interesting, and some would say humorous, events in state history occurred in Lac Qui Parle County. As settlers moved into this western Minnesota county in the 1860s, small towns started popping up throughout the rolling landscape. As the population increased, residents elected a slate of county officials before officially being designated a county.

The battle over which town would get the county seat erupted between the residents of Madison and Lac Qui Parle. The competition finally culminated on the evening of November 12, 1886, when 150 men and 40 teams of horses met on the Leather Breeches farm near Madison. The group went to Lac Qui Parle, put the courthouse on wagons, and moved it 15 miles across the prairie to Madison.

Now Madison had the building and records, while the officials stayed in Lac Qui Parle, stopping any county business for a month. After much political maneuvering—this time in the courts and legislature instead of on the prairie—the county seat finally ended up in Madison.

surrounding the church and the exhibits inside make this prairie oasis well worth a visit.

It was here that the Bible was first translated into the Dakota language in a written alphabet developed by the missionaries. Lac Qui Parle was also the location of the valley's first school and the first place in the state where thread was woven into cloth. During the mission's active years, there were a school, a corn mill, cabins for the missionaries, and a spring. Exhibits in the church, which was constructed in 1841, show the work of the mission; the life of Joseph Renville, an early fur trader in the area; the archaeological excavation of the site; and the history and culture of the Dakota. The site is open daily, free of charge, during the summer. For more information contact the Chippewa County Historical Society, Box 303, Montevideo 56265, or call (320) 269–7636.

Yellow Medicine County

The name of this western Minnesota county comes from the river that flows through it before merging with the Minnesota River near Granite Falls. The Sioux named the river Yellow Medicine for the bitter, yellow roots of the moonseed plant that grows as lush vines in thickets along the river banks. This long, narrow county borders two distinct areas: the prairie of South Dakota and the rugged Minnesota River Valley.

Granite Falls is a pleasant little city. It has an impressive park system, densely wooded residential avenues, and an attractive business district near the banks of the Minnesota River. The community's traditional small-town values are reflected in one of its historic sites: the ***Volstead House,*** at 163 Ninth Avenue, which was the residence of congressional representative Andrew Volstead, author of the bill that instituted Prohibition in 1919.

But that's not all, for beneath the surface of Granite Falls's all-American facade, two of Minnesota's most exotic environmental features have been cleverly hidden. If you're a nature-minded sleuth you can unmask them both by parking your car at the ***Yellow Medicine County Historical Museum,*** at the junction of Minnesota Highways 67 and 23 just south of downtown, where a sign in the parking lot gives one of the secrets away.

WORLD'S OLDEST ROCK, the placard states boldly. You peer behind it to see a lichen-covered clump of Morton gneiss (pronounced "nice")—a protrusion of gray, red, and black bedrock that probably looks no older than any other rock you've seen. But to be fair, when you're face to face with an object that's well over three billion years old, it may take a moment for its significance to sink in. Climb on top, make yourself comfortable, and give yourself a few minutes to think. Consider the sweep of monumental events that have occurred in the world since the time of Christ. Then imagine that if the entire existence of the rock beneath you were reduced to the scale of an average human lifetime, all that has passed in the last 2,000 years would have been experienced by the rock in slightly more than one second.

Prairie and Valley

Two geographic features best define Prairieland. The first is the omnipresent prairie, which stretches for miles and offers the big sky views normally associated with the Dakotas and Montana. The Minnesota River Valley is the other dominant feature of this region, carved by a torrent of glacial meltwater and flowing for more than 300 miles through the rolling prairie and patches of hardwood forest.

The Minnesota River meanders through the wide and often steep-walled valley, a remnant of the waterway that carved this great gash in the landscape. When the glacial flood subsided, it left behind a valley that is up to 5 miles wide and 250 feet deep. The terraced valley walls, irregular channels, and rock ridges form a rare landscape found in few areas. The Columbia River of eastern Washington and parts of Oregon and Idaho shows the same characteristics that formed from a short, but catastrophic, flood. The area around Granite Falls in eastern Yellow Medicine County is a good place to see the unique features left behind by an ancient river.

Lutefisk Capital of the United States

Today Madison claims another important title besides county seat of Lac Qui Parle County. It's also known as the Lutefisk Capital of the United States. As a dish only a Scandinavian could love, lutefisk is cod cured in lye and boiled, before being served with lefse and potatoes. In June 1993 the town dedicated a 25-foot fiberglass model of a cod, named Mr. Lou T. Fisk.

The smell before cooking and texture after are the most distinguishing features of lutefisk. Uncooked lutefisk smells like something that someone forgot about for months in a refrigerator, while mushy comes closest to describing the texture. Despite these less than appetizing traits, diehard Scandinavians love it and feast on it during the holiday season.

Each year during Norsefest at Madison, lutefisk lovers gather to celebrate Scandinavian heritage. Activities include a lutefisk eating contest and the Norsky Outhouse Race. Though it's hard to say if future generations will still eat lutefisk, this delicacy should stay popular in Madison.

When you've had enough of such mind-bending contemplation, stretch your legs by walking west across the highway and into the woods that crown another outcrop of ancient gneiss. You have now entered the **Blue Devil Valley Preserve,** a thirty-five-acre tract of land set aside by The Nature Conservancy as one of the state's five natural habitats for an endangered lizard called—that's right—the blue devil. Also known as the five-lined skink, the blue devil is one of Minnesota's two indigenous lizards. In fall and winter the quick little metallic blue creatures burrow into the crevices in the rock for protection. In spring and summer they tend to prefer cool, damp shelter, such as that offered by rotten logs and humus. Brochures on the blue devil can be found at the County Historical Museum, which has exhibits on local history and is open free of charge Tuesday through Sunday in the afternoons.

Lincoln County

Besides being the windpower capital of the Midwest, this county that borders South Dakota is easy to overlook. And though most travelers won't plan a special trip to this lightly populated area of farms and prairie, two attractions make it worth visiting if passing close by.

Hole-in-the-Mountain Prairie runs south from Lake Benton and offers visitors a look at both virgin and restored prairie. Consisting of 4,300 acres, the prairie runs partially through a valley the Indians called "Mountain Pass" or

"Hole-in-the-Mountain." Though not a mountain pass in the true sense, the valley does cut through the often steep hills of Buffalo Ridge, which is part of the Coteau des Prairies.

Besides having more than 60 species of grasses, sedges, and rushes; 10 species of trees and shrubs; and 200 species of wildflowers, the preserve also provides good habitat for rare prairie-dependent insects. One, the Dakota skipper butterfly, survives on only a few scattered sections of virgin prairie in the Dakotas, Minnesota, and Iowa. For more information call (507) 694–1138 or (800) 442–9854.

Tyler, Home of the Nissemaend, is a fun place to stop. According to Danish lore, *nissemaend* are tiny elves who occupy each Danish home. Cousins to Irish leprechauns, nobody ever sees them, and they are helpful or mischievous depending on how much food their hosts set out. Other attractions in Tyler include the Danebod Complex, one of the few buildings that survived a 1918 tornado that destroyed the town; Aebleskiver (ball pancakes) Days; and three special guided tours through the area. For more information call (507) 247–3905.

Lyon County

Most people who visit this county come to Marshall, one of the largest towns in southwestern Minnesota and home to Southwest State University. Most don't know that the Redwood River, which runs through the county and through a beautiful valley that many years ago was an oasis in the harsh prairie for animals and humans, received its name from Indians.

The name came from the reddish bark of the dogwood that grows along the river. Indians called it *Kinniqkinnic,* and they used the white inner bark as smoking "tobacco." This farming county also has a couple of attractions that are definitely off the beaten path.

Most people think of an oasis as a stand of palm trees surrounding a small pond in the middle of a desert. Ten miles south of Marshall near the town of Lynd lies a different type of oasis—one that sheltered human and animal inhabitants of the plains.

Today this oasis is named Camden State Park, and it's a true anomaly in a region of gentle rolling hills and thousands of acres of corn, soybeans, and pasture. Located in an area called the Coteau des Prairies, the park is a shaded valley with thick stands of deciduous trees. The Redwood River carved this valley eons ago, and animals and humans have long found shelter here from the blazing summer sun and the cold winter winds that whip across the landscape of southwestern Minnesota. Camden State Park still shelters wildlife from the

Coteau des Prairies

One of the most surprising geographic features in Minnesota cuts across the southwestern part of the state from northwestern Iowa to northern South Dakota. The Coteau des Prairies (highland of the prairie) is a plateau made of glacial till piled high on a base of quartzite rock, the remains of an ancient mountain range. Only the hills along Lake Superior are higher than this plateau. While the glacial moraines left some rugged terrain along the edges, the top is mostly smooth and gently rolling.

Many streams flow from the top of the coteau, dropping through steep gorges on both sides of the plateau. To both animals and humans, these wooded valleys provided free-flowing spring water and shelter from the summer heat and winter storms of the prairie. While many species of wildlife still live on the coteau, unfortunately the populations of bison, elk, wolf, prairie chicken, and golden eagle have disappeared within the last one hundred years. In one quirk of geography, trout survive in the Redwood River, an extremely unlikely occurrence in southwestern Minnesota.

The four major rivers that flow from the plateau and into the Minnesota have three distinct stretches. Each has a swift and rocky section as it drops from the coteau, followed by a slow meandering course across the plains, before ending with a fast 200-foot plunge into the Minnesota River. In fact, these rivers resemble streams in northern Minnesota as they tumble down the final stretch. Some of the best places to see the impact of the coteau on the southwestern Minnesota landscape and rivers include: Camden State Park near Marshall (507–865–4530), Upper Sioux Agency State Park near Granite Falls (320– 564–4777), and Alexander Ramsey City Park in Redwood Falls (800–657–7070).

changeable weather of this area. If you find yourself driving through this part of Minnesota, take the time to stop at this oasis of the plains.

In the small town of Minneota, located north of Marshall, visitors will find the Big Store Opera House, which in the 1800s was the only store between Mankato and Watertown, South Dakota. Each September this small town also hosts Box Elder Bug Days, a celebration that revolves around this orange and black insect. Festivities include bug races, a parade, and a concert. Just south of Minneota at Ghent, visitors will find the Silver Dollar Bar, the first bar in Minnesota to open after Prohibition.

Redwood County

One of the big events occurring in the Redwood County seat of **Redwood Falls** each June is the **Minnesota Inventors Congress,** a gathering of creative folks— including children in grades kindergarten through twelve—from around the state who come together to spark ideas and to learn how to market and patent objects of their own invention. Prominent Minnesota inventors—both living and dead—are also recognized at the congress by being inducted into the Minnesota Inventors Hall of Fame. (For information about the convention, contact the Minnesota Inventors Congress, 805 East Bridge Street, Redwood Falls; call 507–637–2344 or check their Web site at www.invent1.org.) Each inductee is immortalized by the placement of a plaque in his or her honor at the **Redwood County Museum,** located on Minnesota Highway 19 just west of downtown; the museum is open afternoons Wednesday through Sunday, May through September, or by special appointment (for information call 507–637–3329 or 637–2828).

The historical museum occupies an imposing building that was constructed in 1908 as the county poor farm. Among a variety of local history exhibits is a room dedicated to the career of Richard W. Sears, founder and first president of Sears, Roebuck and Company. In the early 1880s sixteen-year-old Sears was employed as a station agent with the Minneapolis and St. Louis Railroad in the little community of North Redwood. One day a shipment of watches mistakenly arrived at his depot. Rather than return them to the manufacturer, Sears arranged to sell them himself to other agents up and down the line. The resulting profit spurred the growth of his famous mail-order business, which, by the time he retired in 1908, had achieved an annual sales volume of $50 million.

When Colonel Samuel McPhail and some companions set about founding the town of Redwood Falls in 1864, they had the good taste to establish the community around a beautiful wooded glen formed by the junction of Ramsey Creek and the Redwood River. The creek, named after Minnesota's first territorial governor, tumbles over a steep, narrow waterfall surrounded by pines. The waterfall soon became the focal point of this little oasis of forestland in the heart of the prairie. Today the 217-acre **Alexander Ramsey Park** is the largest municipal park in Minnesota.

A network of trails and roads winds through the rugged terrain, attracting hikers, joggers, cross-country skiers, and those who simply enjoy a drive through inspiring scenery. Visitors will also find a zoo, an exercise course, a public golf course, two playgrounds, and plenty of space for camping and picnicking.

Although the history of the Dakota Indians is integral to the history of the Minnesota River Valley, there are few sites in the area that provide opportunities for visitors to learn about the traditional lifestyle of these Native Americans. An exception is the **Lower Sioux Interpretive Center,** located within the boundaries of the Lower Sioux Indian Reservation on County Road 2, 9 miles southeast of Redwood Falls. Exhibits and films at the center provide an appreciation of the Dakota perspective of the events surrounding the tragic conflict of 1862. Visitors are also given an overview of the past 200 years of Dakota culture, from the time that the Indians were pushed westward out of the woodlands of eastern and central Minnesota by the Ojibway up to the present.

When the **Lower Sioux Agency** was built in the 1850s, it was one of two U.S. government administrative centers along the Minnesota River charged with the task of transforming the nomadic Dakota into Christian farmers. Despite opposition to this program by most Dakota, at the height of its operation the agency's population approached 100 whites and 3,200 Indians. There were stables, storehouses, a blacksmith shop, a school, a boardinghouse, and staff quarters. But by the summer of 1862, following a crop failure the previous year, the Dakota were faced with starvation. The gross insensitivity of the head agent— who refused to allocate food supplies held in storage and, through a representative, admonished the Indians to "eat grass" instead—was more than the Dakota could take. Tribal elders, moved to act against their better judgment by a group of enraged younger braves who had murdered a white family, declared war on the whites. When the fighting ended six weeks later, 300 settlers and soldiers had died, whereas the surviving Dakota (no one knows how many were killed in battle) had been either arrested or driven from their lands.

Today a stone warehouse that predates the conflict still stands behind the interpretive center, which is open free of charge daily, year-round. Call (507) 697–6321 for hours and information on special events.

Once you've had a chance to look backward into Dakota history, you may want to visit several other sites on the reservation that will give you a flavor of life there today. The sporting crowd can check out the **Jackpot Junction** high-stakes bingo and casino facility, replete with Las Vegas–style entertainment. Jackpot Junction is located a couple of miles west of the Lower Sioux Interpretive Center on County Road 2. At the **Lower Sioux Trading Post,** near Jackpot Junction, Indian-made pottery and beadwork are sold and craft demonstrations are given. And across the street in an outdoor staging area next to the community center, a large **powwow** is held in mid-June each year. For information about trading post hours and powwow dates, call (507) 697–6185.

The lack of trees on the prairies of southwestern Minnesota posed an interesting problem for the area's first settlers: how to build a house? The solution most commonly reached was to slice up bricks of topsoil sprouting the ubiquitous prairie grasses and build dwellings made of sod. As strange as the idea may seem today, Stan McCone of Sanborn, in southeastern Redwood County, has proved that, properly made, a sod house is a downright comfortable place to call home.

Stan first tried constructing the **Sod House on the Prairie** of second-growth prairie grass, but he found that without the extensive root system characteristic of virgin prairie, the sod just didn't hold together. Then he spotted an

Sod House on the Prairie

area of virgin prairie grass on an accommodating neighbor's farm and proceeded to plow up strips of the stuff with a special plow. After carefully stacking an estimated 300,000 pounds of sod in a cross-linked pattern and installing a wooden floor, rafters, six windows, and a sod roof (which he says weighs in at about 24,000 pounds), in August of 1987 Stan and his family proudly beheld their creation.

The 36-by-21-foot one-room "soddie"—tastefully appointed with two high-backed antique double beds, a wood-burning cook stove, tables, chairs, and even a leather fainting couch—is as cozy as can be. Two-foot-thick walls keep the place cool in summer, warm in winter, and insulated from the sound of the persistent prairie winds. For adventuresome travelers willing to pay a moderate rate, the place is even for hire. Those just wishing to tour the soddie may do so for a token fee. To find the house, look for the first dirt road on the south side of U.S. Highway 14, 1 mile east of U.S. Highway 71. Stan can be reached at (507) 723–5138, or write him at 12598 Magnolia Avenue, Sanborn 56083. You may also log on to www.sodhouse.org.

A pioneer alternative to the sod house was the "dugout"—a less labor-intensive dwelling built into an embankment or hillside that required fewer sod bricks. One famous resident of Redwood County whose family constructed a prairie dugout in 1874 was Laura Ingalls Wilder, the author of the popular children's book series on pioneer life that gave birth to the *Little House on the Prairie* television series. The site of the **Laura Ingalls Wilder Dugout** on the banks of clear-flowing Plum Creek is open to visitors for a small fee; it is located on the Harold Gordon Farm, a couple of miles north of Walnut Grove on County Road 5. *Little House* fans may want to peruse the Wilder memorabilia at the free **Laura Ingalls Wilder Museum** and gift shop on County Road 5, just south of US 14. Also, *"Fragments of a Dream,"* an effectively staged pageant based on anecdotes drawn from the *Little House* books, is presented the first three weekends of July each year at sunset in a park at County Roads 18 and 20 in Walnut Grove. For more information go to www.walnutgrove.org.

Brown County

The white community most heavily damaged by fighting in the Dakota conflict of 1862 was the eight-year-old German settlement of *New Ulm.* The fledgling city was attacked twice—on August 19 and August 23—and citizens defended themselves behind barricades erected in the streets. By the end of the two battles, thirty-four whites had been killed and 190 structures destroyed by fire. Indian losses were unrecorded.

Today, more than 140 years later, New Ulm's strong German tradition is thriving. To find out just how much of a grip it still has on the town's 14,000 residents, drop in to see the *Brown County Historical Museum*—no doubt the only county museum in the state where exhibit labels are written in German as well as English. An interesting pattern of white-and-red brickwork graces the building's striking German Renaissance exterior, whereas the recently renovated interior of this former post office (circa 1910) has three floors of exhibits dedicated to local art and history. The quality of the displays and their contents is several cuts above that at most county historical societies. One whole floor is dedicated to the interpretation of Dakota culture, and the museum often displays paintings from a large permanent collection of works by nationally renowned artist Wanda Gag. The museum, located at the corner of Center Street and Broadway, is open for a small fee on afternoons Tuesday through Sunday. For more information call (507) 233–2616.

The Victorian era was a time when the construction of large public monuments was very much in vogue, and according to Minnesota architectural historians, in no place was that trend given such grand expression as in New Ulm. *Hermann the Cheruscan,* a sword-wielding, winged-helmeted Teutonic warrior whose stern visage has been looming above the city since 1897, stands in *Hermann Heights Park* (along Center Street on top of the bluff) as further tribute to the city's proud German heritage. The 32-foot copper statue of the Cheruscan tribesman who freed his people from Roman domination in A.D. 9 rests on top of a massive pedestal replete with ten stout Greek columns and a large dome. A circular staircase winds nearly to the top to afford sweeping views of the city.

The *Glockenspiel,* a large carillon clock tower on Fourth and Minnesota Streets, is a more recent and decidedly less Wagnerian public monument in town. At noon, 3:00 P.M., and 5:00 P.M. daily, the Glockenspiel rings out a ten-minute concert, accompanied by the appearance of seven animated figures depicting aspects of the city's history. The figures slowly rotate on a circular stage midway up the 45-foot structure. On special occasions the thirty-seven-bell carillon is played manually as well.

What German-American town worth its salt would be without a brewery, you ask? The answer, of course, is none. And New Ulm amply fulfills this expectation in a beautiful wooded glen along the banks of the Cottonwood River at the south end of town with the **Schell Brewery.** August Schell arrived in New Ulm in 1858 and quickly set up shop, rolling his first barrel of beer onto the delivery wagon within two years' time. His brewery survived the Dakota conflict unscathed (except for the unaccounted-for disappearance of two and a half barrels), and by 1880 Schell had outpaced New Ulm's five other breweries, establishing August as the dominant brewer in the vicinity.

Visitors to the Schell facility today discover that the *gemütlichkeit,* or congenial charm, of the place is arresting. From Memorial Day through Labor Day, they are free to wander through the lovely hillside gardens and beside the deer and peacock pens that surround a large European-style mansion built in 1885. The daily guided tours of the small processing plant, which produces only 25,000 barrels annually, are instructive for those curious about the brewing process. And each tour ends in the tasting room, where visitors can sample the eleven beers and sparkling beverages that the company produces. The brewery is located near the southeastern end of Franklin Street. For more information on tours, which cost a token fee, call (800) 770–5020 or visit www.schellsbrewery.com.

Although it borders on sacrilege to visit New Ulm and not enjoy beer, wine lovers now have a place of their own. **Morgan Creek Vineyards** (507–947–3547 or www.morgancreekvineyards.com) sits in the scenic Minnesota River Valley that cuts through the rolling prairies of this region. While it seems unlikely that a vineyard would operate in southern Minnesota, the hills along the river provide a hospitable location for grape production.

Established in 1993, the vineyard rolled out its first commercial vintage in 1998 and opened the first underground winery in Minnesota. Morgan Creek hosts private wine tasting for groups of five to twenty from May to October and conducts public tours on Saturdays and Sundays from May to December. Who knows, a serious beer drinker might even enjoy a tour of the winery.

Festival-goers with a taste for German culture may want to visit New Ulm during **Heritagefest** in mid-July or for **Oktoberfest,** taking place over two weekends in mid-October. Both festivals feature German food and music, including performances by New Ulm's acclaimed Concord Singers. At Heritagefest there are also a parade, running races, and traditional arts-and-crafts exhibits. For further information call the chamber of commerce at (507) 354–4217.

Nicollet County

In the early 1870s the steamboat was the primary means of transportation for river towns such as New Ulm. As the settlement of the prairies gradually resumed in the wake of the 1862 Dakota conflict, little communities up and down the river looked forward to years of growth and prosperity. Such was the case in the village of **West Newton,** 9 miles upstream of New Ulm on Nicollet County Road 21, where Alexander Harkin opened a general store in 1869.

Today visitors who drop in to the **Harkin Store,** where tours are offered Tuesday through Sunday from Memorial Day through Labor Day, step back to that era of hope and budding economic development—expectations that were dashed for West Newton in 1873, when the railroad was routed through New Ulm, effectively ending the steamboat era, and when a devastating grasshopper plague wiped out crops. The Harkin Store hung on until 1901, when it was closed with most of its merchandise left intact.

Today 40 percent of the items stocking the shelves at the Harkin Store date back to the turn of the twentieth century, though visitors would be hard-pressed to identify anything inauthentic. In keeping with its former function, Harkin's store is a sociable gathering spot where news of the outside world, circa 1873, can be obtained from costumed guides and from notices posted on the walls. Evidence of the store's role as a post office, apothecary, and dry-goods, food, and implement dealer abounds. Coffee is advertised at 35 cents per pound, and bottles of Ayers Tonic promise relief from just about any conceivable ailment. Even the well-used checkerboard, whose hand-carved wooden pieces sit on top of the cracker barrel next to the wood stove, is genuine. For information on tour times (a token fee is charged), call the Brown County Historical Society in New Ulm at (507) 233–2616 or the store at (507) 354–8666.

Fort Ridgely State Park, 9 miles farther upstream at the junction of County Road 21 and Minnesota Highway 4, combines fascinating history with a variety of recreational opportunities. The only Minnesota state park with a golf course, Fort Ridgely also has 11 miles of hiking trails, 4 miles of groomed cross-country-skiing trails, and 7 miles of trails for horseback riders and snowmobilers, in addition to camping, picnicking, and playground facilities.

The partially reconstructed fort occupies a prominent site on a bluff-top field that is surrounded by steep ravines. These natural wooded depressions sheltered hundreds of Dakota warriors during the two battles that took place at the fort on August 20 and 22, 1862. The restored commissary building, which now houses excellent exhibits on the history of the fort, military life in the 1860s, and the role that Ridgely played in the Dakota conflict, is the only historic structure that today appears much as it did originally.

Chances are that nothing at all would have remained of the small garrison had the Dakota decided to attack one day earlier, on August 19, instead of assaulting New Ulm, for on that day only twenty-nine soldiers were stationed at the fort, the rest either having been killed in earlier fighting elsewhere or being out on maneuvers to the north. The recruits who were on duty were almost all fresh volunteers with no fighting experience. But the extra day given

Sleepy Eye

The town of Sleepy Eye got its name from the lake that it sits beside. The lake is named after a peaceful and friendly Dakota Chief named Ish Tak Ha Ba, which translated in English to Sleepy Eyes. Historians believe that his name came from his slightly droopy eyelids.

Born around 1780 at Swan Lake in what became Nicollet County, Ish Tak Ha Ba became chief of the Sissetons by order of the Indian Department. Significantly, he was not a hereditary chief since neither his father nor his grandfather held such a position, but he did sign several treaties with whites.

While reluctantly signing the Traverse des Sioux Treaty, he said he wanted to live the rest of his days in the "Lake of Many Swans." Granted this wish, he lived along the lake until 1857, when some settlers died at the hands of marauding Indians. Ish Tak Ha Ba moved to a lake west of his village, which eventually became the town of Sleepy Eye.

Ish Tak Ha Ba died around 1860 in South Dakota, and in 1902 Sleepy Eye residents disinterred his remains and buried them with proper ceremony in the Minnesota town. Today the park sits in the middle of Sleepy Eye, with a tall obelisk marking the final resting place of the peaceful chief.

the soldiers at Ridgely enabled them to boost their ranks and set up defenses for the attack that they knew was coming. In the end—thanks to the effective use of the fort's cannons, which primarily fired canister shot (collections of small lead balls that disperse when fired, like shot from a shotgun)—180 green-horn soldiers repelled 800 Indians while losing only three of their number. For more information about Fort Ridgely, call (507) 426–7840.

Each year in late June at Ridgely, the middle 1800s are brought back to life through the *Fort Ridgely Historical Festival.* Surrounded by more than a hundred tepees and period tents, the old fort grounds come to life with military and cannon drills by the historic New Ulm Battery, a fur traders' rendezvous encampment, folk arts exhibits, bluegrass and folk music, and traditional foods and beverages. For more information on the festival, for which there is a small daily charge, write the Fort Ridgely Historical Festival, Box 292, Fairfax 55332, or call (507) 426–7840.

St. Peter, a Minnesota River community in eastern Nicollet County, is a town that has had to settle for second best. Following a well-planned, marginally ethical, and ultimately unsuccessful attempt to wrest the state capital from St. Paul in 1857, St. Peter was instead designated the site of Minnesota's first public hospital for the insane. Today at the *St. Peter Regional Treatment*

Center (as the hospital is now called), which is south of downtown on Minnesota Highway 169, an interesting museum chronicles the history of the institution and the sort of care it has provided to its wards since the hospital's construction in 1866.

In contrast to many visitors' notions of the stereotypically primitive "insane asylum," when the state hospital first opened its doors it offered a variety of relatively humane therapeutic services in an effort to rehabilitate its patients. It was only sixty years later, during the Great Depression, that funding for rehabilitative treatment dried up and the hospital essentially became a warehouse for people who couldn't live elsewhere in society. Photographs on display from this period, which lasted until the 1950s, show huge dormlike rooms filled with beds no more than a foot apart. In another section of the museum, mannequins depict a variety of early-twentieth-century treatment methods, including early electric shock technology, insulin shock (whereby patients were sent into temporary comas with large and sometimes fatal doses of insulin), and hydrotherapy (whereby agitated patients were wrapped in wet sheets to dissipate their hysterical energies). Tours of the museum are by appointment only and can be arranged by calling (507) 931–7250.

Though never out of line enough to warrant a visit to the state hospital, the eccentricities of one of St. Peter's more colorful nineteenth-century community leaders, Judge E. St. Julien Cox, did get him into the kind of trouble that made headlines throughout the region. You can learn about the good judge's exploits by visiting the magnificent *E. St. Julien Cox House,* located at 500 Washington Street, a completely restored structure that one historian describes as the "most impressive example of a Gothic Revival dwelling still standing in Minnesota." The house and carriage house, with their high-pitched roofs, board-and-batten walls, tower, and round-hooded windows, were considered flamboyant by community standards when they were built in 1871, though they apparently were well enough suited to the tastes of their builder.

In the midst of an impressive career in public life that included leading a regiment from St. Peter to assist the beleaguered citizens of New Ulm in August of 1862 and serving as St. Peter's first mayor, as a Democratic member of the state legislature and senate, and as a district magistrate, Judge Cox ran afoul of his Republican enemies in 1878. It seems that they took exception to the usual etiquette in the Cox courtroom, which reputedly entailed sending defendants out for a bucket of beer before they were sentenced and staging miniconcerts—on a melodeon—by the judge himself, who was not above stealing an occasional catnap during moments of uninspired testimony. Cox was ousted from the bench following a sensational six-month trial that resulted in a whopping 7,000 pages of proceedings, only to be exonerated and reinstated a few years later by a Democratic-controlled legislature. Costumed guides relate the history of the Cox House and family on Wednesday through Sunday afternoons during summer and on weekends in September. For information call (507) 931–2160 or 931–4309.

Le Sueur County

John Schumacher, the proud owner of **Schumacher's New Prague Hotel,** describes himself as Minnesota's pioneer innkeeper. This "Minnesota German," who grew up on a farm in Wheaton, undertook the creation of his central European–style hotel in 1974, when the nearest bed-and-breakfast establishment was practically across the Atlantic. To this day his New Prague remains one of Minnesota's finest country inns.

A recently completed $300,000 remodeling project in the building—which was designed in 1898 by Cass Gilbert, architect of the Minnesota state capitol—has provided a more cosmopolitan touch to many of the inn's eleven guest rooms. Double whirlpool baths, built-in stereos, and gas fireplaces now accompany the hotel's traditional hand-painted detailing on the antique wooden furnishings and the down-comforter-covered beds.

The German and Czechoslovakian food served in Schumacher's three restaurants, inspired by John's extensive travels throughout the Continent, is outstanding. The hotel also has a gift shop featuring central-European imported furniture, glassware, lace, and linens and a lounge with bar stools hand carved to resemble the booted legs of a row of mountain climbers. Accommodations and meals at Schumacher's are expensive. For reservations at Schumacher's New Prague Hotel, 212 West Main Street, New Prague, call (952) 758–2133 or (800) 283–2049 or log on to www.schumachershotel.com.

After visiting the **W.W. Mayo House** in Le Sueur (north of St. Peter), it's easy to see why rural Minnesotans in the 1850s consulted doctors only with trepidation and as a last resort. There were no licensing procedures for those who wanted to practice medicine, no required course of study beyond several months of internship with another doctor, no minimum required skills. But as costumed guides at the 1859-vintage dwelling explain, in that era's hack-filled medical profession, William Worrall Mayo, founder of Rochester's famed Mayo Clinic, was an exception.

Mayo's upstairs examining room provides some insights into the forty-year-old doctor's far-reaching vision even at that relatively early stage of his stellar career. The primitive microscope on his desk, for example, is similar to his own, which was the first microscope to be used in the state. Meanwhile, the fully functional 1850s kitchen downstairs, which on any given day may well be exuding aromas of fresh-baked bread or muffins, re-creates the home life of the Mayo family. There is a gift shop, and a token fee is charged to visitors for tours, offered Thursday through Sunday in summer; call (507) 665–6965 or 665–3250 for times.

A statue of two mothers and three small children engaged in a delightful dance stands in a little park adjacent to the Mayo House. The statue is known as the **Mothers Louise Sculpture,** and it is Louise Mayo, William's wife, and Louise Cosgrove, a later resident of the Mayo House, who, along with three of their children, have been immortalized in bronze. The Cosgrove family gained prominence in Le Sueur by founding the Minnesota Valley Canning Company— which eventually became Green Giant Company—in 1903.

If the romance and imagery of the steam age—the ponderous metal engines, the billowing smoke and steam, the wide leather belts stretched great distances between wooden pulleys, the sweat and heat of the boiler—catch your imagination, you must pay a visit to the *Geldner Sawmill.* Rounding the eastern shore of Jefferson Lake on County Road 13 a few miles northeast of Mankato, you'll find the weathered, shedlike building with a very tall smokestack on the west side of the road. Inside is a fully operable machine that played an essential role in the rural Minnesota landscape of the late nineteenth century.

The second Sunday afternoon of each month, May through September, engineer John Zimmerman fires up the boiler to raise the pressure in the system.

Traverse Gap

Way up in the northwestern corner of Prairieland, visitors will find a geological site that is both subtle and significant. It's easily missed when passing through this remote area of Minnesota, yet it marks the thin line between the headwaters of the Red River and the Minnesota River and the drainage between Hudson Bay and the Gulf of Mexico.

The *Traverse Gap* marks the point where around 12,000 years ago, Glacial Lake Agassiz broke through the ridge of the Continental Divide and began flowing southeast through central Minnesota. Known as Glacial River Warren, this immense river flowed through this breach for almost 3,000 years and carved out what we now call the Minnesota River Valley.

The gap separates Lake Traverse and Big Stone Lake, bodies of water that form the respective headwaters of the Red and Minnesota Rivers. The channel carved by the ancient river measures 1 mile wide by 130 feet deep. Though not nearly as spectacular as the canyons of the West, it must have been an awesome sight as this torrent of water rushed through the cut in the divide.

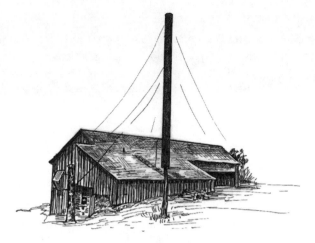

Geldner Sawmill

Sawyer John Ballman and an assistant secure a hardwood log on the carriage, and the sawdust begins to fly. (The mill is also open for tours on the remaining Sunday afternoons throughout the summer.) This bustling activity is as interesting to watch as these men are enlightening to listen to.

As they describe the technical evolution of the machinery, the conditions under which employees worked, and the lifestyles of the farmers who slowly cleared the big maple, basswood, oak, and elm off their land, a picture of Le Sueur County circa 1870 begins to form in your mind's eye. It was a place where the official dirt roads were often so impassable that most hauling of heavy loads took place on an informal network of "winter roads"—primarily the surfaces of frozen lakes. Thanks to places such as the Geldner Mill, the log homes first constructed by the early pioneer farmers were gradually replaced by wood-frame dwellings. It was also a time when Minnesota's Big Woods were slowly giving way to the neat rows of crops that are found today. For information on special sawing demonstrations, call (507) 357–4319.

In *Elysian,* the *Le Sueur County Museum,* located in an 1895 brick school building on top of the largest hill in the middle of town, is of special interest for art-history buffs as well as those curious to learn more about local history. Dorothy I. Hruska, the museum's director and curator, says that more than a quarter of a million dollars' worth of paintings, drawings, and prints are part of the museum's permanent collection. Among these are works on display by several world-renowned artists, including Adolf Dehn and Roger Preuss, who hail from nearby Waterville. These exhibits are complemented by a wide-ranging assortment of historic items: a 10,000-year-old skull of a now-extinct species of bison, 400 glass slippers, a large church vestments collection, and an exhibit dedicated to the work of a NASA scientist from Elysian who developed a meteorite detector for *Explorer 1,* America's first satellite to orbit in space. The museum is open Wednesday through Sunday afternoons in summer, weekend afternoons in May and September, and by special appointment; call (507) 267–4542.

Blue Earth County

The city of *Mankato* grew up around the confluence of the Blue Earth and Minnesota Rivers, drawing its name from the Dakota word for blue earth, *mahkato.* The community of 43,000 occupies the slopes and floodplain of a broad wooded valley at the southernmost point of the Minnesota's run to the Mississippi.

Blue Earth is bluish green clay layer that formed from the decomposition of prairie grasses over the past 9,000 years or so. Indians used the clay for decorating their faces and bodies. It also attracted the attention of French explorer Pierre Charles Le Sueur, who believed that the clay contained copper because its blue-green color resembled copper salts. Le Sueur and some fellow miners dug 30,000 pounds of the clay out of the bluffs overlooking what became known as the Blue Earth River and took some of it back to France. It did not contain copper but ended up becoming known as fool's copper.

Each July the ten-day *Bend of the River Festival,* featuring canoe races, a parade, and other family activities, reflects Mankato's prominent position at the elbow of the long arm of the Minnesota. Then on the third weekend in September, hundreds of Native Americans and others return to ancient Dakota ceremonial grounds at Land of Memories Park for the *Mahkato Mdewakaton Pow Wow.* For more information on these events and others, contact the Mankato Area Convention and Visitors Bureau by calling (507) 345–4519 (toll-free, 800–657–4733) or visit www.mankato.com.

One of the first buildings encountered upon crossing the Minnesota River to enter the heart of Mankato's business district is an unremarkable structure with surprising historical significance. The simple, modern design of the *Blue Earth County Library,* located at 100 East Main Street, gives no hint that the site on which it stands is one of special importance to the history of the Minnesota Valley and the conclusion of the Dakota conflict of 1862. Yet it was here that thirty-eight defeated Dakota warriors were simultaneously hanged from a huge gallows in the largest mass execution in U.S. history. A statue of a sorrowful Dakota chief and a plaque commemorating the event stand outside the northwest corner of the building.

In the children's wing of the library, past the lobby's impressive boulder-filled fountain, is a special collection of books and memorabilia concerning Mankato-born author Maud Hart Lovelace. The Betsy-Tacy book series that

Lovelace wrote in the 1940s and 1950s centered on her Mankato childhood, and many houses, buildings, and geographical landmarks mentioned in the books are recognizable around town today. Betsy-Tacy enthusiasts can visit the library to look through the Lovelace scrapbooks, listen to a taped interview with the now-deceased author, view a video inspired by the books, and chat with Shirley Lieske, librarian of the children's section and Lovelace expert. A ***Betsy-Tacy walking-tour*** guide is also available.

Not long after its incorporation in 1868, Mankato rose to prominence as an important center for flour milling and limestone quarrying. On Minnesota Highway 68, 5 miles west of town, is an interesting site that pays tribute to both aspects of Mankato's economic history. The ***Seppmann Windmill*** was built by Louis Seppmann in 1862 on top of a hill in what is now ***Minneopa State Park.*** The European-inspired conical shape of the mill's limestone base is pleasing to the eye, and its massive beams and burrstones only hint at the tremendous amount of labor that must have been required to build the now-inoperable structure. Thirty-five-square-foot canvas sails were supported by four huge wooden arms until the mill was afflicted by a series of natural disasters late in the nineteenth century: In 1873 Mr. Seppmann's mill was struck by lightning, losing two arms; then in 1880 a tornado took off two arms again; and finally in 1890 another storm wrecked the mill beyond repair.

Before leaving Minneopa State Park, you may want to visit a spectacular double waterfall, along Minneopa Creek (*Minneopa* is translated from Dakota as "water falling twice"). The 45-foot falls, which are a short hike from a picnic area in the southern part of the park, spill into a steep wooded gorge over a protruding lip of Jordan sandstone.

Faribault County

The little town of ***Winnebago*** in northwestern Faribault County (south of Mankato) derives its name from the fact that from 1855 to 1863 a group of Wisconsin's Winnebago Indians, driven from their traditional lands by whites and by other hostile tribes, lived on a reservation nearby. Native American history and prehistory are the main attraction at the ***Winnebago Historical Society*** as well. From postglacial times—when this continent's first human inhabitants migrated southward from the Bering land bridge about 20,000 years ago—until the first contact between Indians and Europeans in the 1700s, the museum chronicles very effectively the evolution of the area's Indian cultures in a changing natural environment. A headdress that once belonged to Chief Red Cloud and some beautiful Ojibway ceremonial beaded clothing bring the prehistory exhibit into historic times. The free museum, located at 36 North Main Street, is open weekday afternoons.

George Bassett is a farmer. He's also a nationally acclaimed sculptor and painter, and when you visit his *Riverside Farm and Studio,* 5 miles south of Winnebago, his doesn't seem to be an incongruous choice of professions at all.

George seems perfectly at home rummaging around in the old sheep barn and the other farmyard buildings that now house his kiln and cluttered studio. And when you study his lost-wax-method brass sculptures—especially the busts he made for the state capitol rotunda that have as their subjects Hubert Humphrey, Martin Luther King Jr., and environmentalist Sigurd Olson—you'll find they have an earthy quality appropriate for a person who has spent many years working the soil. George welcomes visitors, as long as they call him in advance at (507) 526–2065.

A statue of a different kind awaits those who approach the town of Blue Earth (not to be confused with the county of the same name) from the north on U.S. Highway 169 near Interstate 90. Here, sporting a 48-inch smile and wearing size seventy-eight green fiberglass slippers as he gazes contentedly down on a new shopping center, is a 60-foot rendering of the *Jolly Green Giant.* The Minnesota competition for most kitschy roadside attraction is a hot one—what with the many manifestations of Paul Bunyan and Babe the Blue Ox up north and the various civic animal totems elsewhere. But whatever you may say about all the rest, Blue Earth's entry is surely the greenest—though from envy or inexperience (he's only been here since 1979) it's hard to say.

Cottonwood County

This southwestern Minnesota county received its name because the Cotton-wood River touches the northeast corner of the county. The Sioux Indians called the river *Waraju* for the dense stands of cottonwoods that grew on the banks. Sparsely populated, the county remained so until after the Civil War and the end of the bloody Dakota uprising of 1862. *Windom,* the largest town in the county, has two buildings of historic significance. The courthouse is on the National Register of Historic Places, and the power plant is the first municipal building in the United States to be listed in the Art Deco Registry.

Heritage Village in Mountain Lake, northeast of Windom, is essentially a pioneer village—a museum built of a variety of transplanted historic buildings construed to represent a typical bygone town—but it's one with a couple of unusual twists. First, there are an extensive collection of historic telephone equipment and a general store that is stocked much as it was when it went out of business early in the twentieth century. Second, the area's Mennonite traditions are preserved in the **Heritage Ayte Shtade** (literally, "eating place") restaurant, located on the village grounds, which are found on County Road 1, 1 mile south of Minnesota Highway 60.

The inexpensive meals served by costumed staff at the Ayte Shtade reflect the fact that the Mennonites traveled widely throughout Europe in their search for social environments tolerant of their religious beliefs. Such Mennonite dishes as *moos,* a delicious cold fruit soup; *klups,* a meatloaf patty with vegetables; and *perischki,* dumplings with fruit, reflect ethnic influences from much of northern Europe. The restaurant is open summer evenings (it's closed in winter) Thursday through Saturday and at noon on Sunday.

Though the experience is guaranteed to bring you rather abruptly back to the present, there are two contemporary private residences in Mountain Lake that are well worth a drive by. Both were designed in the 1970s by architect Bruce Goff. The **Glen Harder House** is held to the ground by three large, irregularly shaped piles of stones that also serve as chimneys. Each of these is topped by a large sheet-metal cap with swept-up, pointy corners. These anchors are apparently necessary, as the house itself looks as though it's hovering a few feet off the ground, except at the corners, which are pulled earthward as if held down by spikes. The peaked roof has extended pointy eaves, in the style of the chimney caps, and draws attention to itself from miles around with its bright orange color. To find this creation, go south on County Road 1 from Minnesota Highway 60 just over 4 miles to County Road 13, turn east and go 2 miles, and then turn south on a gravel road, from which you can see the house.

The **Jacob Harder House** has been described by one architectural historian as looking like a "pregnant spaceship . . . sheathed in fish-scale shingles which really look more like chicken feathers." Looked at another way, this circular dwelling, with its two bug-eyed bay windows separated by a proboscis-like bulge in the wall, just might be the visage of some extraterrestrial

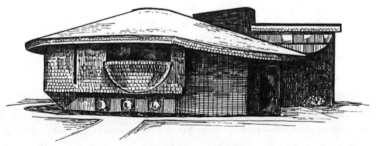

Jacob Harder House

insect. Decide for yourself by driving down Eighth Street between Second and Third Avenues.

Extraterrestrial influences may also come to mind upon visiting the *Jeffers Petroglyphs.* There are nearly 2,000 rock carvings at this site, located several miles east of Jeffers and a couple of miles north of Minnesota Highway 30 on County Road 2. Each figure was chiseled into an exposed ridge of red quartzite bedrock at some undetermined prehistoric date. Together they represent the state's largest group of petroglyphs.

The circular trail begins at a tepee-shaped interpretive center managed by Minnesota Historical Society staff. After picking up a guidebook, visitors are free to wander the quarter-mile walkway, which is surrounded by virgin prairie, at their own pace. Many of the figures encountered seem to have been suggested by aspects of the natural environment, including such animals as bison, bear, wolf, turtle, and elk. Human forms, sometimes wearing what look to be horned headdresses (perhaps similar to those used by Dakota medicine men in historic times), imply the possibility that at least some of the glyphs held spiritual significance. Others are simple geometric designs, hand- or footprints, or so abstract as to defy description. But whatever they may have meant to their creators, it's clear that making these figures required a lot of work. Each of them was pecked into the hard quartzite surface by a pointed rock held in the fist that was struck with a hammerstone.

The site is open daily free of charge during summer and on weekends through September. For more information call (507) 628–5591.

Watonwan County

Named after the Watonwan River, an Indian word meaning "good fish bait" or "where fish abound," this county (east of Cottonwood) has a site related to one of the most infamous events in Minnesota history. On September 21, 1876, Jesse and Frank James, the three Younger brothers, and three other gang members robbed the single bank in Northfield, the only criminal act the gang pulled off in Minnesota. The robbery was also the only real mistake Jesse made as an outlaw.

A gunfight in Northfield killed two gang members, and the James brothers escaped to the Dakota border. Two weeks later the Younger brothers and Charlie Pitts stopped at a farm near St. James for food, but the son of the family recognized them and fled to get help. A posse formed and soon caught up with the gang in the Watonwan River bottoms. In the ensuing gunfight, Pitts died and the Youngers surrendered. *The Younger Brothers Monument* sits one-half mile south of LaSalle on County Road 3. For information call the St. James Chamber of Commerce at (507) 375-3333.

Nobles County

Ask serious windsurfers for their favorite place to ride the wind, and most will say the Columbia River Gorge between Washington and Oregon, Maui, or some big reservoir in the windy western United States. Many midwestern windsurfers probably don't realize that the best wind in the Midwest blows across Lake Okabena in Worthington.

Called "Gorge of the Midwest," this prairie lake has a reputation for strong and consistent winds that some say make it the best windsurfing lake in the Midwest. Entrepreneurs have built electricity-generating windmills throughout southwestern Minnesota, and now windsurfers have discovered this inexhaustible natural resource. For more information call AWOS at (507) 376-9441.

Worthington's **Nobles County Pioneer Village,** more than most other collections of antique, historically furnished buildings in the state, has the feeling of a real town. Practically every institution that a thriving turn-of-the-twentieth-century prairie community would have had is represented among the forty-seven structures. There's a law office, a hospital with an iron lung and a primitive X-ray machine, a train depot, a church, a millinery shop, two life-size grain elevators, a well-equipped schoolhouse, and even a doghouse. Enter most of these establishments, and the furnishings and artifacts arranged casually about create the illusion that everyone has just stepped out to lunch. Walk out on the empty street and you *know* you're in a ghost town.

The village, located just west of the Nobles County Fairgrounds, south of I–90, is open daily in summer for a nominal fee. For further information call (507) 376–3125.

Rock County

As one might expect, Rock County received its name because of rock. In this case, the rock is a ledge of Sioux quartzite (also called red rock or jasper) that starts in Blue Mounds State Park and extends northwest to the town of Jasper. Rock County also has the distinction of being the only county in Minnesota where all its streams flow into the Missouri River, a unique feature in a state dominated by the Mississippi.

Driving north from Luverne on U.S. Highway 75, **Blue Mounds State Park** grabs your attention as soon as it comes into view. In a landscape of largely treeless, boulderless, and flat agricultural fields, suddenly you confront a ridge running at odd angles to the highway, as if a mountain were beginning to emerge from the well-groomed surface of the earth. Against a background of colorful prairie grasses, you can see boulders and protrusions of Sioux quartzite bedrock,

mysteryat bluemound

For avid viewers of the X- Files or anyone who has pondered the origin of Stonehenge and the statues on Easter Island, another such mystery awaits at Blue Mounds State Park. In this prairie park located in Rock County, a 1,250-foot-long line of rocks sits aligned from east to west.

While no one knows who built it or why, on the first day of spring and fall, sunrise and sunset line up on this stone arrangement. Did prehistoric humans align the stones to mark the changing of the seasons? Did visitors from light years away do it to let us know they were here? Or did some locals do it more recently as a hoax? While the first scenario seems the most likely, we'll probably never know definitively. And it's probably better that the mystery remains.

which are covered with lovely constellations of lichens and surrounded by clumps of prickly pear cacti. And as you approach the entrance to the park, a small herd of bison is visible in the distance. The sensation is uncanny: You've returned to the prairie of a hundred years ago.

Approached from the east, as they were by the westward-migrating settlers, the mounds appear bluish against the predominant prairie sky, hence the origin of their name. The face that the Blue Mounds presented to these travelers was a rugged one—a steep escarpment 2.5 miles long and up to 100 feet high, with a ragged line of oak trees at its base. Mound Creek, which flows along the northern edge of the ridge, has been dammed in two places to form small reservoirs; otherwise, little in the park has changed over the centuries.

Hiking trails follow the top and bottom of the cliff and meander across the top of the mounds, offering many vistas of the surrounding countryside and a chance to wallow in the rich prairie environment. Swimming is possible in Lower Mound Lake, and camping and picnic grounds are located nearby. The bison can be viewed from numerous locations. And at the southern edge of the park is an interpretive center containing exhibits on the natural history of the prairie environment.

Pipestone County

The Sioux quartzite formation that gives rise to the geology of Blue Mounds State Park breaks through to the surface again just north of the city of *Pipestone.* But here a second kind of stone, softer than the quartzite and of a distinct reddish color, is visible, too. It is called pipestone, or, after nineteenth-century itinerant artist George Catlin, catlinite. And the site now known as *Pipestone National Monument* has for hundreds of years been a sacred quarry from which raw material was obtained to produce the stone pipes so widely associated with Native Americans.

Despite whatever animosities existed between tribes, throughout most of its history the pipestone quarry was considered neutral territory to which Native Americans from as far as 1,000 miles away would travel on foot and remove the soft clay stone in peace. Pipe makers still quarry and work the stone today, though since 1928 the land has been under National Park Service jurisdiction.

A visit to the monument begins at the interpretive center, where a film on the history of the site is complemented by exhibits of pipestone artifacts, a gift shop, and craft demonstrations by native carvers. A three-quarter-mile footpath leads from this building through the quarry grounds. The trail winds through stands of trees (which have matured in the absence of the once-frequent prairie fires) along Pipestone Creek to beautiful Winnewissa Falls, which was formed where the creek pours over a quartzite ledge. Several quarry pits are passed along the way, appearing as gashes in the ground surrounded by discarded quartzite rubble. Notations chiseled into a trailside boulder are evidence of cartographer Joseph Nicollet's expedition in 1838. Even bird-watching is excellent in this special place.

Pipestone National Monument is found to the west of US 75, adjacent to the north side of the city of Pipestone. Open daily there is a small admission charge.

If you're interested in finding some distinctive overnight accommodations in Pipestone, the hundred-year-old **Historic Calumet Inn** is worth

The Missouri River Connection

It's unfortunate that most people think of southwestern Minnesota as the epitome of flyover country. Although the scenery doesn't have the breathtaking qualities of the north shore of Lake Superior or the bluff country of southeastern Minnesota or the endless vistas of green common to the thick forests of northern Minnesota, the rolling hills that stretch to the horizon have the big sky views more common to the High Plains than the Corn Belt. This part of Minnesota also has a subtle geographic feature that some travelers may find surprising.

While the vast majority of streams and rivers in Minnesota drain into the Mississippi River, Hudson Bay, or Lake Superior, a handful of waterways in the southwestern corner of the state flow into the Missouri River. The largest of these is the Rock River, which originates on the Coteau des Prairies and is the only major stream in Minnesota that drains into the Missouri. So the next time you happen to drive through southwestern Minnesota on your way to somewhere else, enjoy the scenery and take an hour or so to stop, look at, and contemplate some of the unique characteristics of Minnesota's portion of the Great Plains.

exploring. The handsome stone building, located at 104 Main Street, has a crenellated parapet and a large arch above the entrance. The Calumet (507–825–5871; www.calumetinn.com) is moderately priced and comfortably appointed with antique and antique-reproduction Victorian furnishings. A lounge and restaurant with inexpensive to moderately priced American food round out the offerings.

Murray County

When the railroad finally reached the town of *Currie* in 1901, it was faced with a little problem. Like many small Minnesota towns that were off the main rail routes, but still large enough (or politically savvy enough) to warrant being served by the iron horse, Currie was at the end of a spur line. And, having made the 38-mile jaunt from Bingham Lake to the southeast, the engines needed some way to get turned around for their return trip.

The solution was to build a turntable—a section of track resting on a pivot upon which the engine and coal car could be swung around 180 degrees by the efforts of a single worker. When it was built, the Currie turntable was an unremarkable bit of engineering similar to many others of the time. But today it is one of only two still in existence in the state, making the *End-o-Line Railroad Park and Museum* an unusual attraction.

Once you're through marveling at how one puny human could spin a locomotive as if it were a top, there's much more to see in the depot and engine shed. The shed, which originally housed locomotives that weren't in use, is full of antique railroad equipment and memorabilia, such as a full set of section foreman's tools and a couple of track inspector vehicles—including the trusty velocipede.

Nearby, the depot has been restored in detail to its former glory, incorporating such touches as the strategic placement of a tobacco tin in the telegraph set to improve its reception. The building's two waiting rooms reflect a tradition of segregation by sex that was in effect until the 1920s. Under this Victorian arrangement, the men were able to spit tobacco and the women to nurse children without compunction or embarrassment. The depot's baggage room has been devoted to an outstanding HO-scale model train display that depicts the Currie railroad yards as they looked in the 1940s. Outside there's a restored caboose to be explored, the reconstructed Currie Store (the first general store in the area), and the region's first school.

The End-o-Line Museum is open free of charge daily during summer and by special arrangement at other times. For information call the End-o-Line Railroad Park and Museum, (507) 763–3708 or visit www.endoline.com.

Lake Shetek State Park, 2 miles north of Currie on County Road 37, is in the center of what is commonly known as the Great Oasis—a lovely hardwood grove surrounded by a network of lakes amid the dominance of farm and prairie. Within the 1,175-acre park are no fewer than five small lakes and ponds, complemented by extensive footage on the shore of the much larger Lake Shetek. Thus there's lots to do for water-sports enthusiasts besides the usual state park fare of hiking, camping, and picnicking.

But Shetek is also the memorial site of one of the more gruesome encounters between Dakota and settlers in the conflict of 1862. Since 1987—the war's 125th anniversary, which was commemorated as the Year of Reconciliation—staff at the park have held an annual ***Shetek Revisited*** program over a late-August weekend to illuminate the complex tragedy that led to the killing of eleven settlers and several Indians at Slaughter Slough. The program includes a bus tour of sites related to this event. For more information write Lake Shetek State Park, Route 1, Box 164, Currie 56123 or call (507) 763–3256 or, toll-free from within Minnesota, (800) 766–6000 and ask for Department of Natural Resources.

Places to Stay in the Prairieland

LITCHFIELD AND WILLMAR
(27 miles west)
(area code 320)

AmericInn,
1525 Highway 12 East,
Litchfield;
693–1500

AmericInn,
2404 Highway 12 East,
Willmar;
231–1962

Comfort Inn,
2200 Highway 12 East,
Willmar;
231–2601

Holiday Inn,
2100 Highway 12 East,
Willmar;
235–6060

Scotwood Motel,
1017 East Highway 12,
Litchfield;
693–2496

MONTEVIDEO
(area code 320)

Country Inn & Suites,
1805 East Highway 7;
269–8000

Sportsmen Inn,
West Highway 212;
269–8889

Viking Motel,
East Highway 7;
269–6545

GRANITE FALLS
(area code 320)

Super 8 Motel,
845 West Highway 212;
564–4075

REDWOOD FALLS
(area code 507)

Dakota Inn,
Highway 101 North;
637–5444

Morton Inn,
Highways 19 and 71,
Morton;
697–6205

Redwood Valley Lodge,
1382 East Bridge Street;
644–5700

NEW ULM/SLEEPY EYE
(area code 507)

**Deutsche Strasse
Bed & Breakfast,**
404 South German Street,
New Ulm;
354–2005

Holiday Inn,
2101 South Broadway,
New Ulm;
359–2941

Inn of the Seven Gables,
1100 East Main Street,
Sleepy Eye;
794–5390

Super 8 Motel,
1901 South Broadway,
New Ulm;
359–2400

**W.W. Smith Inn
Bed & Breakfast,**
101 Linden Street
Southwest, Sleepy Eye;
794–5661

MANKATO
(area code 507)

**Butler House
Bed & Breakfast,**
704 South Broad Street;
387–5055

Comfort Inn,
131 Apache Place;
388–5107

Holiday Inn Downtown,
101 East Main Street;
345–1234

Super 8 Motel
Highways 169 & 14;
387–4041

BLUE EARTH
(area code 507)

AmericInn,
Highway 169 and I–90;
526–4215

Fering's Guest House,
708 North Main;
526–5054

Super 8 Motel,
Highway 169 North;
526–7376

WINDOM
(area code 507)

Super 8 Motel,
Highway 60 & 71 South;
831–1120

Windom Family Inn,
Highway 60 & 71 North;
831–3111

WORTHINGTON
(area code 507)

AmericInn,
1475 Darling Drive;
376–4500

Days Inn,
207 Oxford Street;
376–6155

Holiday Inn Express,
1250 Ryan's Road;
372–2333

LUVERNE
(area code 507)

Comfort Inn,
801 South Kniss
(Highway 75 South);
283–9488

Super 8 Motel,
I–90 & Highway 75;
283–9541

PIPESTONE
(area code 507)

Arrow Motel,
Highway 75 North;
825–3331

Calumet Inn,
104 West Main Street;
825–5871

Super 8 Motel,
605 Eighth Street Southeast;
825–4217

Places to Eat in the Prairieland

LITCHFIELD
(area code 320)

Dairy Queen,
Highway 12 West;
693–2001

King's Wok (Oriental),
305 Sibley Avenue North;
693–2259

Main Street Cafe
(American),
226 Sibley Avenue North;
693–9067

Original Farmers' Daughter
(American),
915 Highway 12 East;
693–8211

Pizza Ranch,
201 Sibley Avenue North;
693–9393

Taco John's,
719 East Depot Street;
693–3554

WILLMAR
(area code 320)

Frieda's Cafe (American),
511 Benson Avenue West;
235–2865

Green Mill Pizza,
2100 Highway 12 East
(in Holiday Inn);
233–2301

Northern Grounds
(coffee),
1001 South First Street;
235–9775

SELECTED CHAMBERS OF COMMERCE

Blue Earth Area
Chamber of Commerce
(507) 526–2916

Granite Falls Area
Chamber of Commerce
(320) 564–4039

Le Sueur Area
Chamber of Commerce
(507) 665–2501

Lincoln County Promotion & Tourism
(800) 442–9854

Litchfield Chamber of Commerce
(320) 693–8184

Luverne Area Chamber of Commerce
(507) 283–4061

Mankato Area
Chamber of Commerce
(800) 657–4733

Montevideo Area Convention &
Visitors Bureau
(800) 269–5527

New Ulm Chamber of Commerce
(888) 463–9856

Pipestone Convention &
Visitors Bureau
(800) 336–6125

Redwood Falls Tourism &
Convention Bureau
(800) 657–7070

Sleepy Eye Area
Chamber of Commerce
(800) 290–0588

Windom Area
Chamber of Commerce
(800) 794–6366

Worthington Area Convention &
Visitors Bureau
(800) 729–2919

Panda Garden Buffet,
1305 First Street South;
235–1288

Perkins Family Restaurant
(American),
2645 Business Highway 71
South;
235–5957

MONTEVIDEO
(area code 320)

Art's Dairy Freeze,
1307 Black Oak Avenue;
269–6282

Grand Buffet (Chinese),
207 North First Street;
269–6888

Jake's Pizza,
207 South First Street;
269–2115

Java River (coffee),
210 South First Street;
269–7106

Trailway's (American),
605 Highway 212 West;
269–8645

Valentino's Restaurant
(American),
110 South First Street;
269–5106

GRANITE FALLS
(area code 320)

DeToy's (family),
845 Highway 212 West;
564–2280

The Grinder (coffee, lunch),
176 Highway 212 East;
564–4244

Jimmy's Pizza,
776 Prentice Street;
564–3222

Subway,
601 West Highway 212;
564–1842

REDWOOD FALLS
(area code 507)

Calf Fiend Cafe (American),
516 East Bridge Street;
637–3728

Chumly's Burger & Brew,
Highways 19 & 71;
637–2885

Fa Choy,
104 Beachwood Lane;
637–8144

Pizza Ranch,
1370 East Bridge Street;
644–5936

Taco John's,
620 East Bridge Street;
637–8275

NEW ULM
(area code 507)

Backerei, The (coffee),
27 South Minnesota;
354–6011

Corner Stone Coffee,
213 South Minnesota;
354–5552

Doug-Out (American),
706 North German;
359–2018

Joni's Restaurant
(American),
24 North Minnesota Street;
359–2018

Kaiserhoff (German),
221 North Minnesota;
359–2071

Main Jiang House,
206 North Minnesota;
354–1218

Taco John's,
1301 South Broadway;
354–8226

Ulmer Cafe
(breakfast, lunch),
115 North Minnesota;
354–8122

SELECTED WEB SITES IN THE PRAIRIELAND

**Blue Earth Area
Chamber of Commerce**
www.chamber.blue-earth.mn.us

Granite Falls Information
www.granitefalls.com

**Le Sueur Area
Chamber of Commerce**
www.lesueurchamber.org

Litchfield Chamber of Commerce
www.litch.com

Luverne Area Chamber of Commerce
www.luvernemn.com

Mankato Area Chamber of Commerce
www.mankato.com

Milan Visitors Information
www.milanmn.com

**Montevideo Conventions &
Visitors Bureau**
www.montechamber.com

New Ulm Chamber of Commerce
www.newulm.com

**Pipestone Convention &
Visitors Bureau**
www.pipestoneminnesota.com
redwoodfalls.org

Willmar Convention & Visitors Bureau
www.seeyouinwillmar.com

Windom Area Chamber of Commerce
www.winwacc.com

**Worthington Area Convention &
Visitors Bureau**
www.wgtn.net

MANKATO
(area code 507)

Applebee's (American),
1900 Adams Street;
386–1010

Cold Stone Creamery
(ice cream),
1600 Warren Street;
344–8152

The Country Pub,
Highway 22 North;
931–5888

Dairy Queen East,
521 Hope Street;
345–1575

Great Wall Restaurant
(Chinese),
1802 Commerce Drive;
625–5999

Jake's Stadium Pizza,
1614 Monks Avenue;
345–5420

Maggie's Cafe & Saloon
(American),
1600 Monks Avenue;
625–2659

Mexican Village,
1630 Madison Avenue;
387–4455

Neighbor's Italian Bistro,
1812 South Riverfront Drive;
625–6776

BLUE EARTH
(area code 507)

Cedar Inn (American),
326 North Grove Street;
526–5612

Dairy Queen,
Highway 169 North;
526–5402

Hamilton's Restaurant
(American),
209 South Main;
526–3287

Pizza Hut,
1511 Domes Drive;
526–4646

Subway,
702 Eezy Street;
526–2728

WINDOM
(area code 507)

China Restaurant,
Tenth Street and Third
Avenue;
831–5998

Dino's Diner,
2270 Highway 60 East;
831–1183

Godfather's Pizza,
South Highways 60 & 71;
831–4836

Hardee's,
Highway 60 and 71;
831–3429

Taco Depot,
904 Second Avenue;
831–1827

Towne Perk, The
(American,)
965 Third Avenue;
831–0116

WORTHINGTON
(area code 507)

Bangkok Cuisine,
1719 East Avenue;
376–9009

Blue Line Cafe (American),
Highway 60 NE;
372–4038

Coffee Nook, The
(coffee, light lunch),
212 Tenth Street;
376–3330

El Taco Restaurant,
418 Tenth Street;
372–5039

Java Nau,
1304 Oxford Street;
376–4455

Michael's Restaurant
(American),
1305 Spring;
376–3187

Pizza Hut,
1551 North Humiston
Avenue;
372–5512

Top Asian Cafe,
304 Tenth Street;
372–6119

LUVERNE
(area code 507)

Coffey Haus, The
(coffee, sandwiches),
111 East Main Street;
283–8676

Country Kitchen
(American),
South Highway 75;
283–4458

Magnolia Steak House
(American),
South Highway 75;
283–9161

Pizza Ranch,
110 East Main Street;
283–2379

Taco John's,
South Highway 75;
283–4562

PIPESTONE
(area code 507)

Dar's Pizza,
Highway 30 and
Eighth Avenue Southwest;
825–4261

Gannon's (American),
Highway 75 & Highway 23;
825–3114

Lange's Cafe (American),
Highway 75 & Highway 23;
825–4488

Pizza Hut,
413 Eighth Avenue
Southeast;
825–5886

Villager Restaurant
(American),
Highway 75 North;
825–5242

Roads to Take

Highway 23 from
Lynd to Pipestone

U.S. Highway 75 from
Luverne to Pipestone

U.S Highway 212 from
Granite Falls to Montevideo

Highway 7 from Beardsley to
Ortonville

Highway 27 from Browns
Valley to Wheaton

Minnesota River Valley
Scenic Byway (call
800–463–3704 for maps)

WAY, WAY OFF THE BEATEN PATH

Box Elder Bug Days,
mid-September, Minneota

Birthplace of Sears,
North Redwood County
on Highway 101

King Turkey Days,
Second Saturday after Labor Day,
Worthington

Red River Country

This region covers the northwestern corner of Minnesota and has a landscape of dramatic contrasts. The Red River Valley covers the western and northern parts of this region and features some of the flattest landscape found anywhere in the world. The valley is not a valley in the true sense of the word because the river meanders north in a channel that sits only a few feet below the surrounding rich farmland.

East of the flat valley floor, rolling hills left by glaciers form a dramatically different landscape. Tabletop flat becomes endless rolling hills of all shapes and sizes, mile after mile of unbroken cultivated land becomes forest, and a landscape of scattered rivers and lakes turns into one of countless lakes and marshes. The change is not sudden, but it leaves no doubt that you have visited two areas of distinctive geologic characteristics.

Douglas County

Due to its proximity to the Red River Valley, you would think that the lakes and rivers of this popular vacation destination would form part of the watershed of the Red River. But thanks to glaciation, the waters of Douglas County drain north and east to eventually join the Mississippi and south to join the

RED RIVER COUNTRY

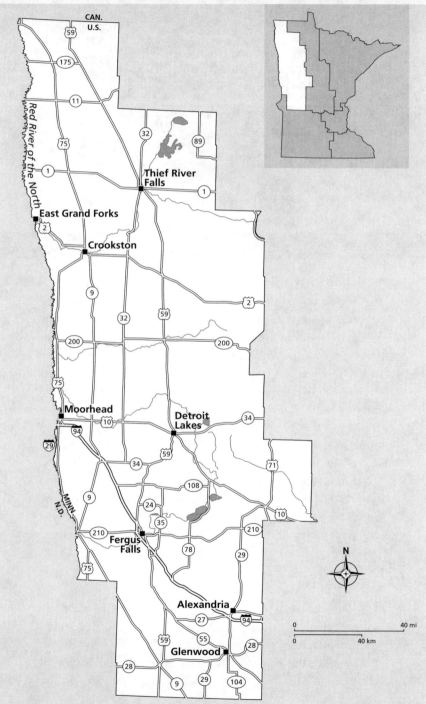

CAN.
U.S.

59

175

11

32

89

75

1

Thief River
Falls

1

East Grand Forks

2

Crookston

9

32

59

200

200

75

Moorhead

10

Detroit
Lakes

34

94

59

29

34

71

9

108

24

10

35

210

210

210

Fergus
Falls

78

29

75

Alexandria

94

27

59

55

28

Glenwood

28

9

29

104

Red River of the North

MINN.

N.D.

N

0   40 mi
0   40 km

Minnesota. Again the often subtle differences in what we see prove the role glaciers had in shaping the landscape of Minnesota.

Standing in the middle of downtown *Alexandria*—an attractive town of 8,800 surrounded by numerous lakes and resorts—is a brightly painted statue of a huge Viking whose shield is inscribed with a brazen claim: ALEXANDRIA/ BIRTHPLACE OF AMERICA. This dubious geographical declaration was inspired by an object housed across the street inside the *Runestone Museum.*

The story goes that in 1897 a large, flat stone with a long inscription of unknown characters was discovered entwined in the roots of an old tree in the nearby community of Kensington. The man who claimed to have found the stone, a Swedish immigrant farmer named Olof Ohaman, forwarded a copy of the inscription to a Scandinavian languages professor at the University of Minnesota. The professor and his colleagues, unable to render a translation of the script, concluded that it was a fraud. But nine years later a historian of Norwegian immigration, Hjalmar Holand, succeeded in deciphering the runic script and became convinced that the Kensington runestone is proof that the Vikings predated Columbus's journey to the New World by at least a hundred years.

Though the stone's authenticity has never enjoyed widespread scientific support, for some residents of Alexandria there exists not even a shadow of a doubt. A visit to the Runestone Museum—where the inscription is translated as describing the activities of a group of "8 Goths [Swedes] and 22 Norwegians" on an "exploration journey from Vinland [the East Coast] through the west" in 1362—will allow you to make up your own mind. The Discovery Room, where the stone is on display, features a video about the Runestone, as well as Viking artifacts. Other exhibits detail the more recent history of Douglas County, including a series of historic log and wood-frame buildings grouped together under the banner of Fort Alexandria. The museum, located

AUTHOR'S FAVORITES

Glacial Lakes State Park at
Glenwood/Starbuck,
(320) 239–2860

Lake country of Otter Tail and Becker
Counties

Lake Minnewaska at Glenwood,
(800) 304–5666

Maplewood State Park,
Pelican Rapids,
(218) 863–8383

Phelps Mill,
Phelps (near Fergus Falls),
(800) 423–4571

TOP ANNUAL EVENTS IN RED RIVER COUNTRY

Polar Fest,
Detroit Lakes, late February,
(800) 542–3992

Detroit Lakes Festival of Birds,
mid-May,
(800) 542–3992

Scandinavian Hjemkomst Festival,
Moorhead, late June,
(800) 235–7654

Ox Cart Days,
Crookston, mid-August,
(800) 809–5997

at 206 North Broadway, is open daily and charges a small admission fee. Call (320) 763–3160 for more information.

When you've had enough musing about the distant past, you may want to stroll south a couple of blocks to *Old Broadway,* a contemporary eatery in an elegantly refurbished nineteenth-century home that offers outstanding food and drink. Normally you just don't find a restaurant like this in a town the size of Alexandria: The delicious nouvelle American cuisine is all made of fresh ingredients, and the late-Victorian decor is resplendent with imported antiques, including an ornate hand-carved hardwood English bar. In summer there's outdoor seating beside a landscaped garden. Prices are moderate, and reservations can be made by calling (320) 763–3999. Old Broadway is located at 319 Broadway, Alexandria.

Pope County

An imposing sight greets travelers arriving in the town of Glenwood from the north or east. The flat roads that pass through the Bonanza Valley, a sand plain formed by a melting glacier, suddenly drop down a steep ridge to Lake Minnewaska. As the thirteenth largest in Minnesota, the lake lies between the flat landscape of glacial outwash and the hilly land of countless glacial deposits of rock and gravel. Surrounded by a ridge that alternates between steep and gradual, the lake doesn't seem to belong in this area of farms. Obviously the glaciers thought otherwise.

Glacial Lakes State Park, located 5 miles south of Starbuck, provides visitors with an exceptional display of the effects glaciers had on this part of Minnesota. Besides the distinct geological formations, the park also sits in a transition zone between prairie and forest. Only one-tenth of 1 percent of the original Minnesota prairie remains, and this park has a section of it. For more information call the park at (320) 239–2860.

The Glacial Ridge Trail provides another way to see the glacier-scoured landscape of west-central Minnesota. This scenic route follows highways and county roads for 220 miles through five counties and traces a ridge left by the last glacier to cover this region. For more information on the trail, call the Glenwood Chamber of Commerce at (800) 304–5666.

When the flour mill was built along the banks of the Chippewa River in the little community of Terrace in 1903, there was trouble in the air. The railroad had passed Terrace by, and with it went the main source of hope and prosperity for Terrace's residents: a mill that had been built by the town fathers in 1870. The new mill was constructed in a doomed attempt to revive the community's economy.

After decades of observing a steady decline in population, the post office finally abandoned Terrace in the early 1970s and the little hamlet was threatened with complete oblivion. Then came a startlingly successful effort to restore the decrepit old mill.

Several times each summer, tens of thousands of people descend on ***Terrace Mill*** for some of the most innovative arts and music festivals to be found anywhere in the state. The internationally acclaimed Minnesota Orchestra has performed an outdoor concert, beside the wooden structure, that culminated in a stirring rendition of Tchaikovsky's "1812 Overture," replete with the firing of sixteen historic cannons. Minnesota's premier theatrical company, the Guthrie, has used the mill's portable stage and nineteenth-century atmosphere for such period productions as the Civil War–era *Red Badge of Courage*. Terrace Mill is also the site of an annual Heritage Festival Art Show in mid-June that showcases Norwegian-inspired rosemaling painting; classes and seminars are offered during the festival in this and other crafts. And each season ends with a concert in late August and

namethatglacier

Most of Minnesota bears the marks of glaciers, the last of which covered much of the state about 10,000 years ago. Although it's not easy for most of us to identify the landscape formations left behind, some are easier to see than others. Some of the more common glacial features in Minnesota include:

Drumlins—a long hill made of glacial debris.

Erratic—a rock carried and deposited by a glacier.

Esker—a long, wormlike ridge formed by debris-laden meltwater. Eskers probably mark the channels of subglacial streams.

Kame—a conical hill of glacial debris deposited in contact with glacial ice. Imagine a snow cone tipped upside down.

Kettle—a depression (which usually becomes a lake or marsh) that formed when a block of ice melted after separating from the glacier and being covered by glacial debris.

an ***Oktoberfest*** celebration and Fiddle Contest the first Sunday in October, which draws fiddlers from far and wide.

Tours of the now fully restored building are given daily during summer (a small donation is requested). Terrace's Historic General Store has been renovated, too, and is now stocked with dry goods and gifts. Restoration of the miller's home and the town's original log cabin qualified most of the community for inclusion on the National Register of Historic Places.

For more information about events at Terrace Mill, write the Terrace Mill Foundation, Terrace Mill 56380 or call (320) 278–3728.

Grant County

Herman is exactly the kind of quiet hamlet preferred by Minnesota's legendary stoic, hard-working bachelor Norwegian farmers. In fact, until recently the tradition had become so entrenched that seeing a woman about town was nearly as unlikely as spying a man without a seed cap. Then the national media decreed there was news in the fact that a town existed where bachelors outnumbered the womenfolk by evolutionarily suicidal odds, and eligible women began to show up in Herman's pool halls and taverns from as far away as Montana and California.

Upon their arrival some of these visitors discovered something else worth noting, namely, a bed-and-breakfast experience unlike any other at Gordon and Gay Ekberg's ***Lawndale Farm,*** 5 miles east of town. Granted, the sort of cozy accommodations offered in the Ekbergs' little two-bedroom wood-frame cottage—which was built by Gordon's grandparents in 1900 and originally sheltered a family of nine—and the delicious Belgian waffles served up for breakfast might be duplicated elsewhere. But the remarkable array of waterfowl from all corners of the earth that thrive in the farm's natural breeding grounds is rare indeed.

Fifty species of ducks, geese, and swans from every continent—totaling more than 800 birds—can be seen in natural-habitat pens and swimming about in an open marsh. Endearing newborns are hatched in large incubators, and guests are welcome to cuddle them in their hands. Surrounding the farmstead are hiking trails that wind through acres of restored prairie.

Some of the nation's top wildlife artists frequent Lawndale Farm to study and photograph such birds as the Siberian red-breasted goose and the brilliantly colored mandarin wood duck. Prints by many of these masters are sold at the Lawndale Gallery, located next to the guest cottage in a converted granary.

Overnight rates at Lawndale Farm are moderate. For more information write Lawndale Farm, Route 2, Box 50, Herman 56248 or call (320) 677–2687.

Otter Tail County

This popular vacation area sits in a scenic pocket on the edge of the Red River Valley. Many lakes dot the rolling landscape, as fields of corn, soybeans, and forage grasses form a patchwork with thick stands of stately hardwoods. Some archaeologists think that humans may have lived here as long as 10,000 years ago along the shores of Glacial Lake Pelican. Today the glacier-scoured landscape attracts many visitors to this watery playground.

Though newspaper magnate William Randolph Hearst Jr. may not have been intending to start a trend when he imported the first South American llamas to the United States in the early 1920s, these graceful, woolly domesticated pack animals have found a fast-growing niche in American society. A visit to **Horseshoe Valley Llamas,** 3 miles south of Fergus Falls on County Road 25, gives travelers a sense of why.

A couple of dozen llamas serenely chew their cuds while monitoring with an attentive gaze everything that transpires in the surrounding pasture. They have long necks, skinny legs, dignified faces, and slender, curved ears that resemble bananas. Like their distant cousin, the camel, llamas walk with a peculiar lateral gait, swinging both legs on one side forward simultaneously. With one touch it's easy to see why their wonderfully soft wool, which makes

Transition Zones

Besides having thousands of lakes and a landscape shaped by glaciers, Minnesota also has a geographic feature unique to this area. Unlike any other state, Minnesota straddles two transition zones: one that runs north and south, with another running east and west. The zone that runs north-south divides the state into prairie and forest, with the northern part of this line cutting through Red River Country.

Much of western Minnesota has the traits of the prairies, including few trees or lakes, less precipitation, and flat to gently rolling terrain. One area near Granite Falls in western Minnesota even has cactus. Moving east through the zone, rainfall increases, thick forest replaces grassland, river valleys get deeper, and lakes and wetlands begin to dominate the landscape.

On the Minnesota prairies, Indians hunted buffalo and traveled by horse, while settlers built sod houses as they turned the fertile soil. In the forested eastern and northern parts of Minnesota, Indians used canoes to travel through the labyrinth of lakes and rivers, while whites exploited the vast tracts of huge white pine to form a lumber boom. Even today, the sizes of farms and cities reflect the type of geography, the amount of yearly precipitation, and the proximity of large rivers suitable for transportation.

the animals' bodies look much bigger than they actually are, is prized for making fine wool sweaters. Call (218) 736–4707 to arrange for a visit.

When you find your way back to **Fergus Falls** from Horseshoe Valley Llamas, awaiting you is one of the best county-history museums in the state. Exhibits at the **Otter Tail County Historical Society Museum,** located at 1110 West Lincoln, are laid out in a labyrinth of passageways that traverse the distance from early prehistory to the present—all within the confines of a single large new building.

The well-interpreted exhibits begin with the glacial events that helped give Otter Tail County its lake-strewn character. This sequence is followed by interesting displays on the Dakota and Ojibway, activities related to the fur trade, a scaled-down logging operation, and an impressive section on agricultural history that includes a life-size harvest scene in a shimmering "field" of real wheat. Victorian lifestyles are displayed in a winding "street" of homes and diverse businesses, each appointed in detail with appropriate furnishings and artifacts. By offering such a fine representation of Otter Tail County's past, the museum, which is open daily year-round, also gives visitors a good overview of western Minnesota history. A small fee is charged to adults for admission. Call (218) 736–6038 for more information.

One of the pinnacles in Minnesota's less-than-alpine landscape is found about 25 miles southeast of Fergus Falls, near the tiny town of Urbank. **Inspiration Peak,** as the conical hilltop is known, is part of what geologists call a terminal moraine that was formed by ice-age glaciers depositing quantities of sediment in a formation recognized today as the Leaf Hills. Along the wooded flanks of Inspiration Peak is a wayside rest and picnic area accessible from County Road 38 about 10 miles east of Minnesota Highway 78. Two asphalt footpaths ascend from the parking lot somewhat steeply to a clearing at the summit, 1,750 feet above sea level and 400 feet above Spitzer Lake immediately to the west.

The grand view from the top is well worth the half-mile round-trip hike. The Leaf Hills, covered with oak and other hardwoods, run in a rugged north-south line. To the east and west, rolling forest- and farmland stretch to the horizons. More than a half-dozen lakes are visible, and numerous grain silos reflect the sunlight.

In mid-July each year, artists gather for the Phelps Mill Summer Festival in the tiny town of Phelps, 25 miles northeast of Fergus Falls on County Road 45. At the center of this celebration sits **Phelps Mill** itself, which is open for self-guided tours throughout the summer season. From 1889 to 1931 turbines in this well-preserved wooden structure drew power from the clear-flowing Otter Tail River to grind wheat into flour. Farmers brought their wheat to Phelps from

Kames

Red River Country lies in a geographical transition zone between Minnesota's western prairies and eastern forests. Maplewood State Park, located near Pelican Rapids, provides an excellent example of a transition landscape. It sits in the Alexandria Moraine, a band of glacial drift 200 miles long by 10 to 20 miles wide. The park offers a startling change of scenery, as the terrain changes from flat to dramatically rolling.

Approaching the park, the observant visitor will notice many cone-shaped hills, known as *kames,* Maplewood has one of the best displays in Minnesota of this distinctive geologic formation. If you drive on Otter Tail County Road 24 along the southern edge of the park, not only will you see an awesome collection of kames, but you will also find some unusual road signs marking places where the road curves around these huge mounds. In an age where technology seems to carve through any hill or under any mountain, it's refreshing to see that humans deferred to nature and rerouted a road.

up to a hundred miles away, often seeking overnight accommodations at the mill's "Farmers Roost" while waiting to collect their flour. The mill remained popular during the heyday of the Non-Partisan League, when farmers didn't want to patronize the large mills owned by "capitalists" in Minneapolis. Finally the drought of the 1930s brought an end to milling activities at Phelps.

Now the mill, which is complemented by a historic country store and log cabin, is part of the Otter Tail County park system. Swimming, picnicking, and limited camping are possible just downstream of the dam. For more information about the park and the arts festival, write the Fergus Falls Chamber of Commerce, P.O. Box 868, Fergus Falls 56538; call (218) 763–6951 or (800) 726–8959; or visit www.fergusfalls.com.

One of the ethnic groups well represented in eastern Otter Tail County is the Finns, and a good place to explore their heritage is **Finn Creek Museum,** found off Minnesota Highway 106 about 3 miles southeast of New York Mills (look for signs on Highway 106). The museum consists of a complete farmstead that was built by Siffert and Wilhelmina Tapio in 1900.

The family's house—originally a one-room log building that was later expanded and covered with wood siding—is furnished much as it would have been at the turn of the twentieth century. A hand pump supplies water in the kitchen, wood stoves heat each room, and straw mattresses cover the beds, including one on an adjacent porch that was slept in by a tuberculosis-afflicted daughter whose treatment called for lots of fresh air. Among the many smaller household items displayed is a sinister-looking collection of bloodletting

Finn Creek Museum

equipment, including a razorlike instrument for making incisions and several hollowed-out animal horns that were sucked on to draw blood.

Outside there's a well with a large hand-hewn beam serving as a counter-balance to the bucket—an arrangement known in Finnish as a *vintti kaivo.* Other buildings include a blacksmith shop, two small barns full of historic farm implements, a summer kitchen, and two log saunas, one of which is roofed in birchbark and called a *savu,* or smoke, sauna. This building was heated by a chimneyless wood stove. Once the rocks surrounding the stove were hot, the building was aired out and used for its intended purposes—which included birthing babies.

An annual **Summer Folk Festival,** celebrating Finnish culture with tradi-tional music, craft demonstrations, and food, is held at Finn Creek the fourth weekend in August. A slight fee is charged for this event; otherwise, the museum, which is open afternoons in summer, charges no admission.

Clay County

Not far over the Otter Tail County line on Minnesota Highway 32 is a tiny ham-let called Rollag, which consists primarily of three institutions. First is the ***Rol-lag Store,*** a wooden structure with peeling paint that is set back into the bushes next to an ancient kerosene pump. This quintessential general store provides its community with just about anything anyone could want that isn't found at Rollag's second institution: a large and thoroughly modern farm-imple-ment dealership. Finally, just north of "downtown" on a dusty hilltop is a sprawling collection of mismatched buildings, unrecognizable pieces of heavy iron machinery, and a couple of steam railroad engines that seem, by the lay of the tracks, to go no place special.

On Labor Day weekend each year, this ghost town, known locally as Threshermen's Hill, comes roaring to life for the **Western Minnesota Steam Threshers Reunion,** an event that some claim is the largest gathering of steam-engine enthusiasts in the world (that's what they'll tell you at the Rollag Store, anyway). In truth, up to 80,000 people converge on little Rollag for a celebration that includes just about every artifact ever made that ran on steam. There are steam threshers, of course, three steam-powered "Trains to Nowhere," merry-go-rounds that run on steam, steam-powered sawmills, and several monstrous steam engines with whirring flywheels up to 17 feet in diameter. There are also more than a hundred antique tractors engaged in pulling matches, a pioneer farm, an antique flour mill, traditional craft demonstrations, shows of long-outdated fashions, threshermen's breakfasts, and a fiddlers' jamboree each evening.

There is a modest fee for adults to participate in this gala festival; for children, it's free. For more information go to www.rollag.com for a complete listing of exhibits, schedules, etc.

Driving from Rollag toward Moorhead, it is impossible to escape noticing how very flat the landscape becomes—a sign that you've entered the valley of the Red River of the North. The river's floodplain has some of the most fertile agricultural land on Earth. And for those who are interested in learning how modern-day farmers work the land in this area, three-hour farm tours are offered through **Agricultural Expeditions USA,** a program of the Fargo-Moorhead Convention and Visitor's Bureau. These tours, scheduled weekday mornings Memorial Day through Labor Day, involve a visit to one of the area's family-owned dairy or sugar-beet farms and a tour of an agricultural products

The Red River

Although most rivers flood at one time or another, few do it with the vengeance of the Red River. In this land of incredibly fertile soil and agricultural bounty, two geographic features cause the meandering and mostly insignificant Red to change from mild-mannered to malevolent.

First, because the river flows north, when the spring melt starts upstream (which in this case is south), the lower reaches remain frozen, and the water has nowhere to go but out of its banks. Second, the Red flows in a small channel through the cutting board–flat lake bottom of Glacial Lake Agassiz, and when it floods the water spreads out over hundreds of square miles. In the devastating flood of 1997, the swollen river reached a width of more than 30 miles. Someone once said that the Red is the only river that runs amok while standing still.

processing plant. Reservations, which should be secured at least a day in advance, can be made by calling the visitors' bureau at (701) 282–3653 or (800) 235–7654.

Despite the fact that almost anywhere you look in the Red River Valley you'll see row after row of crops running toward the horizon, not all the land around Moorhead is dedicated to farming. Here and there, patches of restored prairie have been maintained, partly in an effort to preserve environmental enclaves for the performance of one of the most unusual spectacles to be witnessed in Minnesota's animal kingdom.

The ***courtship of the prairie chicken*** is a fascinating annual event in these parts that demands certain rigors of those who want to see it. Having made the necessary arrangements well beforehand, you must arise an hour or so before dawn and find your way to a "blind"—a cubelike canvas tent staked securely to the ground—somewhere in the middle of a field that seems as big as the endless prairie sky. Then you sit tight and wait. If all goes well (and it usually does if the blind is well placed), about a half-hour before sunrise the chickens will begin stirring.

Probably before you can see anything at all, you'll hear a peculiar deep-throated whooping sound that hits three distinct notes. This is the "booming" that these birds are so well known for. When making this sound, the male chickens lift up special pinnae (feathers) on the backs of their necks into a vertical position while inflating the bright yellow air bags that the feathers normally hide; thus posed, in the dim light they could be mistaken for jowly rabbits. The booming, which is given off as the air bags deflate, is often followed by some frantic foot stomping, complete with appropriate sound effects and a sudden leap into the air, usually performed in tandem by two males against each other in a head-to-head duel.

Chicken Blind

These histrionics are accompanied by a wide range of other noises, resembling, among other things, tropical bird calls, meows, the cooing of pigeons, an old woman's cackle, and an infant's forlorn crying. No one knows exactly what all this means, but the show you're watching has to do with each male defending his oval breeding territory against other males while trying to attract the amorous attention of any females in the vicinity.

Once they get started, the chickens usually occupy themselves in this way for two or three hours, providing plenty of opportunities for you to preserve it all on film if you like. Active season on the booming grounds begins in late March and runs through April. For more information contact Brian or Sonia Winter, a representative of the Nature Conservancy, Route 2, Box 240, Glyndon 56547 (218–498–2679).

Two historic sites in *Moorhead* offer visitors distinctly different views of the community's early history. The first is the *Bergquist Cabin,* Moorhead's oldest permanent dwelling, which is located in a wooded glade on the banks of the Red River of the North. A small log building with simple period furnishings, the cabin accurately conveys the humble beginnings of its remarkable builder.

John G. Bergquist decided to leave Smaland, Sweden, for the New World in 1868 after receiving a severe beating from his father for having been caught playing a forbidden musical instrument, an accordion, in the woods near his home. He traveled westward by rail to Brainerd and then set out alone on foot, first to a land office in Alexandria and then northwest along the Red River Trail to what was eventually to become Moorhead. He arrived in the Red River Valley in midwinter and took shelter in the only building within sight—an abandoned stagecoach stop, which he shared with a fellow traveler who spoke only English. John, whose sole tongue was Swedish, undertook all this at the tender age of eighteen.

The following summer, in 1870, he built his cabin and set up a modest farm. Within five years the town was beginning to take shape around him, and he eventually started a successful brick manufacturing business, using the clay he found in the riverbank near his home. Tours of the Bergquist Cabin, which is found on a dirt road near the west end of Eleventh Avenue, can be arranged by contacting the Clay County Historical Society; call (218) 299–5520.

The *Comstock House,* at 506 Eighth Street South, is a well-preserved example of the kind of society to which the likes of John Bergquist might have aspired. Solomon G. Comstock built this gracious, eleven-room, Queen Anne–style home—whose foundation was provided by the Bergquist brickworks—in 1883 after having established himself as one of the community's most prominent residents. During a sixty-year public career, Solomon served Moorhead as the Clay County attorney, a state representative and senator, and a member of the Fifty-seventh U.S. Congress. His relationship with railroad baron James J. Hill helped secure an extensive railroad system in the Red River Valley. And he was pivotal in the establishment of a state normal school in Moorhead, which later became Moorhead State College.

Owned and maintained by the Minnesota Historical Society, the Comstock House still has most of the family's original furnishings, reflecting a well-to-do lifestyle that nevertheless falls short of the opulence found in some grand homes elsewhere in the state. The house is open to the public on weekends in summer and by appointment at other times. A small admission fee is charged. Call (218) 291–4211 for more information.

Not far from the Bergquist Cabin, in a wooded park on the banks of the Red River, is a monument that stands quite literally in recognition of a dream come true. With its high-peaked twin towers and white tentlike shape, it even looks a little dreamy. But the ***Heritage Hjemkomst Interpretive Center*** is real enough, as is the magnificent wooden vessel within it.

Hjemkomst (pronounced "yemkomst") means "homecoming" in Norwegian, and it was the vision of paying a dramatic tribute to the seafaring Vikings of his homeland that inspired a local teacher, Robert Asp, to begin work in 1971 on a project that dominated the last years of his life. His plan was to build

Too Wet, Too Dry

To the casual observer or traveler, the Red River Valley is a boring place to pass through as fast as possible on the way to some other place. And though this flat, lakeless area doesn't inspire comments about its beauty, it occupies one of the most remarkable places in North America, if not the world.

This incredibly flat valley was formed courtesy of Glacial Lake Agassiz, a lake that at one time or another covered more than 200,000 square miles. Formed by the last glacier that covered northwestern Minnesota, the lake covered parts of Minnesota, South Dakota, North Dakota, Saskatchewan, Manitoba, and Ontario. It extended more than 700 miles from its southern tip in western Minnesota to near Hudson Bay.

While eastern parts of the ancient lake bottom became impassable wetlands, the western section drained better, becoming fertile farmland. Today residents curse and praise the landscape left behind. They curse the region when the Red River floods because the extremely flat landscape causes the floodwaters to spread incredible distances. And they undoubtedly praise the area when farmers harvest bountiful crops of sugar beets. Because it was a lake bottom, the thick clay soil that formed from decayed vegetation is difficult to farm. Soil scientist Jim Richardson summed it up best when he said, "We believe there is about one day a year when it isn't too wet or too dry, so you better be out there working on that day."

an authentic Viking sailing ship, the *Hjemkomst,* and to sail it from Duluth to Norway. It was nine years before Robert was able to stand at the ship's helm on its maiden voyage in Duluth Harbor, and not long afterward he died of leukemia. But several members of his family saw his dream through to fruition, landing the *Hjemkomst* in Bergen, Norway, on July 19, 1982.

The multimillion-dollar interpretive center that has been built in the *Hjemkomst*'s honor is an impressive site. Beneath the building's steeply pitched fiberglass roof, the ship is displayed fully rigged, along with many artifacts associated with its construction and sailing. The well-interpreted displays are complemented by a moving twenty-minute documentary, shown in an adjacent auditorium, on the construction and voyage of the *Hjemkomst.*

In addition to this exhibit are a large space for traveling exhibitions and a gallery for items from the Clay County Historical Museum's permanent collection. The Heritage Hjemkomst Interpretive Center is open daily year-round; a small fee is charged (for information on special exhibits, call 218–299–5511 or visit www.hjemkomst-center.com). It can be found at 202 First Avenue North.

A visit to the **Plains Art Museum** in Fargo, North Dakota, quickly reveals the lie behind the common misconception that cultural life in rural Minnesota is as arid as the land is flat. Occupying a renovated turn-of-the-twentieth-century warehouse in downtown Fargo, the museum displays works by prominent contemporary artists who have been professionally or personally associated with the upper Midwest. The influence of the northern plains environment is evident in some paintings in the permanent collection, as are historic and cultural themes expressed by Dakota and Ojibway artists. A large gallery downstairs provides space for traveling exhibits. The Plains Art Museum, located at 704 First Avenue North, (701) 293–0903 or www.plainsart.org, is open Tuesday through Saturday year-round. Admission is free.

Becker County

Besides being a popular summer vacation spot, the Becker County seat of Detroit Lakes happens to be the annual site of the Midwest's largest country-and-western music festival. During the **WE Fest,** held the first weekend in August, the likes of Waylon Jennings and Willie Nelson get together with many of their star-studded buddies for three days of outdoor music and fun.

It all happens at the **Soo Pass Ranch,** 3 miles south of Detroit Lakes on Route 59. Campgrounds at the ranch, including one just for families, provide space for 5,000 campers. A rock-and-roll Fourth of July celebration called **Celebrate America** is also held at the ranch each year. Tickets and camping reservations for the WE Fest and Celebrate America, which start at about $70 per person, can be ordered by mail (write WE Fest Tickets, Box 625, Detroit Lakes 56501). Or call (218) 847–1681 or (800) 4–WEFEST (800–493–3378) or go to www.wefest.com.

A nearby alternative to the festivities at Soo Pass is a lovely 43,000-acre wilderness area 18 miles northeast of Detroit Lakes that's teeming with wildlife. The rolling wooded terrain and numerous lakes and marshes of **Tamarac National Wildlife Refuge** are popular with anglers, hikers, birders, and those looking for a pleasant drive through a fine stretch of northern Minnesota landscape. The refuge headquarters, at the junction of County Highways 26 and 29, features a beautiful new interpretive center with an excellent multimedia presentation on the history and wildlife of Tamarac. Wilderness-oriented films are shown on summer weekend afternoons; for titles and show times, call (218) 847–2641.

There's a self-guided auto tour of the refuge that starts and ends at the headquarters, too. The drive follows winding gravel roads past duck wetlands, stands of wild rice, and peat bogs that support clusters of tamarac—Minnesota's only "evergreen" that drops its needles each fall. You may even see trumpeter swans that claim the refuge as a summer home. In winter the swans will be gone, but the refuge's 8 miles of cross-country ski trails offer their own special appeal.

Polk County

The regular customers of **Joe DiMaggio's** bar and pizza joint in **Erskine** will tell you that they don't care much for big-city life. One says he last traveled to St. Paul in 1965 and hasn't been drawn back since. Another claims he even avoids cities the size of Moorhead as much as possible. But clearly both of them and many of their fellow citizens are very much at home in a tavern that radiates as much New York City nostalgia—most of which has to do with the mighty Yankees—as a Coney Island hot-dog stand.

Dozens of historic photographs of the likes of Babe Ruth, Lou Gehrig, and, of course, Joe DiMaggio himself are scattered about the crowded walls. There are jerseys, hats, banners, and baseballs signed by mighty sluggers and fielders. Painted above each booth are boldface headlines lifted from the sports pages on historic occasions in Yankee Stadium. And dominating a large wall by the pool table is a delightfully rendered mural of one of the most famous moments in Yankee baseball history: Don Larsen is shown unloading the final pitch of his World Series "perfect" game on October 8, 1956.

Ask Joe DiMaggio, the establishment's owner (no kidding—that's his real name), what inspired all this and he tells about his baseball-oriented boyhood in the Bronx, where he and his father (Joe Sr.) were often reminded that fate had placed them in the shadow of greatness. Mail and phone calls intended for their namesake were frequently misdirected to Joe's house. Thus in 1983, when Joe and his wife opened up a pizza place and tavern in Erskine, he decided to dedicate the place to a subject that had captured his imagination long ago. The story of how a city boy like Joe wound up in Erskine is another tale worth telling—ask him about it when you belly up to the bar.

Red Lake County

Red Lake County is not only the smallest county in Minnesota; it also happens to be one of the flattest. And despite its size, passing through on U.S. Highway 59 or some lesser road is a little like traversing the boundless waters of an ocean. There are few landmarks to gauge the passing of the miles besides an occasional stand of trees rising like an island above the distant horizon.

But when you've just about decided that this monotony will never quit, all of a sudden you stumble onto a pleasant surprise. The **Red Lake River** winds across the prairie like a beautiful wooded oasis—one that offers clear, cool flowing water and the kind of recreational opportunities that you'd expect to find only in a more woodsy environment.

The 20-mile stretch of river from St. Hilaire in Pennington County to Red Lake Falls, which flows through steep clay banks lined with hardwoods, is fine for easy canoeing and fishing, particularly for channel catfish. Then just above Red Lake Falls, the pace picks up. Three miles of nonstop rapids support Minnesota's largest commercially developed inner-tube-float-trip industry.

Minnesota Woman

In 1931, a road repair crew found a skeleton along Highway 59 north of Pelican Rapids. Originally called Minnesota Man, researchers finally determined that he was a she, and changed the name to Minnesota Woman. Although not all experts agree on her age, no one disputes that her remains date back thousands of years.

Archaeologists estimated the age of the skeleton at 10,000 years old, which makes it the oldest human remains ever found in North America. Experts surmise that Minnesota Woman was fifteen years old when she drowned in Glacial Lake Pelican, a massive body of water that adjoined the even larger Glacial Lake Agassiz. Two artifacts found with the skeleton—a dagger made of elk horn and a conch shell—led archaeologists to believe that she fell in the lake while gathering food.

The first outfitter to begin full-scale operations along the banks of the Red Lake, *Voyageur's View,* claims to have hosted the world's largest inner-tubing flotilla. Some 749 persons, clinging to one another's tubes on a sunny day in 1986, made newspaper headlines as far away as Korea. This feat, however, belies the fact that most of the time tubing on the Red Lake is relatively uncrowded. Also, due to a stiff deposit required on all beverage cans, the tubing experience has managed to preserve the quality of this fine natural resource. Voyageur's View also offers camping facilities. For more information write Voyageur's View, Box 48B, Red Lake Falls 56750 or call (218) 253–4329 (summer only) or 253–2031.

Pennington County

If official recognition were given to the most populous creature found roaming the countryside during even the coldest or roughest of Minnesota winters, the snowmobile might well be the uncontested recipient. In many rural communities there are sometimes more "sleds" parked on the streets and in front of taverns than cars and trucks, and Minnesota's backcountry is literally crisscrossed with snowmobile trails.

For those intrigued by the legacy of the snow machine, the Pennington County seat of Thief River Falls, where *Artco Corporation* turns out the Arctic Cat snowmobile line, is likely to be an interesting summer destination, for it's during the snowless months that the following season's machines are being assembled. Visitors are welcome to stop in at the plant, located on Minnesota Highway 32 just south of town, for scheduled tours given every workday (call 218–681–8558 or visit www.arctic-cat.com for times).

Hundreds of employees on the assembly line turn out an average of 130 snowmobiles per eight-hour shift. Nearby dozens of welders are at work in a row of cubicles that collectively emit more dazzling explosions of light than a fireworks show. In another room men and women are dressed in what appear to be inflated space suits to protect themselves from a cloud of dust generated as they take the rough edges off various fiberglass parts. Also, a couple of delightfully primitive-looking Arctic Cats that hark back to the snowmobile's infancy in the early 1960s are on display in the lobby.

Marshall County

If you're staying the night in Thief River Falls and don't mind rising at the crack of dawn, a drive to the *Agassiz National Wildlife Refuge*—located on County Road 7, 18 miles northeast of town—may well result in a chance to see one of Minnesota's grandest mammals: the moose. The extensive upland and wetland areas of the 100-square-mile refuge are maintained to provide an optimal habitat for this largest member of the deer family, as well as for 280 bird species and 49 other mammals. Opportunities for observing these creatures are provided by a network of roads that wind along dikes through the extensive marshes; a booklet outlining a self-guided auto tour is available at the headquarters. There is also a 100-foot observation tower that commands a magnificent view of the flat countryside in all directions. For more information call (218) 681–3720 or 449–4115.

Thirty miles west of Agassiz, along the banks of the lazy Middle River, is one of Minnesota's most obscure state parks. ***Old Mill State Park*** provides an attractive setting in which to hike among the trees (a rare commodity in these parts), swim in a clear swimming hole, picnic, and camp. But perhaps its greatest attraction is a historic steam-powered gristmill that still works.

The simple, small wooden structure near the banks of the river next to a settler's log cabin is actually the last of nearly a half-dozen mills built near this site by the Larson family. The first of these was a water-powered mill constructed in 1886. This building was destroyed in a flood a couple of years later and replaced by a wind-powered mill. When that didn't prove very effective, the Larsons went back to water power, moving the mill a couple of times to new locations, and then finally they converted to steam about 1896.

The steam engine is fired up several times each summer on special occasions to demonstrate the milling process. The large machine, which looks a little like a railroad engine, is surprisingly quiet as it turns the 2,700-pound French burrstones, which were hauled to the site by ox cart. For more information about grinding demonstrations, write Old Mill State Park, Route 1, Box 43, Argyle 56713, or call (218) 437–8174 or, toll-free from within Minnesota, (888) 646–6367 and ask for Department of Natural Resources.

Places to Stay in Red River Country

ALEXANDRIA
(area code 320)

AmericInn,
4520 Highway 29 South;
763–6808

Cedar Rose Inn
Bed & Breakfast,
422 Seventh Avenue West;
762–8430

Country Inn & Suites,
5304 Highway 29 South;
763–9900

Holiday Inn,
5637 Highway 29 South;
763–6577

The Pillars
Bed & Breakfast,
1004 Elm Street;
762–2700

GLENWOOD
(area code 320)

Little Norway Resort,
Route 3;
(800) 290–3453

Scotwood Motel,
Highways 55 and 28;
634–5105

FERGUS FALLS
(area code 218)

AmericInn,
526 Western Avenue;
739–3900

Bakketop Hus,
Route 2, Box 187A,
Fergus Falls 56538;
739–2915

Comfort Inn,
425 Western Avenue;
736–5787

Days Inn,
610 Western Avenue;
739–3311

**Forest Lodge Farms
Bed & Breakfast,**
RR 3, Box 111,
Fergus Falls 56538;
(800) 950–0306

MOORHEAD
(all lodging in Fargo, ND;
area code 701)

AmericInn,
1423 35th Street Southwest,
Fargo, ND;
234–9946

C'mon Inn,
4338 20th Avenue
Southwest,
Fargo, ND;
277–9944

Comfort Inn East,
1407 35th Street South,
Fargo, ND;
280–9666

Super 8 Motel & Suites,
I–29 and Thirteenth Avenue
South,
Fargo, ND;
232–9202

Note: There are 36 motels in
the Fargo/Moorhead area.

DETROIT LAKES
(area code 218)

AmericInn,
777 Highway 10 East;
847–8795

**Best Western
Holland House,**
615 Highway 10 East;
847–4483

Castaway Inn & Resort,
1226 East Shore Drive;
847–4449

Detroit Lakes Lodge,
1334 Washington Avenue;
847–4458

Fairyland Cottages,
410 West Lake Drive;
841–1588

CROOKSTON
(area code 218)

AmericInn,
1821 University Avenue;
281–7800

Northland Inn,
2200 University Avenue;
281–5210

THIEF RIVER FALLS
(area code 218)

Best Western Inn,
Highway 32 South;
681–7555

C'mon Inn,
1586 Highway 59 Southeast;
681–3000

Super 8 Motel,
1915 Highway 59 Southeast;
681–6205

SELECTED CHAMBERS OF COMMERCE

**Alexandria Lakes Area
Chamber of Commerce**
(800) 235–9441

Crookston Chamber of Commerce
(800) 809–5997

Detroit Lakes Tourism Bureau
(800) 542–3992

Fergus Falls Chamber of Commerce
(800) 726–8959

**Glenwood Area
Chamber of Commerce**
(800) 304–5666

**Moorhead-Fargo Convention &
Visitors Bureau**
(800) 235–7654

**Thief River Falls Visitors &
Convention Bureau**
(800) 827–1629

SELECTED WEB SITES IN RED RIVER COUNTRY

**Alexandria Lakes Area
Chamber of Commerce**
www.alexandriamn.org

Detroit Lakes Tourism Bureau
www.visitdetroitlakes.com

Fergus Falls Chamber of Commerce
www.fergusfalls.com

Moorhead Chamber of Commerce
www.fargomoorhead.org

**Thief River Falls Convention &
Visitors Bureau**
www.ci.thief-river-falls.mn.us

Places to Eat in Red River Country

ALEXANDRIA
(area code 320)

Angelina's Restaurant
(American),
1215 Highway 29 North;
762–1324

**The Daily Grind
House of Java,**
518 Broadway;
762–7240

**Great Hunan Chinese
Restaurant,**
2919 Highway 29 South;
763–6288

Old Broadway,
319 Broadway;
763–3999

Pizza Hut,
1518 Broadway Street;
763–6669

Taco John's,
1702 Broadway;
763–7885

Time Square Bagels
(coffee),
203 Twenty-second Avenue
West;
762–8463

Traveler's Inn Restaurant
(American, Italian),
511 Broadway Street;
763–4000

Weston Station (American),
4417 East Highway 27;
763–6677

GLENWOOD
(area code 320)

A & W Restaurant
(American),
Highways 28 and 55;
634–4320

Franklin Street Diner
(American),
9 North Franklin Street;
634–3371

Gingerbread House Cafe
(American),
3 Franklin Street;
634–4969

The Pastry Shoppe Bakery,
1 North Franklin Street;
634–3105

The Pizza Ranch,
14 Minnesota Avenue;
634–4261

FERGUS FALLS
(area code 218)

Mabel Murphy's
(American),
Highway 210 West;
739–4406

**Thomas Kao Chinese
Restaurant,**
419 West Lincoln Avenue;
739–3800

Tomacelli's Pizza & Pasta,
121 West Cavour Avenue;
739–6373

Viking Cafe (American),
203 West Lincoln Avenue;
736–6660

MOORHEAD/FARGO, ND
Acapulco (Mexican),
1303 Thirty-fourth Street
Southwest,
Fargo, ND;
(701) 297–0355

Ember's University Diner
(American),
2130 University Drive South,
Fargo, ND;
(701) 280–0414

Giant Panda (Oriental),
1331 Gateway Drive,
Fargo, ND;
(701) 298–8558

Luna Coffee,
1545 University Drive South,
Fargo, ND;
(701) 293–8818

Santa Lucia (Mediterranean),
505 Fortieth Street
Southwest,
Fargo, ND;
(701) 281–8656

Speak Easy
(Italian, American),
1001 Thirtieth Avenue South,
Moorhead;
(218) 233–1326

Taste of India,
855 Forty-fifth Street
Southwest,
Fargo, ND;
(701) 281–1500

Note: The Fargo/Moorhead
area publishes a Gourmet
Guide that lists all restaurants
in the two cities. Call the
Convention & Visitors
Bureau at (800) 235–7645
or check their Web site at
www.fargomoorhead.org.

DETROIT LAKES
(area code 218)

Chinese Dragon,
Washington Square Mall;
847–2177

Giovanni's Pizza,
100 West Lake Drive;
847–7711

Main Steet Restaurant

(American),
900 Washington Avenue;
847–3344

Zorbaz at the Beach
(Mexican),
402 West Lake Drive;
847–5305

CROOKSTON
(area code 218)

China Moon Restaurant,
114 South Broadway;
281–3136

**Happy Joe's Pizza &
Ice Cream Parlor,**
705 East Robert Street;
281–5141

Mugoo's Pizza,
1500 University Avenue;
281–3130

The Novel Cup (coffee),
101 West Robert Street;
281–4830

RBJ's Restaurant
(American),
1601 University Avenue;
281–3636

Taco John's,
605 North Main;
281–7357

THIEF RIVER FALLS
(area code 218)

**Danny's Pizza & Italian
Restaurant,**
203 Third Street West;
681–8544

Dee's Kitchen (American),
811 Atlantic Avenue North;
681–9907

**Handy Farms Country
Cookin'** (American, pizza),
Highway 59 South;
681–7686

Johnnie's Cafe,
304 Main Avenue North;
681–8102

Lantern Restaurant
(American),
1910 Highway 59 South;
681–8211

Roads to Take

Glacial Ridge Trail,
(800) 304–5666
or (800) 845–8747 for maps
and information

Otter Tail Scenic Byway,
(800) 423–4571 for maps
and information

Highway 104 from
Glenwood to Highway 12

Highway 108 from Pelican
Rapids to Highway 78 near
Perham

Highway 34 from Detroit
Lakes to Park Rapids

Otter Tail County Road 24
from County Road 35 to
Erhard

Otter Tail County Road 35
from I–94 to Dent on
Highway 108

ALSO WORTH SEEING

Red River Valley

Headwaters

In this region of north-central Minnesota, the Mississippi River begins its 2,350-mile journey to the Gulf of Mexico. From a humble start in Lake Itasca, the Mississippi grows to become North America's largest and longest river, draining all or part of thirty-one states and two Canadian provinces. In addition to the mighty river, the Headwaters region contains a good portion of Minnesota's 10,000 lakes.

The landscape ranges from fields of corn and soybeans in the southern part of this region to thick pine and deciduous forests dotted with lakes, rivers, and wetlands in the north. It's a land of amazing quantities of water. Rivers rise out of the massive network of bogs that covers a large part of northern Minnesota and gradually make their way out of state. It's an impressive landscape, more subtle than the mountains and canyons of the West, yet spectacular in a quiet way because of the volume of water.

Sherburne County

From any major highway through this county southeast of St. Cloud, it doesn't look like anything special. It's mostly flat to slightly rolling, with a patchwork of farm fields, small sections of

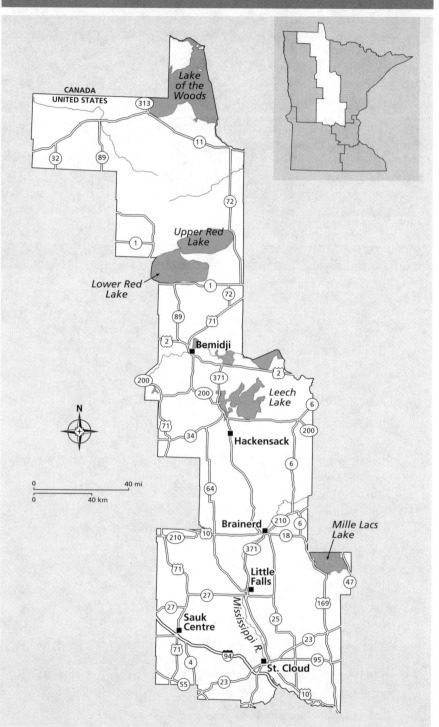

HEADWATERS

CANADA
UNITED STATES

313

Lake of the Woods

32   89   11

72

1

Upper Red Lake

Lower Red Lake

1   72

89   71

2   Bemidji

2

200

371   Leech Lake

200   6

N

71   34

Hackensack

200

6

0   40 mi
0   40 km

64

6

Brainerd   210   6

Mille Lacs Lake

210   10   18

371   47

71

Little Falls   169

27

27   Mississippi R.   25

Sauk Centre   23

71   95

4   94

55   23   St. Cloud

10

forest, and towns that have grown as more urbanites move from the Twin Cities. Most people don't realize that this county in central Minnesota sits in a unique geologic area called the Anoka Sandplain. As the last glaciers melted, outwash from the massive glacial rivers deposited fine material that eventually formed the largest area of sand dunes in Minnesota. Although it's not the best farmland, irrigation has helped it become reasonably productive.

When Minnesota was organized into a territory in 1849, most of the 6,000 settlers who lived within it practiced a kind of subsistence farming. Following an agricultural tradition nearly as old as civilization, they grew a variety of crops to feed themselves, and whatever surplus there was supported a few nonfarming villagers.

Upon this scene came a young, educated son of a Boston tailor named Oliver Hudson Kelley, who staked a claim—the *Oliver Kelley Farm*—along the banks of the Mississippi River (3 miles southeast of Elk River along Route 10). What he lacked in experience as a farmer Kelley made up for by reading everything he could find about the new technology and crops just becoming available. He was a natural organizer and began to propagate information on "modern" farming through numerous newspaper articles and letters. His organizational efforts culminated in the founding of the Order of the Patrons of Husbandry—or, more commonly, the Grange—a national fraternal organization of farmers whose purpose was to advance the practice of agriculture and to promote the interests of farmers.

A visit to the Kelley Farm, which is now managed by the Minnesota Historical Society, is a step back in time to this turbulent period in American agriculture when subsistence farming began to give way to the raising of large

AUTHOR'S FAVORITES

Brainerd Lakes Area,
(800) 450–2838 ext. 400

Heartland Bicycle Trail,
Park Rapids,
(800) 247–0054,
or Walker,
(800) 833–1113

Itasca State Park,
Lake Itasca,
(218) 266–2114

Leech Lake Area,
Walker,
(800) 833–1118

Paul Bunyan Bicycle Trail,
Brainerd,
(800) 450–2838 ext. 400

Oliver Kelley Farm

single crops for shipment to fast-growing urban centers. Kelley's organization had a spectacular, if brief, popularity. The intentions of the Grange struck a chord with farmers across the land—more than a million of them quickly became members—but when their most pressing economic concerns weren't effectively addressed, membership dropped off sharply.

Exhibits and multimedia presentations at a modern interpretive center chronicle this populist agriculture movement, while costumed interpretive staff at Kelley's historic farm and farmhouse bring to life the farming practices of the time. Visitors can help feed animals and sample foods prepared on the cook-stove in the kitchen. Outside, men wearing wool pants even on the hottest summer days demonstrate horse-powered plowing, planting, and harvesting. Special events, such as a Victorian wedding day and period games at the annual *Independence Day celebration,* make for great educational family fun. For more information call (763) 441–6896.

Stearns County

For a city with such an ethereal name, it's ironic that the Stearns County seat of **St. Cloud** has such a down-to-earth nickname: The Granite City. But make no mistake, this growing urban center of 50,000 has its feet firmly on the ground, where the quarrying and processing of the area's distinctive red, pink, and gray granite have been a primary economic activity for much of the century.

The story of St. Cloud's contribution to the granite industry is told through several creative displays at the *Stearns County Heritage Center,* one of the best county historical museums in the state. Inside the spacious, modern building is a convincing two-story replica of a 1930s quarry site that illustrates how the rock was drilled and blasted free in huge chunks weighing many tons. There are also exhibits on the area's natural history, early farming, immigration, and settlement, as well as revolving displays on other aspects of local culture. Thorough research in the museum's extensive archives combines with professional design and display techniques to result in the outstanding quality of the center's exhibits. There is also a nature center, with trails for skiing and hiking, that shares the 106-acre wooded grounds with the Heritage Center. To get there, go 3 blocks south of Division Street to 235 South Thirty-third Avenue. For more information on programs and hours (the museum is open most days of the week, year-round, and charges a small fee), call (320) 253–8424.

If a romantic dinner for two or a fun outing with friends is what you're up to, head to **D.B. Searle's** at 18 Fifth Avenue South in downtown St. Cloud. This tall, narrow Victorian Eastlake building, which is named for a nineteenth-century St. Cloud lawyer and judge who happened to have witnessed the shooting of President Lincoln, has been transformed into a well-designed bistro that serves delicious food and oozes charm and good taste. The top floor, reserved "for lovers only" (call for reservations *at least* three months in advance), is actually a labyrinthine loft with interconnected platforms supporting a network of private booths. The third floor has a more traditional layout, accentuated by the omnipresent tones of the building's handsome woodwork. There is more dining space on the second floor, and a wonderful tavern on the ground floor is watched over by a life-size statue of a bear. The moderately priced menu features sandwiches, good steaks, and Cajun-style seafood and poultry dishes. For reservations call (320) 253–0655.

One of the most devastating natural disasters that confronted the early settlers of the Minnesota prairie was the periodic invasion of huge clouds of crop-destroying locusts. In response to a second consecutive year of this "grasshopper plague," in 1877 German Catholic farmers near the town of Cold Spring sought respite from their troubles by pledging to construct a chapel in honor of the Assumption of the Blessed Virgin. They made the vow, and as history has it, the grasshoppers disappeared the next day.

The wood-frame, Gothic Revival–style Locust Chapel built that very year survived until 1894, when it was destroyed by another violent prairie phenomenon: a tornado. In 1951 the Assumption Chapel—or, as it's commonly known, the **Grasshopper Chapel**—was reconstructed on the original site at the top of a lovely secluded knoll surrounded by oaks on Pilgrimage Road, just south of Minnesota 23 in Cold Spring, about 20 miles southwest of St. Cloud. The new chapel is built of locally quarried granite left rough on the buttressed exterior and polished to a glistening sheen inside, where a statue of the Virgin and Christ child is the only remaining article from the original building. Over the entrance is a plaque depicting the Virgin Mary ascending into heaven on a cloud, with two grasshoppers below. The chapel is open for visitation spring through fall.

There is another sacred site in the St. Cloud area that is as grand and imposing as the Grasshopper Chapel is intimate and secluded. The famous bell banner above the entrance of **St. John's Abbey and University Church** can be seen for miles protruding above the wooded slope upon which the church stands. This architectural marvel has attracted such acclaim that, for the first ten years following its completion in 1961, it received more visitors than the state capitol did.

From among proposals by fifteen of the world's greatest architects, including Frank Lloyd Wright, the monks of the Benedictine Abbey selected a design for their church by Marcel Breuer, an Orthodox Jew. Breuer's concept of an unadorned, pillar-free sanctuary with walls of exposed poured concrete reflects the simplicity with which the monks carry on their lives. The prominence of the altar, near the center of the sanctuary beneath a cloudlike canopy, is a natural focal point. Illumination comes primarily from the north wall, where, behind a fantastic cantilevered, self-supported balcony, the largest stained-glass window in the world radiates magnificently. This abstract, honeycombed design was created by a member of the St. John's University art faculty, Branislaw Bak. His intent was to represent the seasons of the liturgical year—Advent, Christmas, Lent, Easter, and the Ordinary Time—through different vertical bands of color and subtly varied patterns of glass. Unifying this panorama is a series of roughly concentric circles, representing God, which draws the eye to the top and center of the window.

Outside, the bell banner stands as a monumental piece of modern poured-cement sculpture, 112 feet above ground and 100 feet across at the top, that is supported by four gracefully sweeping legs. High up in the center of this 2,500-ton creation are a large white oak cross and five bells that ring on the quarter-hour.

You're welcome to drop in and visit the church anytime and to worship with the monks if you so desire. Inside the front entrance by the beautiful granite baptismal font, you can pick up a brochure for a self-guided tour. After touring the church, you may also walk the pathways of the surrounding 2,400-acre wooded grounds, which have been designated as a wildlife sanctuary (no pets or fires are allowed). Finding St. John's church is easy: Just take the Collegeville exit off Interstate 94 and look for the bell banner to the south.

Sauk Centre has had a love-hate relationship with its most famous citizen ever since 1920, when Sinclair Lewis put the town on the world map with the publication of his American masterpiece, *Main Street*. The first reaction to the book's less-than-flattering portrayal of life in "Gopher Prairie" was outrage—apparently many citizens thought they could see themselves in Lewis's scathing critique of small-town middle-class life. But *Main Street* and its author, who in 1930 received America's first Nobel Prize in literature, gave Sauk Centre a certain notoriety, the value of which has not escaped the notice of at least some in this otherwise undistinguished dairy town of 7,000. Today signs on I–94 point the way to the Sinclair Lewis Interpretive Center, and what was once the intersection of Third Avenue and Main Street—a crossing governed by Sauk Centre's only stoplight—is now the junction of The Original Main Street and Sinclair Lewis Avenue. Even the athletes at Sauk Centre Senior High, who compete as the Mainstreeters, honor the town's literary heritage.

Four sites in Sauk Centre relate to the life and work of its best-known native son. At a rest area near the freeway you can find the **Sinclair Lewis Interpretive Center,** which also serves as a local history museum and the chamber of commerce. The small exhibit area features samples of Lewis's writing in various stages of the publishing process, as well as first editions of his published works and historic photographs of the town and its founders. There is also a short videotape on Lewis's life.

Sauk Centre's celebrated main intersection is dominated by the **Palmer House Hotel,** which has been restored to surpass its former state of modest elegance with the recent addition of private baths in each of the twenty-two rooms, including several Jacuzzi-equipped suites. The appeal of the place is enhanced by the fact that Sinclair Lewis worked here as a night clerk while he was in high school, though the malcontent lad was fired for daydreaming and reading on the job. Nonetheless, the hotel found its way into literary history as the "Minniemashie House" in *Main Street* and as the "American House" in *Work of Art.*

Local legend has it that when it was built in 1901, the Palmer House was the first Minnesota hotel outside the Twin Cities to offer its guests hot and cold running water and electricity in every room. The traveling salesmen who frequented the hotel during its early years were reportedly so impressed with these novelties that they wore out the light switches in six months by playing with them so incessantly. The tin ceiling and chairs in the lobby, the furniture in many of the guest rooms, the wainscoting, and the stained glass in the arched first-floor windows fared better and have survived to the present day. The Palmer House charges modest to expensive rates. For reservations write the Palmer House Hotel, 500 Sinclair Lewis Avenue, Sauk Centre 56378, or call (320) 352–3431.

A pilgrimage to Sauk Centre would be incomplete without a visit to the **Sinclair Lewis Boyhood Home,** located 3 blocks west of the Palmer House on Sinclair Lewis Avenue. This simple Eastlake cottage has been restored and appointed with period furnishings, earning a spot on the National Register of Historic Places. Some of the household items on display actually belonged to the Lewis family, including a junior-size bed that was occupied by Sinclair, who was often sick during his youth. The house is open for tours daily Memorial Day through Labor Day and by arrangement the rest of the year; call the Sauk Centre Chamber of Commerce at (320) 352–5201, or visit www.saukcentrechamber.com.

Morrison County

In central Minnesota the Mississippi River pauses. The Ojibway called this spot *KaKaBikans,* the little squarely cut-off rock, which was a place where the river dropped over an outcrop of granite to form a waterfall. The Ojibway, Sioux, and Winnebago Indians at times fought near the falls, and many fur traders, missionaries, and explorers wrote of it in their journals. Today Little Falls, the boyhood home of Charles A. Lindbergh, sits at this special place along the great river.

In one of Lindbergh's fond memories from his boyhood summers on a farm near Little Falls, he's lying on his back in tall grass, gazing for hours up at the sky. Oblivious to everything happening around him on Earth, he marvels at the passing cumulus clouds, imagining what it would be like to soar among them, birdlike, in an airplane. His early dreaming about flight was nourished in a family whose members had for generations excelled at everything they undertook. Lindbergh's father was a successful lawyer and congressional representative, and his grandfather had been a prominent member of the Swedish Parliament before immigrating to the Minnesota frontier in 1860. Lindbergh, following his own path to greatness, at age twenty-five climbed aboard the single-engine *Spirit of St. Louis* on an overcast day in May 1927 and in thirty-three-and-a-half hours completed the first nonstop solo flight from New York to Paris. To his own surprise, Lindy became an international hero overnight.

Still, as you'll learn for yourself upon visiting the **Lindbergh House History Center,** the crossing of the Atlantic was only one of many accomplishments in the lifetime of this remarkable person. Exhibits at the modern interpretive center, which is situated on the wooded banks of the Mississippi River, embrace the full range of Lindbergh's various achievements and interests. Parts of his first airplane, a World War I–vintage Jenny, are on display, as is a device Lindbergh helped design that is used to keep animal organs alive outside the body for the purposes of medical research. Lindy's political activities—initially he was a vocal opponent to the United States entering World War II, just as his father had argued against America's involvement in the Great War—and his later concern with ecology are also well documented. The center houses a library of films on Lindbergh, his family, and the history of human

Little Elk Heritage Preserve

When I first glanced at the brochure for the **Little Elk Heritage Preserve,** I dismissed it as either a petting zoo filled with semitame animals in pens or a large farm field with elk sauntering around. Closer inspection revealed this site near Little Falls to be the largest privately owned archaeological preserve of its kind in the Midwest. Stretching along 1 mile of undeveloped Mississippi River frontage, the Little Elk Heritage Preserve contains archaeological sites dating from at least 3,000 B.C.

Visitors to this fascinating place—situated in an area where the prairie-forest transition zone meets the Mississippi River Valley—can take a self-guided hike through the preserve. Stops at seventeen points provide many details on important events and milestones of this patch of land. For more information contact the Institute for Minnesota Archaeology, 287 East Sixth Street, Suite 260, St. Paul, Minnesota 55101, (651) 848–0095, or www.imnarch.org.

flight and offers an attractive theater for viewing them. Admission is charged to the center, located on Minnesota 238 just south of town. It is open daily from May through Labor Day and on weekends the rest of the year. Tours of the nearby **Lindbergh Boyhood Home** are also offered. For more information call (320) 616–5421.

You'll find the entrance to **Charles A. Lindbergh State Park,** named for the aviation hero's father, immediately across the street from the history center. Charles Jr., before he died in 1974, praised the establishment of this park as symbolic of civilization's greatest advancement: the valuing of life itself over the achievements of science and technology, such as the satellites now visible in the nighttime sky overhead.

Not far upstream of the Lindbergh home is an excellent museum dedicated to the Minnesota military experience. Located on the historic grounds of 53,000-acre **Camp Ripley**—the largest National Guard training site in the country—the **Minnesota Military Museum** features professionally developed exhibits, including a series of displays illustrating the role Minnesota soldiers have played in every war since statehood in 1858. Another display area concerns Minnesota frontier forts, of which the original Old Fort Ripley was one. Elsewhere in the building are an exhibit on the development of small arms and a collection of war souvenirs brought home by Minnesotans from overseas. Among the latter are a handkerchief and napkin monogrammed *AH*—authenticated, says the label, as having once belonged to Adolf Hitler. The museum, located 7 miles north of Little Falls on Minnesota 115, is open free of charge Wednesday through Sunday from Memorial Day through Labor Day. Call (320) 632–7374, extension 374, for more information.

Crow Wing County

If any area of Minnesota defines lake country, this north central county does it perfectly. As the home of many extremely popular lakes and countless resorts of all sizes, this region ranks as a favorite vacation spot for several generations of Minnesotans. The Crow Wing River enters the Mississippi barely after crossing the county line and splits into two parts. An island sits between the channels, and prehistoric Indians thought that it resembled the wing of a raven. Eventually their name for the river, Raven's Wing, through multiple translations became Crow Wing, which also became the name of the county.

Besides the Mississippi River, Crow Wing County is also home to the Brainerd lakes, a collection of lakes ranging from large to small and from crowded to quiet. The past decade or so has seen the area transformed from one of small family-owned, nothing fancy resorts and cabins into one of expensive resorts with highly rated golf courses and lake homes the size and price of upper-end suburban houses.

Although the Brainerd lakes are busier nowadays than in the past, it's still possible to get away from the crowds. Taking a bike ride on the Paul Bunyan Bicycle Trail is one of the best ways to find peace and quiet in this increasingly busy area. The trail currently runs 100 miles from Brainerd to the town of Bemidji and is paved for 57 miles from Brainerd to Hackensack. It passes twenty-one lakes, goes through sixteen small towns and weaves through countless acres of forest and wetlands. Plans call for this recreational trail

Brainerd Pitted Outwash Plain

In a state covered with thousands of lakes, the area around Brainerd in north central Minnesota has become a favorite among many people. The lakes in this area are shallow, warm, and clear, with gentle and sandy shores. Although thousands of tourists visit this area every summer, few probably give a thought about how the lakes in this region were formed.

Geologists call this area the Brainerd Pitted Outwash Plain, a mouthful for sure, but a simple idea to understand. As the glaciers receded, ice blocks of various sizes fell off, made depressions in the landscape, got buried by sand and gravel, and eventually melted. These dents became lakes and marshes, and the hundreds of such pits in the soil surrounding Brainerd represent a unique find. The ice blocks varied in size and formed depressions ranging from a few feet to several miles across. Geologists also estimate that 80 to 85 percent of Minnesota's lakes formed in ice-block depressions, providing further evidence of the role glaciers had in shaping our landscape.

TOP ANNUAL EVENTS IN THE HEADWATERS

Perch Jerk,
Walker, late March,
(800) 833–1118

Wheels, Wings and Water Festival,
St. Cloud, early July,
(800) 264–2940 ext. 129

Sinclair Lewis Days,
Sauk Centre, mid-July,
(320) 352–5201

Taste of Dorset,
Dorset, early August,
(800) 247–0054

Lindbergh Symposium and Celebration,
Little Falls, mid-August,
(800) 325–5916

eventually to be paved all the way to Walker where it will hook up with the Heartland Trail. For more information on this gorgeous trail, check the Web site at www.paulbunyantrail.com.

The Cuyuna Iron Range is sometimes called Minnesota's forgotten iron range. Smaller than the larger ranges to the north, late to be discovered and early to be abandoned, the Cuyuna for seventy years was nevertheless a significant producer of iron ore and, during World War II, manganese. To commemorate the history of mining on the Cuyuna, two sites in Crosby are open to the public, both of them found by following signs along Minnesota 6 in the heart of town. The *Croft Mine and Historical Park* will take visitors on a simulated tour of the type of underground mine that was common in the area until the 1940s (for more information call 218–546–5466).

At the *Cuyuna Range Historical Society Museum,* housed in Crosby's old train depot, a collection of mining artifacts and photographs is augmented by other local-history displays. The museum has photographs and memorabilia related to Cuyler Adams, who discovered iron on the range and named the area by combining his own name with that of his dog, Una. Also of interest are newspaper accounts and photographs of the famous 1924 Crosby mine disaster, in which forty-one miners died when their underground mine suddenly became inundated with water through an underground passage from a nearby lake. The museum is open Monday through Saturday in summer. For more information call (218) 546–5435.

Most of the historic industries that come to mind in association with the woods and lakes of northern Minnesota—trading for furs, logging the huge red and white pines, commercial fishing, mining—have come and gone relatively quickly. But in the background there has persisted a humble economic pursuit that is as long-lived as it is pervasive today: the ma-and-pa resort. And along the shore of Whitefish Lake, east of Pine River, one such establishment has dedicated a museum to this modest Minnesota institution.

The **Minnesota Resort Museum** grew out of the historical interests of the Leagjeld family, who have owned the **Driftwood Resort** since 1958. Eventually their collection of artifacts and photographs warranted construction of the exhibit hall that today re-creates aspects of resort life through the decades. Featured are a well-equipped, woodstove-fired kitchen and pantry, a shop area, an icehouse, a laundry, an office, and all the fixings for a traditional "shore lunch." To find the museum, go east of Pine River about 5 miles into Crow Wing County on County Road 1; then turn south on County Road 15 for 3 miles and look for signs for the Driftwood Resort. The museum, open daily in summer, charges a modest admission. For more information call (218) 568–4221.

Cass County

If you're heading north through Brainerd and need a break from the sometimes heavy traffic, or if you're searching for something a bit more restful and refined than the sort of action found at Brainerd's International Raceway and the Paul Bunyan Amusement Center, you may want to stop by **Maddens Resort** on Gull Lake for a game of croquet. Now this is not exactly the kind of backyard "guerilla croquet" that you may have played as a kid. Many players on the close-cropped bent-grass courts at Maddens will be dressed all in white. The hefty wooden mallets that they swing with strategic precision cost upward of $250. They may even be drinking champagne while engaging in convivial patter between shots. This is croquet in the grand tradition of the sport, and Maddens is one of two such places in the state where the public is welcome to join in the fun.

Guest lawn fees, including equipment rental, at Maddens are moderate, and free clinics are offered several times each week. Stop by in mid-June to see some of the nation's best players compete in the Madden Invitational and Minnesota Championship tournaments. Maddens is located 12 miles northwest of Brainerd on County Road 77. For further information call (218) 829–2811 or, toll-free from within Minnesota, (800) 642–5363, or log on to www.maddens.com.

The 6,100-acre **Deep-Portage Conservation Reserve,** located about 10 miles east of Hackensack on County Road 46, is a beautiful natural haven offering recreational and educational activities for individuals, families, and groups. There are 40 kilometers (25 miles) of trails wandering over a hilly, wooded terrain shaped by the action of two ice-age glaciers. The trails are equally divided for use between skiers and snowmobilers in the winter and are available for hiking the rest of the year. Naturalists operating out of the attractive interpretive

River Pigs and Long Drives

While immigrant settlers plowed the rich soil of the prairie to form the farms that now cover most of the state, a different natural resource drew people to this area. Much of the Headwaters region lies in a part of Minnesota blanketed by thick forest. Huge old-growth white pines covered much of this area and lured the lumberjacks and future lumber barons who thought they had found an inexhaustible supply of trees.

From around 1855 until the last major log drive down the Mississippi in 1919, loggers hauled incredible amounts of timber from the forests. As in much of Minnesota, water also played an important role in the lumber industry. Teams of horses would drag out huge loads of logs on frozen roads, workers would pile them along river banks, and once the ice melted, huge log drives to sawmills downriver would begin.

Working a river drive was a dangerous job, and the crews even had to bear the indignity of being tagged with the less than complimentary title of river pig. Hopping from rolling log to rolling log, the river crews occupied one of three positions. The driving crew worked at the front of the huge log rafts to keep the logs moving and out of side channels. The jam crew had the most dangerous duty, and the others considered them the elite of the three crews as they worked to prevent and remove jams. Finally, the rear crew brought up the back and gathered stray logs caught on snags or in backwater swamps.

Eventually the virgin timber ran out and the logging industry modernized, which changed the products and methods of this major Minnesota business.

center offer weekday and weekend programs using the surrounding lakes and forests as a classroom. For directions and information about special events, call (218) 682–2325 or visit www.deep-portage.org.

Hikers may also want to explore a recently opened section of the *North Country Trail*, which, when completed, will provide a continuous footpath from New Hampshire to North Dakota. A 68-mile stretch of the trail now runs east and west through *Chippewa National Forest* between Remer and Walker. It may be accessed from Minnesota 371 about 5 miles north of Hackensack or from a Chippewa National Forest road near Longville. Contact the forest supervisor of the Chippewa National Forest at Walker 56484 (218–547–1044) for maps and further information.

One weekend each winter everyone in Walker gets especially excited about an event that revolves around what is commonly regarded as one of the ugliest fish in the world. The *Eelpout Festival*, held every February, brings thousands of anglers to the frozen reaches of Leech Lake to try for cash prizes awarded to those able to "bag a burbot." Information on the Eelpout Festival can be obtained by calling the Leech Lake Area Chamber of Commerce at (218) 547–1313.

Hubbard County

Food lovers will find a special treat in this county located in the heart of lake country. The town of **Dorset** boasts of having the most restaurants per capita in the United States. Of course that's not too difficult with a population of twenty-two, but Dorset still has four restaurants in its short downtown. During their annual **Taste of Dorset festival** or any busy summer weekend, the town may seem anything but off the beaten path, but it still ranks as one of the most surprising finds in Minnesota.

After you've eaten your fill at the Taste of Dorset, you may want to wear some of it off with a leisurely bicycle ride on the Heartland Trail. This trail runs 49 miles from Park Rapids to Cass Lake, with the 27 miles from Park Rapids to Walker paved. It goes through the scenic lake country of Hubbard and Cass Counties, cutting through miles of northern forest and several small towns before coming to Walker, which sits on the shore of Leech Lake, one of the largest lakes in Minnesota.

Leech Lake is a reservoir and attracts anglers in pursuit of walleye (the state fish) and the elusive and aggressive muskie. The lake is so huge that there are several places along the shore where you cannot see across it, not unusual for the Great Lakes but uncommon for an inland lake. The town of Walker has a city dock that gives it a coastal feel as people staying on the lake more often than not take their boat instead of their car to town.

The headwaters of the Mississippi River are a destination of such international renown that the point could be made that they don't belong in a guidebook dedicated to undiscovered—or at least untrammeled—places. **Itasca State Park,** in which the Father of Waters begins its epic journey south by flowing northward at a mere trickle, has within it a number of genuinely obscure attractions that most people discover only by stumbling upon them.

Perhaps more than any other of Minnesota's sixty-four state parks, Itasca, the oldest in the state, has the feeling of a national park. The massive hand-hewn-log and stone construction of the Forest Inn Interpretive Center and the Douglas Lodge (Itasca is the only Minnesota state park to offer meals and accommodations) are reminiscent of Yosemite or Yellowstone. The scale of these buildings reflects the size of the trees to be found in the surrounding forests, too. In fact, Itasca boasts the largest white and red pines on record in the state.

Both of these trees are found at marked locations along Wilderness Drive, a one-way road that winds through the northwestern quarter of the park. Having survived the past 300 years, including the onslaughts of loggers near the turn of the twentieth century, the giant white today looms 112 feet high, protruding above the surrounding forest canopy. Its trunk is massive—55 inches in diameter—and its limbs somewhat diminished, suggesting that this tree has spent most of its energy growing up, not out. Nearby, the big red, or Norway, pine tops out at 120 feet above ground. The bark of its 300-year-old trunk has a scaly, reptilelike appearance, and visible at its base are scars from six different fires. Far overhead, a tangle of branches twists out in all directions like a frozen burst from a fireworks display.

The short path leading to the big red pine also passes by one of the state's more interesting archaeological landmarks. A plaque along the banks of a small creek marks a **bison kill site** where 8,000 years ago a group of prehistoric hunters slaughtered sixteen giant bison en masse, perhaps by driving them off a now-nonexistent cliff.

For more information about lodging, meals, recreational opportunities, and the extensive naturalist programs offered at Itasca, write the park manager at Itasca State Park, Lake Itasca 56460 or call (218) 266–2114 or, toll-free from within Minnesota, (888) 646–6367 and ask for DNR.

One tourist-oriented destination near Park Rapids provides visitors with insights into the era that saw the transformation of Minnesota's woodlands from magnificent pine climax forests into a mixed bag of second-growth species such as aspen, birch, spruce, and balsam fir. The *Rapid River Logging Camp,* located 5 miles north of town on County Road 18, features several logging exhibits and an all-you-can-eat lumberjack cook shanty—the camp's main attraction—that provides three inexpensive meals daily, Memorial Day through Labor Day. For more information about the camp, call (218) 732–3444.

Beltrami County

Around 1700, explorers started searching for the source of the Mississippi. Some of the explorers included Du Charleville, a relative of New Orleans founder Bienville; Zebulon Pike for whom Pikes Peak is named; and Lewis Cass, governor of the Michigan Territory and namesake of both Cass Lake and Cass County. Perhaps the most flashy explorer to search for the source, Count Giacomo Beltrami, arrived at Fort Snelling in 1823.

His route took him up the Minnesota River and down the Red River of the North. He got as far as Pembina, North Dakota, before heading southeast on foot and canoe. He ultimately named Lake Julia near Bemidji as the source but didn't explore another lake a Chippewa guide told him about. That lake, Lac la Biche, later became known as Lake Itasca, the source of the great river.

Though they're miles from the United Nations, one day each summer Bemidji's *Concordia Language Villages* explode in a polylingual, multicultural celebration of world unity that casts a shadow all the way to the UN Plaza

Red Lake Peatland

One of the most striking geologic features of the Headwaters region, and for that matter, of the United States, is also one of the most difficult to see. Found in only a few places in the world, patterned peatlands cover a large chunk of northern Minnesota. The Red Lake Peatland covers about 450 square miles of Beltrami, Koochiching, Lake of the Woods, and Roseau Counties and ranks as one of the largest continuous mires in the forty-eight states.

This massive wetland occupies the eastern part of the Glacial Lake Agassiz plain, and travelers can see a good example of it in northern Beltrami County. Follow Highway 72 north from Blackduck along the east side of Upper and Lower Red Lake. Go about 10 miles north of unincorporated Waskish and you will see an obvious example of the peatland. Large open areas of low shrubs and coarse grasses give way to patches of tamarack, black spruce, and dwarf birch.

Although most people who drive the few roads that traverse these marshes think of them as boring swamp, observant travelers will appreciate nature's work. Peat up to 10 feet thick covers much of this swamp, as water aimlessly and slowly moves through the thick vegetation, discouraging humans from entering, but making it a rich habitat for wildlife.

While not spectacular like mountains and deep canyons, patterned peatlands have a more subtle way of displaying nature's power.

in New York City. For one day in July or August, hundreds of young people participating in the nine Concordia Language Villages programs throughout Minnesota converge on Bemidji for an *international festival.*

Participants in the acclaimed Concordia College–sponsored program live in Russian, Finnish, Chinese, Norwegian, French, Swedish, Danish, German, Japanese, or Spanish "villages," in which their American belongings have been surrendered upon arrival at "customs." Students exchange their familiar language, their currency, and even their own names for those derived from their new culture.

Guests of the festival (it is open to the public free of charge) can participate in this experience as the young people emerge from their adopted cultures to share ethnic foods, crafts, music, and gifts. Professional folk dancers and musicians add to the entertainment. Festival revelers also have an opportunity to see the traditional German and Norwegian architecture of the Bemidji Language Villages sites. For more information call (218) 299–4544 or (800) 222–4750, or visit www.cord.edu.

As you're passing through downtown Bemidji, you're bound to catch sight of one of Minnesota's classic pieces of oversize civic roadside "art." Paul Bunyan and Babe the Blue Ox stand so stiffly at attention at the intersection of Third Street and Bemidji Avenue that your limbs ache just looking at them. This structure, built in 1937, is one of the most photographed statues in the United States—or at least that's what they'll tell you at the chamber of commerce next door.

Before leaving town you may want to stop for a bite to eat at **_Union Station,_** a restaurant and bar in the historic depot building at First Street and Beltrami Avenue. Employing much tasteful woodwork and featuring a dramatic railroad mural of grand proportions in the main dining room, Union Station serves good, moderately priced Italian and American food. Champagne brunch is offered on Sundays. For information or reservations call (218) 444–9261.

One doesn't have to attend too many of the Gopher State's historic festivals before encountering a peculiar species of Minnesotan. He is dressed from head to toe in buckskin and furs; he assumes a historically derived manner that can, with generosity, best be described as uncouth; and he dotes on his bowie knife and black-powder musket.

Those taken by the presence of this character—or perhaps just curious about his origins—may want to pay a visit to an obscure shop called **_Antle's Long Guns and Accessories,_** located on U.S. Highway 2 just west of Bemidji. The approach to this humble establishment follows a bumpy gravel road through a wooded graveyard of decomposing automobiles. Displayed inside is a varied assortment of muskets, beads and other clothing accessories, muzzle-cleaning supplies, and gunpowder, as well as a selection of books on how to become an authentic black-powder buff. Roy Antle is available to instruct the unenlightened regarding the safe use of his muskets on the shooting range out back.

Pequot Lakes Legends

As you drive into the small resort town of Pequot Lakes, you may notice that the town's water tower resembles a large fishing bobber. Local tradition says that it belonged to Paul Bunyan, the mythical lumberjack whose footprints formed many of the lakes in this region. Legend claims that Paul lost the bobber during a fight with a 40-foot northern pike and that he flipped it and the fish 7 miles from Whitefish Lake to downtown Pequot Lakes.

One story also says that Paul's longtime companion, Babe the Blue Ox, helped form the Mississippi. According to the tale, a huge tank wagon being towed by Babe sprung a leak. The rushing water formed Lakes Bemidji and Itasca, while the overflow trickled down to New Orleans to form the great river. It's only fitting that Minnesota legend revolves around fishing and water. Of course, now that Minnesotans have added golf to their list of summer obsessions, some residents of Pequot Lakes want to build a new water tower modeled after a golf ball.

As its owner is a member in good standing of the Bemidji Hangfires Black Powder Club, Roy's shop is also a good source of information on the northland's largest **Black Powder Rendezvous,** held each June somewhere near Bemidji. Those attending can look forward to "paper punchin', primitive shooting, gun trading, and knife and spear throwing" among other activities, only some of which are claimed to be suitable for kids and women. For more information call Antle's at (218) 751–4752.

Lake of the Woods County

As one of the most northern counties in Minnesota, this sparsely populated region borders Ontario and its namesake, Lake of the Woods. As part of the watery boundary between Canada and the United States, much of this remote region remains as it was during the time of the voyageurs. It's a land of water dotted by land instead of land dotted by lakes.

When French explorer Pierre La Verendrye built **Fort St. Charles** in 1732 on an island in what is now called Lake of the Woods, it was the most northwesterly settlement of Europeans in North America. For ten years the fort was an important fur trading post for La Verendrye and his sons, who used it as a base of operations for their explorations of the Canadian Northwest. The fort also became the burial place of a French Jesuit priest, Father Jean Aulneau, and nineteen of his companions, who were killed on another island by a Dakota war party in 1736.

Walleye Season

Mention walleye to any avid angler in Minnesota and he or she will likely regale you with passionate stories about their pursuit of this tasty fish. When walleye season opens, more than one million residents drop most of what they're doing and go fishing.

Harvesting the walleye has caused conflicts in several parts of the state. At Lake Mille Lacs in central Minnesota, tense standoffs have developed between Indians exercising their historic treaty rights to spear walleye and anglers and resort owners who oppose spearing. Talk by resource officials about closing part of the lake to sport fishing borders on sacrilege for anglers.

On Lake of the Woods, a huge lake that covers most of the northwest angle of Minnesota and ranks as the state's most productive walleye lake, conflicts have erupted between sport and commercial anglers as both groups compete for this prized fish. In such a water-blessed (or obsessed) state, it comes as no surprise that vehement arguments develop over fish.

Northwest Angle

Look at a map of Minnesota and you'll see a small point sticking up from the top. Called the Northwest Angle, it doesn't seem to fit with the rest of the state. In the 1783 Treaty of Paris, the border between Canada and the United States was traced along the old voyageurs route to the northwest corner of Lake of the Woods and then west to the Mississippi. There was only one problem. No one knew the exact source of the Mississippi.

After explorers found the source of the great river, the two countries modified the border. After the War of 1812, a boundary commission decided that the 49th parallel would be the new border from Lake of the Woods to the Pacific Ocean. This didn't intersect in the right place near the lake, so the plotters dropped a line straight south to close the gap. Thus the Northwest Angle, now separated from the rest of Minnesota, became the northernmost point of the lower forty-eight states.

Visitors can reach the fort by boat from Warroad or Baudette (about a 50-mile ride) or by car from Warroad, 63 miles (the final 23 of which are gravel) through a section of Manitoba to Minnesota's Northwest Angle, where a number of resorts can provide easy boat access to Magnusson Island. A reconstructed palisade and log chapel stand today on the site of the original fort, and markers show where other buildings once stood. For more information on the fort, go to www.entreeltd.com/fortStCharles.htm or www.lakeofthewoods.com.

Places to Stay in the Headwaters Region

ST. CLOUD
(area code 320)

Budget Inn,
420 Highway 10 Southeast;
253–0500

Comfort Inn,
4040 Second Street South;
251–1500

Edelbrook House B&B,
216 North Fourteenth
Avenue;
259–0071

Holiday Inn Express,
4322 Clearwater Road;
240–8000

Victorian Oaks
Bed and Breakfast,
404 Ninth Avenue South;
202–1404

LITTLE FALLS
(area code 320)

AmericInn,
306 LeMieur Street;
632–1964

Country Inn and Suites,
209 Northeast Sixteenth
Street;
632–1000

**Lottie Lee Bed
and Breakfast,**
206 Southeast Third Street;
632–8641

Randall House B&B,
200 Southeast Fourth Street;
616–5815

Super 8 Motel,
300 Northeast Twelfth Street;
632–2351

BRAINERD/NISSWA
(area code 218)

Comfort Suites,
1221 Edgewood Drive,
Baxter;
825–7234

Country Inn & Suites,
1220 Dellwood Drive North,
Brainerd;
828–2161

Econolodge,
2655 Highway 371 South,
Brainerd;
828–0027

Hawthorn Suites,
2300 Fairview Road,
Baxter;
822–1133

CROSSLAKE
(area code 218)

**Birch Hill Inne Bed &
Breakfast,**
P.O. Box 468,
Crosslake 56442;
692–4857

WALKER
(area code 218)

AmericInn,
Highway 371 North;
547–2200

**Horseshoe Bay &
Pioneer Inn,**
8098 Hawthorn Trail;
547–1366

**Peace Cliff Bed &
Breakfast,**
Route 73;
547–2832

PARK RAPIDS
(area code 218)

AmericInn,
Highway 34 East;
732–1234

Super 8 Motel,
Highway 34 East;
732–9704

Wildwood Lodge B&B,
HC 06 Box 45A,
Park Rapids 56470;
732–1176

Note: The Park Rapids area
has seven B&B inns. Call the
chamber of commerce for a
complete list at (800)
247–0054 or check their
Web site at www.park
rapids.com.

BEMIDJI
(area code 218)

AmericInn,
1200 Paul Bunyan Drive
Northwest;
751–3000

Beltrami Shores B&B,
Route 5, Box 201, Bemidji
56619;
(888) 746–7373

Holiday Inn Express,
2422 Ridgeway Avenue
Northwest;
751–2487

Super 8 Motel,
1815 Paul Bunyan Drive;
751–8481

Places to Eat in the Headwaters Region

ST. CLOUD
(area code 320)

Ciatti's (Italian),
660 Mall Germain,
Centre Square;
251–5255

SELECTED CHAMBERS OF COMMERCE

Bemidji Chamber of Commerce
(800) 458–2223

**Brainerd Lakes Area Chamber of
Commerce**
(800) 450–2838 ext. 400

**Leech Lake Area Chamber of
Commerce**
(Walker) (800) 833–1118

Little Falls Chamber of Commerce
(800) 325–5916

Park Rapids Chamber of Commerce
(800) 247–0054

**St. Cloud Convention &
Visitors Bureau**
(800) 264–2940 ext. 129

SELECTED WEB SITES IN THE HEADWATERS

Bemidji Chamber of Commerce
www.bemidji.org

**Brainerd Lakes Area
Chamber of Commerce**
www.brainerd.com

**Leech Lake Area Chamber of
Commerce** (Walker)
www.leech-lake.com

Little Falls Chamber of Commerce:
www.littlefallsmn.com

Park Rapids Chamber of Commerce
www.parkrapids.com

**St. Cloud Convention &
Visitors Bureau**
www.stcloudcvb.com

Green Mill (pizza),
1 Sunwood Drive;
259–6455

Mexican Village,
509 Mall Germain;
252–7134

**O'Hara's Brew Pub
& Restaurant** (American),
Thirty-third & Third Streets;
251–9877

Park Diner (American),
1531 Division Street,
Waite Park;
252–0080

LITTLE FALLS
(area code 320)

**Black & White
Hamburger Shop,**
114 Southeast First Street;
632–5374

Charlie's Pizza,
1006 Northeast Fifth Street;
632–6727

China Dragon,
110 Northeast;
632–6727

Pete & Joy's Bakery
(coffee),
121 East Broadway;
632–6388

Royal Cafe (American),
120 West Broadway;
632–6401

BRAINERD/NISSWA
(area code 218)

Eclectic Cafe,
717 Laurel Street,
Brainerd; 825–4880

Ganley's Nisswa Inn
(American),
Main Street, Nisswa;
963–2993

Giovanni's Pizza,
625 Oak Street, Brainerd;
828–4978

Great Wall,
704 Laurel Street,
Brainerd;
825–8636

Log Cabin Restaurant
(American),
320 South Seventh Street,
Brainerd;
829–3431

Lost Lake Lodge
(American),
6415 Lost Lake Road,
Nisswa;
963–2681

**Nisswa Grille,
Coffee & Raw Bar**
(American),
25477 Main Street,
Nisswa; 963–4717

**Northwind Grille
Family Restaurant**
(American),
603 Laurel Street, Brainerd;
829–1551

WALKER
(area code 218)

Blue Loon Express,
Main Street; 547–1456

Cafe Zona Rosa (Mexican),
Front Street and Fifth;
547–3558

Jimmy's Restaurant
(American), Highway 371
North;
547–3334

Margarita Mulligan's
(American),
1812 Merit Road Northwest;
836–2062

Village Square Ice Cream,
Main Street;
547–1456

Wharf, The (American),
Main Street;
547–3777

PARK RAPIDS
(area code 218)

Great Northern Cafe
(American),
218 East First;
732–9565

Khan's Mongolian Barbecue,
Highway 34 East;
732–4474

Long-Van Oriental Restaurant,
Highway 34 East;
732–5491

MinneSoda Fountain
(ice cream),
205 South Main Street;
732–3240

Pizza Ranch, The,
Highway 34 East;
732–4229

DORSET
(area code 218)

Companeros (Mexican),
Route 3;
732–7624

Dorset Cafe (American),
Route 3;
732–4072

Dorset House (American),
Route 3;
732–5556

La Pasta Italian Eatery,
Dorset General Store;
732–0275

BEMIDJI
(area code 218)

Cabin Coffee House & Cafe,
214 Third Street Northwest;
444–2899

Keith's Pizza & Restaurant
(pizza, American),
110 Paul Bunyan Drive
Southeast;
751–7940

Raphaels Bakery Cafe
(American),
319 Minnesota Avenue;
444–2867

Tutto Bene Italian Ristorante,
300 Beltrami Avenue
Northwest;
751–1100

T. Juan's Restaurante
(Mexican),
Third and Park Avenue;
751–6879

Uptown Caffé,
532 Minnesota Street;
444–5282

Roads to Take

Highway 200 from Walker to Remer

Highway 6 from Remer to U.S. Highway 2

Highway 2 from Bemidji to Grand Rapids

Highway 47 from Isle to Malmo along east shore of Mille Lacs Lake

U.S. Highway 169, County Road 35 along south and west shore of Mille Lacs Lake

WAY, WAY OFF THE BEATEN PATH

Wood Tick Race,
Cuyuna, middle of June. Open to "family pets." They encourage novice entries; the champions never return.

Arrowhead

If any part of Minnesota occupies a special place in the hearts of many residents, this is it. The appropriately named Arrowhead region encompasses thousands of square miles of untouched forest and impenetrable bogs, thousands of lakes, and the big lake itself, Superior. Nowhere else in the state will a traveler see such spectacular scenery. And though you will see countless scenic vistas of forest and water throughout the region, the Lake Superior shoreline truly defines the Arrowhead: rugged, isolated, and inhabited by people of hardy stock.

Drive along the shore of Lake Superior (we natives call it the North Shore, no other description needed) and you'll see the vast body of icy freshwater bordered by thundering rivers toppling through narrow gorges, rocky outcrops that soar a thousand feet above the lake, and a vast forest of pine, birch, and maple. This region also has patches of the boreal forest, a special northern ecosystem that covers Canada up to the Arctic.

From Interstate 35, the most direct route from the Twin Cities to Duluth, travelers will find a variety of roads from which to explore the Arrowhead. The best scenery in the region is along Highway 61 as it hugs the shore of Lake Superior. Highway 1 climbs north from Highway 61 into the hills

ARROWHEAD

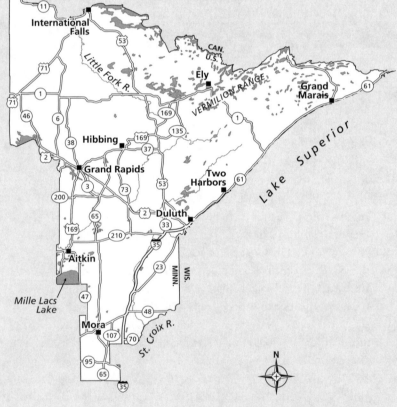

International Falls

11

53

71

71

1

46

6

38

Hibbing

169

169

37

135

Grand Rapids

2

200

3

73

53

65

169

210

2

Duluth

33

35

Aitkin

23

Mora

47

48

107

70

95

65

35

Little Fork R.

CAN.
U.S.

Ely

VERMILION RANGE

Grand
Marais

61

1

Two
Harbors

61

Lake Superior

Mille Lacs
Lake

MINN.

WIS.

St. Croix R.

N

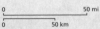

bordering the big lake and runs to Ely through thousands of square miles of pine forest. Leaving Lake Superior behind, many other highways cut through the countless square miles of tamarack swamp, forest, and lakes.

Aitkin County

Aitkin, the largest town in the county, sits on the Mississippi River (at U.S. Highway 169 and Route 210) and owes its settlement in 1870 to a combination of the lumber industry, riverboats, and the railroad. It's also the site of the only diversion channel on the Mississippi. Although the town lacks a large tourist attraction, the residents have a sense of humor.

In 1991 Aitkin merchants, discouraged by the exodus of residents on shopping excursions to malls in bigger cities, and tired of shoveling snow after a huge Thanksgiving Day storm, decided that a parade would draw people into town. And so began the *Aitkin Fish House Parade*, held annually the Friday after Thanksgiving. Each year the parade grows as word spreads. Entrants show up with fish houses of all shapes and sizes to help celebrate the return of winter.

Besides the whimsical, Aitkin also has an important bird habitat at nearby *Rice Lake National Wildlife Refuge* and throughout the county. *Wildbird* magazine called this area the "best little unsung birding spot in America," and Aitkin County is becoming an important stop for serious bird-watchers. According to experts, the area has excellent bird-watching potential year-round. Harsh Canadian winters often force several species of owls south in search of food, and the low glacial hills of this region provide good habitat. Besides these winter visitors, many other species stop during their migration.

After spending a day bird-watching or fish-house watching, you may be ready to kick back with a glass of fine wine. Surprisingly, there's no need to drive to some fancy restaurant with an extensive wine cellar. *Minnesota Wild Winery and Gift Shop,* located about one-half mile north of McGregor on

AUTHOR'S FAVORITES

Cascade River State Park,
west of Lutsen,
(218) 387–3053

Iron Range, Hibbing,
Chisholm, Eveleth, Virginia, etc.,
(800) 777–8497

Lake Superior

Temperance River State Park,
east of Schroeder,
(218) 663–7476

Fun in Aitkin County

While most chamber of commerce and convention bureau representatives tend to be friendly, some take themselves much too seriously. You won't find that the case with the Aitkin Area Chamber of Commerce. Besides having a very friendly and helpful executive director, the town's sense of humor comes through in their area guide. The partial list that follows shows you what I mean:

Useful Facts for First-time Visitors

Distance to Lake Wobegon: 1,200 miles and 16 toll booths

Electricity: Yes

Telephone: Yes

Highest curb: Curb at Potter Bridge (Minnesota Avenue)

Cable TV: Yup

Parking meters: Nope

Most creative use of surveyor's transit: Minnesota Avenue

Indoor plumbing: Yes

Climate: Yes

Most famous landmark: Our stoplight (only one in Aitkin County)

Sense of humor: Yooou-Bet!

Highway 65, (800) 328–6731, can take care of that craving. This winery located in the bog country of northern Minnesota bottles several varieties of wild berry wine, as well as one made from honey. They provide samples but do not have a restaurant or lounge.

Kanabec County

This county received its name in 1858 after being part of three other Minnesota counties and one Wisconsin county. *Kanabec* (Kay-Nay-Bec) is the Ojibway Indian word for "snake," which is also the name of the winding river that runs through the county before emptying into the St. Croix. The unremarkable landscape in this part of Minnesota is a mostly flat mix of wetlands and varied forest. In fact, more than 80 percent of the original wetlands of Kanabec County remain untouched.

Mora, named after its sister city of Mora, Sweden, is the largest town in the county and home to several fun athletic events. Cross-country ski racers know it as the home of the Mora Vasaloppet, the second-largest ski race in the United States and part of the three-race international Vasa series. This ski series has become more than a group of races. It has led to educational and cultural exchanges between the United States and the other two countries that hold Vasa races, Sweden and Japan.

Besides the Vasaloppet, Mora also hosts a half marathon, a canoe race, and a bicycle tour for the athletically inclined. For those looking for less active endeavors, Kanabec and neighboring Isanti County host many other events, from the **Braham Pie Day** in Braham to the **Corn on the Curb** celebration in Ogilvie.

Along with a schedule of athletic events, Mora is also home to the **Kanabec History Center.** This local museum features rotating exhibits that tell the story of the Swedish settlers who arrived in the area with virtually nothing and began a new life. An authentic rural school also occupies the museum site. For more information contact Kanabec History Center, 805 West Forest, Mora 55051; (320) 679–1665; or www.kanabechistory.org.

People from other parts of the country often comment about our Minnesota (Meen-eh-sootah to us natives) accents, which apparently came from our Scandinavian ancestors. If you doubt the significance of Swedish heritage in this area, take a look at the festival brochure the county prints. It's printed in Swedish as well as in English.

Pine County

This north central county defines the term "geographic transition zone." As you drive from south to north in Minnesota, you will notice that the farms get smaller, the patches of forest get bigger, and the mix of crops changes. Pine County provides a perfect micro view of this transition. Although it's not prime agricultural land, the southern part of the county has some decent-size dairy and livestock farms. In northern Pine County, the farms become fewer and smaller, while forests and bogs take over the landscape. Eastern Pine County borders the federally protected upper St. Croix River, one of the most scenic rivers in Minnesota.

While it's easy to see the influences of logging and agriculture in Pine County, it's much more difficult to see evidence of stone quarrying. The **Sandstone History and Art Center** has interesting displays showing the quarrying of sandstone from the banks of the Kettle River, Minnesota's first wild and scenic river. For more information contact Sandstone History and Art Center, 402 Main Street, Sandstone 55072, (320) 245–5241.

As the first Europeans began making their way west to the land that was to become Minnesota, they arrived via a mode of travel that was true to the old adage "When in Rome, do as the Romans do." The birchbark canoes of Indian design that these explorers used proved so well suited to the watery landscape that the canoe remained essential to the region's first commercial enterprise— the fur trade. Thus, the banks of a river like the Snake would have been the perfect place for an operation like the **North West Company Fur Post,** which

dalahorses

In 1972 Mora erected a large Dala Horse to reflect its Swedish heritage and sister-city ties. Measuring 22 feet high and 18 feet long, this landmark is a replica of the wooden Dala Horses carved by Swedish craftsmen.

The carving of Dala Horses began in the 1840s. Although two versions exist about who exactly started it, all seem to agree that the carvers chose the horse because they considered it the most valuable farm animal a family could own. The distinctive orange color and floral patterns painted on the Dala Horse came from the Dala paintings that decorated furniture and interior walls of Swedish homes. Carvers still do most of the work by hand, and because of this no two horses are exactly alike.

today stands in all its early nineteenth-century splendor north of Country Road 7, about 2 miles west of Pine City.

This living-history site, managed by the Minnesota Historical Society, offers you an intriguing immersion into one of the state's most romantic eras. The French Canadian voyageurs whom you will find "living" inside the exactingly re-created rough log palisade were a notoriously colorful and lusty bunch. Paddling heavily ladened canoes and portaging loads of 180 pounds and up from dawn to dusk throughout summer, the voyageurs were so high-spirited that they reputedly could not be kept from singing. In their boisterous way they will teach you how to throw a tomahawk and start a fire using flint and steel while spinning tales about how they spent their time at the post (which was occupied in the winter of 1804) trading guns, blankets, beads, and metal cookware with trappers belonging to local Ojibway bands.

The North West Company Fur Post—which is open free of charge Tuesday through Saturday, May through early September—also gives you a glimpse into the incredibly vast scale of this Canadian-controlled fur trade empire. When the men at the post paddled to Grand Portage in early summer for their company's annual rendezvous, they were joined by compatriots from as far away as Montreal and the arctic tundra of the Canadian Northwest. For more information call (320) 629–6356 or go to www.mnhs.org.

Perhaps the most tragic legacy of Minnesota's turn-of-the-century logging boom was the devastating fire that completely consumed Hinckley and five other towns nearby in the hot, dry summer of 1894. The **Hinckley Fire Museum**—located in the town's defunct train depot at 106 Old Highway 61 and open daily for a small fee May through October—has been dedicated to this singularly destructive event. Because of an accumulated effect of years of clear-cut logging, in which a thick mantle of limbs from the felled giant pines was left like tinder on the ground, there had been a number of small fires ignited through the summer, many by sparks from passing steam locomotives. Finally, on September 1 conditions were at their driest and a strong wind fanned one of these blazes into a firestorm that swept across 320,000 acres of land, destroying everything in its path. The museum's multimedia presentation, photographs, mural, and static displays of melted household artifacts recount the fate of the 418 persons killed in the conflagration, as well as those few who escaped by fleeing to nearby rivers and ponds.

Carlton County

By the time you reach Carlton County, which sits just south of Duluth, the transition from farm to forest is almost complete. While a few stubborn Scandinavians hang on to their small farms, logging and tourism begin to dominate the economy. Main attractions in the county include Jay Cooke State Park, which encompasses a wild section of the St. Louis River, and the Willard Munger State Trail, a beautiful bike trail that starts in Duluth.

Ask a knowledgeable Minnesotan to steer you toward the Grand Portage and you're likely to find yourself cruising along Lake Superior's spectacular north shore, headed for the Canadian border. The 9-mile climb from the shores of Gitche Gumee up and over the Sawtooth Mountains that was made famous by the voyageurs (see the section on Cook County) isn't the only grand portage in the state. The spectacular cataracts of the St. Louis River in its final descent before entering a placid estuary that leads to Duluth harbor also precipitated a major carrying place for early explorers and fur traders seeking passage from the Great Lakes to the Mississippi watershed. This rugged valley, too, was known as the Grand Portage.

Today the area surrounding the St. Louis River Dalles is preserved as *Jay Cooke State Park,* which offers great hiking and skiing trails, camping, and picnicking along the banks of the river. But if you haven't the time or inclination to explore the area under your own locomotion, there's much to be gained by a drive along Minnesota Highway 210 between I–35 and Minnesota 23, which parallels the river on the north side. The road winds up and over the rugged contours of the valley for 9 miles and could almost fool you into thinking you've been detoured onto an Appalachian highway.

If hiking isn't adventuresome enough for your tastes, stop by *Superior Whitewater,* just 1 or 2 miles east of Carlton on Highway 210. Spring through fall, Superior Whitewater conducts professionally guided whitewater-rafting trips down an undeveloped stretch of the St. Louis just upstream of Jay Cooke State Park. The rafts accommodate six paddle-wielding passengers, each outfitted with a life jacket and instructed by experienced guides in the skills required

Fish Houses

In the north country, when the lakes develop a thick enough coating of ice, people tow little square shelters onto the lakes, drill holes through the ice, and fish. Obviously it's not a sight you'll see in warmer climates. Fish houses come in all different sizes and run the gamut from one-person canvas shelters to solidly built wood units that hold up to ten or more. The larger ones often have received substantial upgrades and may have a television, stereo, kitchen, bunk beds, and carpet. Whatever the size, all fish houses come with an important feature: a hole, or holes, in the floor.

Clusters of fish houses on lakes will resemble an Arctic settlement, and on large lakes such as Mille Lacs, resort owners plow wide roads from shore to the temporary towns and put bridges over cracks in the ice. Although people fish everywhere, few go to such lengths to pursue their passion when the weather changes so drastically. Should you see a motley assortment of fish houses on some vast frozen wasteland, don't take pity on the inhabitants. They may be catching their limit of walleye.

to pilot the vessel; two-person inflatable kayaks are also available. The rapids on this section of the river begin gently enough and then grow in size and intensity as you progress downstream. By the time you reach Electric Ledge— a thrilling 6-foot chute formed where the water tumbles over a riverwide bedrock dike—you're ready for the exhilarating splash in the face that you're likely to get.

The excitement of Minnesota's only whitewater-rafting experience lasts about two and a half hours and is expensively priced. You should make reservations in advance by writing Superior Whitewater, 950 Chestnut Street, Carlton 55718 or by calling (218) 384–4637 or checking out www.minnesotawhitewater.com.

Before you disappear into the northern forests, a final stop in Carlton County should be made at the southeast corner of the junction of Minnesota Highways 45 and 33 in Cloquet. Here, amid gas fumes and the honking of cars, stands the world's only ***Frank Lloyd Wright–designed service station.*** Since 1957 this Phillips 66 franchise has been humbly serving the fossil-fuel needs of countless customers who have pulled up beneath the steep, angular, cantilevered roof, perhaps unaware that they were in the presence of architectural greatness. Thus forewarned, you won't make the same mistake.

Itasca County

In the land of 10,000 lakes, this northern Minnesota county has its own monopoly on water. More than 1,000 lakes surround Grand Rapids, which is the largest town in the county, and the Mississippi River flows through town as it begins its journey south. Although the two main highways that meet in Grand Rapids, U.S. Highway 2 and US 169, aren't especially scenic, a special treat awaits travelers. Highway 38 runs north from Grand Rapids to Effie and is designated The Edge of the Wilderness Scenic Byway, one of the first of twenty National Scenic Byways.

Grand Rapids, the Itasca County seat, is an attractive old logging town that hasn't quit. The looming buildings of the **_Blandin Paper Company,_** which line the banks of a not-yet-so-mighty Mississippi River in the heart of the city, stand as living testament to the days when the decimated giant pine gave way to the cutting of pulpwood. Free tours of the facility are offered regularly and follow the high-tech, step-by-step transformation of locally harvested balsam and poplar into fifteen-ton spools of glossy magazine stock that may eventually find its way into your home as _Time_ or _Newsweek._ For more information on tours, call (218) 327–6302.

Back when pine was king, of course, life was a whole lot simpler, as you'll discover for yourself if you pay a visit to the Minnesota Historical Society's wonderful **_Forest History Center._** You'll find this painstakingly resurrected turn-of-the-twentieth-century logging camp and interpretive center a few miles west of town on County Road 70, near Golf Course Road.

The modern interpretive center houses an excellent exhibit on the history of mankind's relationship with Minnesota's forests. From now-extinct Native American cultural traditions to the most recent trends in conservation, this story is told through multimedia presentations, static displays, and photographs. A highlight is a short film of the last logging drive in Minnesota, which took place on the Little Fork River in 1937. Expert "whitewater men" can be seen hopping nimbly from log to log, while others guide huge "wanigans"—rafts supporting the crew's kitchen and bunkhouse—through the rapids.

Even though it may look like summer outside to you, it's December 15, 1900, in the **_Northwoods Logging Company camp,_** located a short hike through the woods from the interpretive center. In fact, as your guide explains before you enter the first of several hand-hewn–log buildings, the crew is still looking for some hardy men and women to fill a few jobs for the season. Highly entertaining and extremely knowledgeable costumed characters populating the camp provide opportunities for a little on-the-job training to help you decide if spending the winter as a "road monkey," assistant cook, or sawyer is for you. Unfortunately, as most folks quickly learn, their backwoods savvy qualifies them only for the bottom-rung position of road monkey, whose job it was to throw straw in front of log-burdened sleighs on the icy downhills and collect the "road apples" dropped in the wake of the powerful draft horses.

Besides visiting the bunkhouse, the notoriously ornery cook and her humble assistants, the earthy barn boss and blacksmith, and the solitary saw sharpener, you also get a chance to chat with a 1930s Forest Service ranger in his nearby cabin. Finally, you can visit a replica floating kitchen, or wanigan, of the type once used by logging crews as they drove their logs downstream. All facilities at the center are open daily mid-May through mid-October, and special events, such as a kids' weekend in mid-June and a woodcrafts festival in mid-July, are scheduled annually. The interpretive center is open afternoons through winter. There is a small admission fee. For more information call (218) 327–4482.

Since its construction in 1902, **Central School**—located at the intersection of US 2 and US 169 in **Grand Rapids** has no doubt seen a lot of students gazing wistfully out of its Romanesque Revival arched windows. Today the attractive building has been preserved as a center for the area's historic heritage and the arts. Also, on the first floor, in what for many years was actually the first-grade room, is the **First Grade,** an inexpensive restaurant serving very good homemade soups, sandwiches, and pies in an atmosphere likely to rekindle some long-forgotten grade-school memories.

Even more nostalgia is in store on the building's third floor, where the **Itasca County Historical Museum** has dedicated considerable space to Grand Rapids' most famous citizen. Judy Garland—born Francis Gumm in 1922 to Grand Rapids movie-theater owner Frank Gumm—lived in town only until she was four. But by then she had already gotten a taste for the limelight, having delighted her father's customers by dancing on the movie-house stage at age two-and-a-half. Commemorating her career are videos of *The Wizard of Oz* and other Garland films, a yellow brick road outside the building, and a collection of photographs, albums, and what is claimed to be the nation's largest display of Garland memorabilia. (**The Gumm House,** not open to the public, can be seen a few blocks away at 727 Second Avenue Northeast. Also, an annual festival in honor of Judy Garland is held in Grand Rapids.) Other exhibits in the museum—which charges a modest admission fee and is open year-round most days of the week—focus on aspects of Itasca County history. Elsewhere in the building a large art gallery features works of local artists.

In Ojibway mythology there is a sleeping giant called "Mesabi," and it was believed that the huge ridge of ancient granite stretching 50 miles north and east of Grand Rapids was its home. Though they may not have been able to conceive of just how their giant was to be awakened or what it would mean to America's burgeoning twentieth-century industries, the Mesabi and the adjacent Vermilion Iron Range did indeed house a giant that for decades yielded vast quantities of the richest iron ore on Earth.

In Calumet—at the western end of the Mesabi, 18 miles east of Grand Rapids on US 169—there is a must-visit site for anyone who wants to gain a firsthand perspective on just how Minnesota's iron-ore giant was shaken to life. The ***Hill Annex Mine*** was in continuous operation from 1903 to 1978, when it was shut down practically overnight and sold to the state for a token fee. Run since 1988 by the Department of Natural Resources as Minnesota's sixty-fourth and newest state park, Hill Annex allows visitors to examine every aspect of the mining process—from the bottom of the pit to the top of the waste-rock piles looming more than 500 feet overhead.

The tour begins at the old Hill Annex Clubhouse, which was built in the 1930s as a gathering place for managers who lived with their families in adjacent company houses at this "location" (a worker-habitation site) near the edge of the ever-growing pit; the miners, by contrast, kept to their own kind in bunkhouses on the other side of the tracks. Well-designed exhibits and excellent larger-than-life photographs in the clubhouse chronicle changing lifestyles and technologies at the mine. Upstairs are re-created living quarters, a chemistry lab, and a foreman's office. Another room has an oral-history library and a computer-operated photograph file, all open to visitors.

This orientation complete, the visitor should get ready to board a colorful bus for a ninety-minute tour of the mine itself. Much of this time is spent exploring the processing plant, which separated ore from waste rock, and the complex network of conveyors that carried these materials to their respective destinations.

Though the Hill Annex was relatively small compared to other mines on the range, it is an awesome sight nonetheless. More than sixty-three million tons of ore were extracted from the 640-acre pit, whose bottom is now flooded with water. The decades of blasting and carving required to move all that rock have created a landscape that is simultaneously beautiful and discomforting to behold. Looking out from the rim, one sees the water glistening far below as if from the bottom of a spectacular desert canyon. But the place is also raw and desolate, occupied here and there by rusting hulks of machinery that look puny from afar and cumbersome and lifeless up close.

Bus tours at the Hill Annex are run on the hour, for a small fee, daily from Memorial Day through September. For information on special geology tours or for group reservations, write the Hill Annex Mine, Box 376, Calumet 55716 or call (218) 247–7215.

There are so few serious practitioners of the lost art of birchbark-canoe building in the United States that they can practically be counted on one hand. But as is only appropriate to a state whose history is so deeply indebted to the canoe, one of the nation's greatest builders can be found in the heart of

Minnesota's northwoods. As you're cruising north on Minnesota 6 from Deer River, passing the settlements of Bowstring and Talmoon in a blur, the thick forests on either side of the road are suddenly interrupted by the Big Fork River and a large tar-paper shed on its banks, with a couple of graceful-looking bark vessels displayed out front. The sign above the door reads HAFEMAN BOAT WORKS.

Ray Boessel inherited this canoe-building business from his grandfather-in-law, Bill Hafeman, in 1981, and since then he has supported himself by producing up to seventeen canoes a year. The elder master learned the trade by necessity after moving to Big Fork in 1920, when the river route to town was a far better option than the area's rudimentary roads. Although Bill's maiden voyage in his first canoe carried him to town in four hours, it took him two *days* to get home. Over the years he greatly refined the canoe-building skills that Ray, in his gentle, friendly way, is glad to share with you. You'll learn all that's involved in his ancient trade—from cutting bark from live birches when the sap is flowing in early summer to collecting the long spruce roots for lashing the canoe together to completing the final stages of assembly. You can even test-paddle one of the finished products on the river to discover how strong, pliable, and lovely these canoes truly are.

In case you want to take one of these watercraft home with you to join the ranks of such proud owners as Charles Kuralt and Lady Bird Johnson, be prepared for a four-figure price tag. For more information you can write Ray at RR 1, Box 187, Big Fork 56628 or call (218) 743–3709.

Koochiching County

Koochiching, the Indian name for the Rainy River, referred to mist and spray from Koochiching Falls. As part of the great network of lakes and rivers that formed a portion of the Voyageur's Highway, the river played an important role in the settlement of this remote northern county, first as a watery highway and later as a source of power for industry. Made up of bogs, forest, and lakes, the county lies in a region blessed with a million acres of wilderness and cursed with long and often harsh winters.

The Big Fork River has been a heavily traveled river throughout most of the human era. Its prominent role in the 12,000-year human history of the north country is revealed by a visit to the ***Grand Mound Interpretive Center,*** located at the confluence of the Big Fork and Rainy Rivers on Minnesota Highway 11, 17 miles west of International Falls.

At the end of a short trail leading from the Grand Mound Interpretive Center building toward the heavily wooded banks of the Rainy, the forest canopy suddenly opens up to reveal a huge dome-shaped earthwork covered with ferns. This mysterious cultural creation that masquerades as a hillock is surrounded by four smaller ancient burial mounds. Several large trees growing on the Grand Mound's flanks only hint at how old the structure actually is. To plumb the depths of its age and to gain some idea of the mound's significance, you would do well to spend an hour or so at the interpretive center, where an excellent video and labyrinthine exhibit on northern Minnesota prehistory flesh out the story.

The Grand Mound was the largest of some 10,000 burial mounds that the first Europeans encountered upon exploring the land that was to become Minnesota. Some of these mounds resembled animal or human forms, others were linear or cone-shaped, and many were located at the junctions of rivers. Apparently the Indians of the time had no explanation as to when or by whom the mounds were made. This reinforced a common belief of early scholars that the "simple savages" then living in North America were incapable of building the mounds, and there was wild speculation as to who should be credited with their creation. The bones and simple artifacts unearthed by enthusiastic investigators and curio hunters were attributed to druids, ancient Egyptians, prehistoric Chinese, and even pioneers from the lost city of Atlantis.

More recent excavations by contemporary archaeologists have produced evidence that the Grand Mound was built by a number of different prehistoric Indian cultures from 200 B.C. to A.D. 1400. Not much is known about what significance mound burials may have had for these peoples, though scientists suggest that the societies that produced the mounds were relatively complex and hierarchical (only selected, hence presumably more important, individuals were entombed) and that their members seem to have been greatly preoccupied with death.

The Grand Mound Interpretive Center is open free of charge Tuesday through Sunday, May through early September. Call (218) 279–3332 for more information.

In winter the Rainy River border town of *International Falls* often receives the dubious distinction of being identified as the nation's "cold spot." But when summer comes, the area around "Frostbite Falls" shows another face altogether. Eleven miles east of downtown, the magnificent 219,000-acre expanse of *Voyageurs National Park,* Minnesota's only national park, draws visitors seeking a full spectrum of water-borne recreational opportunities. So much of this relatively unknown park is covered with water—there are more than thirty lakes, five of which are large—that no roads lead into its interior. Thus the most common means of travel are by motorboat, houseboat, sailboat, canoe, kayak, and floatplane. Excellent hiking routes are found on the densely forested Kabetogama Peninsula in the interior, but the only access to the peninsula on the U.S. side requires the services of an air- or waterborne ferry. During the chilly winter months, Voyageurs' thick lake ice and plentiful snow invite exploration by snowmobile and on skis.

If you don't happen to have your own watercraft along on your visit to Voyageurs, don't despair. Departing at least once daily during most of the summer from the Rainy Lake Visitor Center on Black Bay, 11 miles east of International Falls on County Road 11, is the *Pride of Rainy Lake*. Many excursions on this large cruiser are narrated by Park Service naturalists who tell tales of the lively human history of the park—including exploits of Indians, voyageurs, gold miners, and lumberjacks—as they interpret aspects of the park's pristine boreal forest environment (prices for these trips are inexpensive to moderate). Excursions across Black Bay via large fur trade canoes are also offered for no charge. The historic exhibits, orientation video, and bookstore at the visitors' center are also well worth an hour of your time.

For more information about the park, write the Superintendent, Voyageurs National Park, Box 50, International Falls 56649 or call (218) 283–9821. For general information on cruises aboard the *Pride of Rainy Lake,* call Rainy Lake Visitor Center at (218) 286–5258; for information about naturalist-guided trips on the same boat, call the Rainy Lake Visitors Center at (218) 286–5258.

St. Louis County

As the largest county in Minnesota, St. Louis County stretches from Lake Superior to the Canadian border. Its hundreds of square miles of forest and bogs have made it an inhospitable place to try to carve out a living. But two features make it unique among northern counties. It has almost 30 miles of Lake Superior shoreline and can lay claim to two of the richest iron ore deposits in the world in the Mesabi and Vermilion ranges. This combination of abundant natural resources and access to the big lake contributed to the growth of Duluth as the largest inland port in the world.

Much of Voyageurs National Park also is accessible from northwestern St. Louis County. The end of the Ash River Trail, County Road 129, is a jumping-off place for the backcountry lakes of the Kabetogama Peninsula, which is also the site of the park's most unusual civilized attraction: Minnesota's remotest and perhaps most historically colorful hotel.

The **Kettle Falls Hotel** landing (travel by boat is the only means of getting here) is close to the now-dammed Kettle Falls, which marks the international border and connects the Kabetogama Peninsula with Canadian soil. Following a comprehensive Park Service–funded restoration that was completed in 1988, the hotel sits proudly among the tall pines at the end of a long

Kettle Falls Hotel

wooded walkway. The building gleams with fresh white paint, and cheerful red-and-white striped awnings adorn each window. A huge wraparound screened porch embraces the lower level and provides a pleasant site for dining, reading, or taking in the evening air. The rooms upstairs, which command a moderate price, are appointed with simple antiques and antique reproductions (all share common bathroom facilities). And then there's the bar . . .

According to its brochure, the Kettle Falls was built in 1910 to provide a "stopping place" for loggers who were endeavoring to rout the surrounding forests of the ubiquitous giant red and white pines. But corner the hotel manager, and you may learn just what induced those loggers to frequent the place. He can tell you about the extensive bootlegging and smuggling operations that were run out of the hotel during Prohibition (the woods on the Canadian side of the border provided an ideal site for a still). He may mention something of the pervasive gambling that took place, and he might just hint at another enterprise that was once central to the Kettle Falls's appeal.

But if the manager leaves some gaps in the story, just find your way to the hotel bar and, with luck, the bartender will fill in the rest. This room is adorned with signed photographs of leering sirens and framed calendar girls of a bygone era—perhaps the same faces that gazed down on the lumberjacks as they waited to take their turns upstairs with some of the hotel's female employees. In their exuberance these customers danced on top of the bar until it was reduced to splinters under their hobnailed boots.

If, after hearing about all this, you find that you have a little trouble walking straight and the surroundings seem a bit out of kilter, console yourself with the knowledge that the barroom floor really does slope rather drastically toward the door. The reconstruction preserved in the warped foundation a 2-foot drop in elevation when measured from the summit of a hump near the pool table (which appears to be desperately maintaining its equilibrium) to the distant corner.

The Kettle Falls has several housekeeping cabins available, as well as boat and canoe rentals. Home-cooked meals from a limited menu are served daily in the dining room. For more information contact the Kettle Falls Hotel, 10502 Gamma Road, Lake Kabetogama 56669; call (218) 374–4404 or (888) 534–6835; or go to www.kettlefallshotel.com.

Renting a houseboat from *Ebel's Voyageur Houseboats* is another way to gain access to the distant bays and numerous fishing holes of the park. Equipped with every convenience a landlubber could ask for, these floating mobile homes cruise at slow speed by day and are nosed up on protected beaches at night. Depending on size of party, length of trip, and degree of luxury sought, houseboat rentals are moderately to expensively priced. Contact Ebel's Voyageur Houseboats at 10326 Ash River Trail, Orr 55771 or call (218) 374–3571 or (888) 883–2357; www.ebels.com.

The *Echo Trail* is a remote Minnesota back road that delivers all of the pristine enchantment conjured up by its name. Flanked on both sides for most of its 60 winding, hilly miles by the famed million-acre Boundary Waters Canoe Area (BWCA) wilderness, the Echo can afford drivers glimpses of deer, moose, bear, and possibly even the elusive eastern timber wolf. As it meanders between Echo Lake, about 6 miles south of the little town of Crane Lake on County Road 24, and the north shore of Shagawa Lake near Ely, the Echo Trail skirts several lakeshores from which, on a calm summer evening, you may hear the resonant call of a loon across the water.

St. Paul YMCA Camp du Nord is one Echo Trail establishment that beckons families in search of an unusual summer vacation experience. Du Nord, located on County Road 644 (also known as the

thegreatlake superior

I don't remember my first visit to the north shore of Lake Superior. After my birth in November, my parents took me along when they vacationed along the shore in June. Even though I don't remember that first trip, it must have ingrained in me a special affinity with that part of Minnesota. And while I still have not taken a canoe into the Boundary Waters Canoe Area (considered by some to be positively un-Minnesotan, especially for someone born and raised here), I have faithfully visited the big lake every year and in every season.

Besides good memories of the shore, I also have a poignant one. Because it had always been my mother's favorite place to vacation, we spread her ashes in the lake near the village of Grand Marais. From the beginning of life to the end, Lake Superior continues to draw my family to its rugged coast.

North Arm Road) about 9 miles down the Echo from its eastern terminus, is a family camp—meaning that it combines many of the features typically found at a resort with a creative variety of program activities for all ages. Upholding a strong wilderness ethic, du Nord staff lead families on canoe trips into the BWCA and offer naturalist-guided hikes and other environmentally oriented activities. Campwide cookouts and campfires develop a robust sense of community spirit, while daily activities for different age groups provide parents and kids with opportunities to mix with their peers. Families who attend the inexpensive, weeklong summer sessions (advance reservations are required) can camp out or stay in rustic housekeeping cabins, many of which are perched along the rugged shore of the north arm of Burntside Lake. For more information write Camp du Nord, 2125 East Hennepin Avenue, Minneapolis 55413; call (612) 465–0450; or visit www.dunord.org.

Does Camp du Nord sound too wholesome for your tastes? Then retrace your steps about a half-mile east along the Echo Trail from the North Arm Road to where a track disappears into the forest, this time to the north. FOREST SERVICE ROAD 459, as it's designated by a small sign, will give you a progressively certain sense that you're headed for oblivion, particularly after mile 3, when you turn left at the intersection to join a ragged, two-tire track whose bumps will nearly slow you to a crawl. Then you cross a little creek on a dubious-looking wooden bridge—the kind where you pray that your car is wide enough as you blindly aim your tires so that they might be supported by the separate wooden planks beneath—and the road suddenly ends.

The simple wood-frame building in front of you with the plastic flamingos in the yard is the **Chainsaw Sisters Saloon.** Tending bar you will probably find owner Michelle Carlson, one of a pair of brawny twins who gained their genteel alias while employed by the Forest Service to keep BWCA portages clear of deadfalls (Michelle's sister and former tavern-owning partner, Marlene, has moved on to other adventures). Following a blowout land-acquisition celebration in September 1987—during which, it is rumored, one of the twins broke some guy's arm while mud wrestling—these two women literally carved their establishment out of the surrounding woods. There's no electricity at the Chainsaw Sisters, nor is there a telephone. But the beer is cold, and there's enough light given off by the gas wall lamps to inform your contemplations of a local legend concerning the two friendly women behind the bar: Did they or did they not outlast the entire all-male Ely ice-rescue squad in a contest to see who could remain submerged the longest in the ice-capped waters of Shagawa Lake?

The Chainsaw Sisters aren't likely to be the only characters you'll meet if you spend some time visiting the wilderness frontier town of Ely. The community's past and present are thick with the exploits of prospectors, lumberjacks, and miners against a backdrop of prehistoric activity that stretches back thousands of years.

To get a sense of the breadth and depth of Ely's past, you may want to pay a visit to the *Vermilion Interpretive Center* at Vermilion Community College, located at 1900 East Camp Street. Exhibits at the center capture the many ways that Ojibway Indians, French Canadian voyageurs, Swedish loggers, and Finnish miners have interacted among themselves and left their mark on the woodlands that dominate the landscape. There is also an exhibit commemorating Ely resident Will Steger, leader of a spectacularly successful self-contained international dogsled expedition to the North Pole in 1986. The interpretive center is open Wednesday through Saturday from October through April and daily in the summer. A modest admission fee is charged.

The howl of a lone wolf echoing across a lake conjures up images of the northern wilderness like nothing else. And the Minnesota legislature, which presides over a state graced with the largest population of wolves in the lower forty-eight (1997–98 estimates place the population at 1,995–2,905), has decreed that an interpretive center be built to honor the wolf and educate people about this much abused and misunderstood creature. Ely's *International Wolf Center,* on Route 169 just east of town, gives people the straight scoop about wolves through imaginative hands-on programs and an award-winning exhibit on the relationship of wolves to humans of all cultures.

Art, literature, interactive videos, a large diorama of a wolf pack bringing down a white-tailed deer, and other displays at the Wolf Center stimulate thinking about the many ways humans have mythologized and romanticized the wolf over the centuries and across the continents. Fables and images range from St. Francis of Assisi to Adolf Hitler, from Lon Chaney to Romulus and Remus.

Several times each day wolf handlers enter an enclosure and introduce visitors (who watch from behind glass windows) to the center's resident pack. A wolf-ecology day camp for children, summer howling trips for families, and hands-on research expeditions for adults round out the offerings. The center charges a modest fee and is open daily, May through mid-October, and on Tuesday and weekends the rest of the year. For more information about programs, call toll-free (800) ELY–WOLF (359–9653) or visit www.wolf.org.

Adjacent to the Wolf Center on Highway 169 stand two log buildings that commemorate the life and times of a most unusual wilderness pioneer. Every log in the *Dorothy Molter Museum* was moved by volunteers, without mechanical assistance, from its original location on the Isle of Pines on Knife Lake in the heart of the Boundary Waters Canoe Area wilderness. Here, from 1934 until her death in 1986, Dorothy lived a quiet life of service surrounded by nature's magnificence. As the Boundary Waters grew in popularity among

TOP ANNUAL EVENTS

John Beargrease Dogsled Marathon,
Duluth, January,
(800) 4–Duluth

Mora Vasaloppet cross-country ski race,
Mora, second Sunday in February,
(800) 368–6672,
e-mail: vasaloppet@ncis.co

Summer Finnish Festival,
Embarrass, early June,
(800) 777–7281

Fisherman's Picnic,
Grand Marais, late July/early August,
(218) 387–1400

Braham Pie Day,
Braham, first Friday in August,
(612) 689–4229

Bayfront Blues Festival,
Duluth, second weekend of August,
(800) 4–Duluth

Aitkin Fish House Parade,
Friday after Thanksgiving,
(800) 526–8342,
www.aitkin.com

canoeists, "The Root-beer Lady," as she became known, also sold homemade brew to many of the 6,000 visitors who paddled to her door each year (her guest books, dutifully signed by all visitors, are available for your perusal).

Walk through the simple rooms of her two cabins and view portions of an excellent documentary video about her life, and you may come to appreciate the many subtle things that make Dorothy's life remarkable. She evidently loved the long silences and solitary rigors of winter life at her island retreat, yet her summers were filled with enough uninvited visitors to make her one of the area's main tourist attractions. Without ever charging a fee, she used her training as a nurse to help wilderness travelers who were injured and sick. She even paid for an emergency float-plane evacuation for a man suffering from hypothermia whose party was unable to afford the flight. Perhaps that explains why an avalanche of signatures was easily gathered to petition the USDA Forest Service to allow her to remain on her island home in the late 1970s, when the Boundary Waters became closed to residents. Appropriately enough she was allowed the privilege of living out her days in the heart of canoe country.

The Dorothy Molter Museum is open weekends from her birthday, May 6, to Memorial Day each spring, then daily through September. Call (218) 365–4451 for more information and to make an appointment for visits outside normal hours.

Numerous resorts and outfitters in town can help even the most inexperienced adventurers gain access to the surrounding wilderness. Though the usual modes of travel in the BWCA are by canoe, skis, and snowshoes, explorers with more exotic tastes can arrange for kayak trips through **Piragis North Woods Company** (call toll-free 800–223–6565 or visit www.piragis.com). In winter they can assume command at the helm of a sled-dog team under the guidance of polar explorer Paul Schurke at **Wintergreen Lodge;** call (218) 365–6022 or visit www.dogsledding.com.

Scandinavians have made a fascinating ritual of the sauna—a ritual that has elements both sacred and profane—and there is no better place to partake of its traditions than the **Ely Steam Bath.** For more than fifty years, work-worn loggers and miners, grimy from a day's labor in the area's once-great open-pit mines, have made the trek into town to catch up on local gossip, cleanse their bodies, and replenish their spirits in the steam bath's penetrating vapors. A visit to this humble landmark institution, found on Harvey Street near First Avenue, will have the same effects on you, as well as providing a unique window to one of Minnesota's most engaging off-the-beaten-path communities.

The steam bath has separate public facilities for men and women, as well as smaller rooms available exclusively for couples. But for the full sociological experience, the public baths are the way to go. Typically the natives prolong their convivial ablutions by working up a sweat in the steam room, showering, and then sitting for a while in the antechamber to enjoy a cold drink before repeating the cycle a couple more times. By their last visit to the steam room, the men are so well softened up that they often shave their bristly beards without need of shaving cream. Newcomers, however, may find themselves similarly poached after only one or two doses of Scandinavian heat.

Open for business Wednesday and Friday from 4:00 to 8:30 P.M. and on Saturdays from 2:00 to 8:30 P.M. year-round, the Ely Steam Bath boasts extremely modest prices. Towels are provided.

The **Vermilion Iron Range,** which runs south and west of Ely, is a small relative to the famous Mesabi Range farther west. But what it lacked in size, the Vermilion made up for in the purity of its ore and in its stature as the place where Minnesota's iron-ore rush began. The start of this world-class industrial bonanza was the **Soudan Underground Mine**—the oldest, richest, and deepest mine in the state and now one of Minnesota's most fascinating tourist attractions.

Run by the Department of Natural Resources as a historic state park since mining operations ceased in 1962, the mine's several modest above-ground buildings and the 1924-vintage hoist (a huge cable, drum, and engine system that hauls loads up and down the Soudan's main shaft) are maintained in top working order. But instead of raising six-ton bins of dense reddish-brown hematite ore up to the surface every three to five minutes, as it has done for most of its working life, the hoist now transports rattling steel elevators, or "cages," full of visitors wearing hard hats.

After viewing a short film on the history of the Soudan, prepare yourself for a quick descent 2,341 feet below ground to level 27—the mine's deepest horizontal "drift," or passage, where the temperature year-round is a cool fifty degrees. The guide explains that the ride down will take three minutes traveling at about 10 miles per hour, but the dizzying blur of rock and steel visible through the elevator's single window gives the impression of much greater speed. The elevator finally comes to a noisy halt, the door opens, and a small train awaits to take you a quarter of a mile down a dark tunnel to a reconstructed mining site.

The reality of what it was like to work in such a place dawns on you slowly. Solitary mannequins placed far apart in a large cavern stand poised to drill holes with deafening, carbide-tipped, air-powered drills (the guide turns them on briefly). Under working conditions the headlamps that the miners wore were the only sources of light (other lights illuminating the scene are momentarily turned off so that you can appreciate the gloom), and a pervasive unhealthy dust frequently limited visibility even more. During lunch breaks and shift changes, the freshly drilled 10-foot-deep holes were filled with explosives, and the caverns were enlarged by blasting. Then, using heavy equipment, the laborers would load the ore into small railroad cars for the trip to the elevator. The best paid among the miners of this "Cadillac of underground mines" (conditions were considered excellent, and, with only thirteen deaths, the Soudan's safety record was very good) were the men who drilled and blasted the ceilings of vertical shafts that were up to 200 feet high. In 1962 each eight-hour shift that these men worked yielded a $24 wage.

If that sounds like no fun, consider the days before electricity and unionization brought their improvements. In the early 1890s, when the possibilities of open-pit mining at the Soudan site were exhausted and the enterprise went underground, miners wielded pickaxes for the duration of each twelve-hour shift. Illumination was cast by candles, one to a man. The mules that hauled the ore to the hoist stayed underground for six months at a time, and when they arrived at the surface for a well-earned six-month vacation, their eyes were wrapped in layers of gauze that were removed gradually over the course of a week to prevent blindness.

Underground tours of the Soudan mine are offered daily for a modest fee throughout the summer; they leave the surface each half-hour and take about an hour. The interpretive film lasts ten minutes, there are aboveground exhibits in the information building, and the giant hoist can be seen in operation. Also, hiking trails lead to several of the Soudan's original open pits. For more information call toll-free within Minnesota (800) 652–9747; outside Minnesota call (218) 753–2245.

Miners long ago discovered that nothing takes the chill off after a shift in the bowels of the earth than an authentic, home-cooked pasty—a delicious culinary tradition on the range that reflects the influence of immigrant Cornish miners. And the **Tower Bakery,** just a mile west of the Soudan Underground Mine on Minnesota 169 in the heart of Tower, has a reputation for some of the best pasties around. Park yourself at the counter, order a cup of coffee, and enjoy your vegetable, pork, and beef pie shaped like a half-moon. The crust is flaky, and the bill is so cheap that you may be inclined to buy a couple more for the road.

Detour about a dozen miles south of Tower on Highway 169 for an exploration of the Finnish heritage and architecture that characterizes much of the region's settlement history. **Sisu Heritage,** in the little town of **Embarrass** (occasionally noted for having the coldest temperature in the lower forty-eight states), provides visitors with two-hour guided tours of several preserved pioneer homesteads. The informative guides strike a balance between explaining subtle differences in log-building techniques developed by Finnish master builders and providing insights into cultural traditions, like the sauna, that were brought by the Finns to the northwoods. The tours are inexpensive and are offered during summer from Monday through Saturday. For reservations write Sisu Heritage, Inc., P.O. Box 127, Embarrass 55733.

Ice-hockey fans will want to pay a visit to a cube-shaped building on a prominent hill overlooking U.S. Highway 53 in downtown Eveleth. The **United States Hockey Hall of Fame** stands as a tribute both to the sport and to the prominence it has enjoyed on the iron range since 1903, when the first game was played in Eveleth. Giants of the sport are immortalized in the Great Hall downstairs, where each star has his own pillar, plaque, and photograph. Upstairs a room dedicated to the U.S. Olympic hockey team contains special artifacts commemorating the gold-medal teams of 1960 and 1980. There is also a continually running video of the much-celebrated U.S. victory over the USSR in 1980.

A tunnel-like exhibit with illustrations and audiotapes traces the history of hockey from its roots in 478 B.C. Other displays are dedicated to modern amateur, collegiate, and high school competition. If, after all this adoration of the game, you're itching to knock the puck around, you can do so at a mock shooting gallery wherein an electronic goalie defends a life-size goal from your best shots. The Hall of Fame is open year-round, seven days a week, except holidays, and charges a modest admission fee. For more information call (218) 744–5167 or log on to www.ushockeyhall.com.

As you're traveling west on US 169 from Eveleth, you may notice that the landscape along both sides of the highway has a slightly unnatural appearance.

There are trees, lakes, and occasionally rugged hills and valleys—just as you'd see elsewhere in northeastern Minnesota—but still, you think, something isn't quite right.

A visit to the interpretive center at **Ironworld Discovery Center** in **Chisholm,** 20 miles west of Eveleth, will clear up the mystery straight away, for at this fantastic historical museum, research library, and entertainment complex, which was completed in 1985 at a cost of $8.5 million, you'll learn that you've been traveling down the backbone of the Ojibway's Mesabi—the sleeping iron-ore giant. And the seventy-five-year endeavor to remove this creature from his resting place has left its mark on virtually everything in sight.

The spectacular views from Ironworld's several observation decks, historic trolley, and tourist railroad are typical. In all directions stands of second-growth timber mask flat-topped piles of discarded low-grade ore and other waste rock. And the lake you see at the bottom of a steeply terraced valley is actually an abandoned open-pit mine.

Ironworld Discovery Center, which was built to celebrate the special ethnic history of the iron range, will leave an indelible impression of the tremendous scope of Minnesota's iron-ore industry and the impact that it has had on the world. Wonderfully creative exhibits at the interpretive center chronicle the cultural traditions brought to the iron range by the masses of immigrants who came from all over Europe at the turn of the twentieth century. Everywhere in the building music and professionally crafted displays complement historic films and audiotapes of miners and their families describing their experiences. There are demonstrations of ethnic cooking and folk art traditions. Large exhibits bring to life the geological history of the area and the technology of taconite mining.

Meanwhile, outside there are regular ethnic music and dance performances in a beautifully landscaped garden. Food booths offer specialties that are traditional to the iron range's historic cultures. Special concerts are held throughout summer in an acoustically superb, 1,600-seat outdoor amphitheater. Also a half-dozen festivals are held at Ironworld each year, drawing internationally renowned performers and musicians. Ironworld's entertainment areas and interpretive center are open daily from May through September for a small fee, whereas the research library, with its extensive genealogy archives, is open year-round. For more information write Ironworld Discovery Center, 801 SW Highway 169, Chisholm 55719 or call (218) 254–7959 or, toll-free from within Minnesota, (800) 372– 6437. Also, you can visit www.ironworld.com.

Across US 169 from Ironworld, on the edge of downtown Chisholm, the **Minnesota Museum of Mining** provides a slightly different perspective on the area's industrial history. Surrounding a building of rambling indoor exhibits, where a detailed scale model of a taconite processing plant is displayed prominently, are several monstrous steam shovels, a railroad engine, and an evolutionary progression of trucks that culminates in one of today's 127-ton behemoths. Nearby, a twenty-ton drag bucket, once used to scrape up car-sized chunks of Mesabi ore, rusts in isolation on the grass, only hinting at the size of the crane that was its companion. The museum is open daily from mid-May through September and charges a small fee. Call (218) 254–5543 for more information.

Travel a few more miles west along the iron range's forested moonscape and you'll arrive at *Hibbing.* Follow the signs at the northeast edge of town for the *Hull-Rust-Mahoning Mine overlook,* where you can watch gigantic trucks and cranes removing what ore remains in the world's largest open-pit iron mine. The pit yawns 2 miles across, 3 miles long, and more than 500 feet deep from the overlook interpretive center, where a short video and volunteer interpreters explain the operation. Blasting in the mine is frequently scheduled for Thursday at 11:00 A.M.

Retracing your steps toward downtown Hibbing, you'll pass through a skeleton of a ghost town. A grid of streets flanked by sidewalks with weeds growing in the cracks and an occasional lamppost is all that's left of what was once a thriving mining settlement called Hibbing. Like most communities on the iron range, Hibbing grew up on the edge of a mine. By 1918 industry managers determined that the town itself and all its inhabitants had to make way for the gaping pit that was to become the Hull-Rust-Mahoning Mine. The town site of Alice, 2 miles to the south, was selected as a suitable location for the transplanted population.

To make this move more palatable, the mining bosses built the town a high school that would match the immigrant miners' towering desire to better the lot of their children through education. Inexpensive tours of the fortresslike *Hibbing High School,* which was completed in 1923 at a cost of almost $4 million, are given Monday through Saturday throughout summer (call 218–263–3675 for more information). Among Hibbing High's most noted alumni is Bobby Zimmerman, a musically talented student now known to the world as *Bob Dylan;* Dylan's boyhood home, not open to the public, can be seen at 2425 Seventh Avenue South.

The state-of-the-art *Paulucci Space Theatre* in Hibbing draws crowds year-round for mind-boggling multimedia programs on subjects that range from dinosaurs to outer space. Using a computer-driven arsenal of twenty-six slide projectors, a Spitz 512 Starball for stargazing, and a Cinema 360 fish-eye movie system that projects images all over the theater's domed ceiling, the Paulucci is among the top two-dozen planetariums in the nation. There is also an interesting gift shop. For information on the theater's inexpensive shows, call (218) 262–6720.

Cozy and hospitable bed-and-breakfast accommodations in Hibbing can be found at the **Adams House.** Marlene and Merrill Widmark, current owners of this 1927 English Tudor–style home, serve a continental breakfast and charge moderate rates. For reservations, write the Widmarks at 201 East Twenty-third Street, Hibbing 55746; or visit www.adamshousebedandbreakfast.com call (218) 263–9742.

Great Lakes shipping is the main economic force that put, and has kept, the city of **Duluth** on the map, and at this head-of-the-lakes international port, shipping primarily means iron ore. On any given day, spring through fall, there may be at anchor in the harbor several huge freighters from South America, Asia, or Europe. A good place to see them is from the breakwater that juts out into the lake from **Canal Park,** found at the south end of Canal Park Drive and next to Duluth's most famous landmark, the aerial lift bridge. Ocean-size waves break against the shore, seagulls call stridently while winging overhead, and the exotic associations conjured up by the flags and foreign names on the ships can all conspire to transport your imagination far from the American heartland.

The **Lake Superior Marine Museum,** which faces the park and the breakwater, is an excellent first stop if you want to learn more about Lake Superior and the global shipping industry that it supports. Upon entering the building you'll pass down a sloping hallway lined above and on the walls with weathered signs bearing the names of ships that once traveled the lakes. The lower floor has an auditorium that shows films about shipping and the Lake Superior environment several times daily. Large maps identify shipwreck sites and graphically depict the bottom contour of the world's largest freshwater lake. There are also exhibits on current underwater research projects and on the history of marine engine technology.

Upstairs three reconstructed staterooms, occupied by mannequins in period dress, convey a sense of what life belowdecks was like in the time of the Great Lakes steamer; also on display are numerous well-crafted models of historic ships. Another film-viewing area offers continually running shows on the U.S. Army Corps of Engineers, which operates the museum, and on the modern bulk-loading process for freighters. The information desk on the second floor will alert you to the origin of any ships moored in the harbor, and against the plate-glass windows facing the lake, telescopes are available for studying these big vessels. The museum is open year-round free of charge. For information about the arrival of ships in Duluth Harbor, call (218) 727–2497 or visit www.lsmma.com.

Great Lakes Aquarium is a second Duluth waterfront destination that provides insights into Lake Superior's importance among the world's freshwater resources. Since opening in July 2000, the aquarium has continued to add exhibits. Besides displays of assorted birds and 100,000 gallons of freshwater exhibits that contain many varieties of fish, the aquarium has several hands-on displays. A dune-making machine lets visitors turn a wheel and change the structure of dunes when the wind changes direction. Although most of us don't think of sand dunes around the Great Lakes, they are found along the eastern shore of Lake Michigan and on a smaller scale along Park Point near downtown Duluth. Another interactive exhibit, the *Great Lakes Water Table,* allows visitors to experience various hydrologic aspects of Lake Superior. For information call (218) 740–FISH (740–3474) or visit www.glaquarium.org.

The Great Lakes Aquarium has had some financial difficulties in the past, which resulted in the facility closing during the winter of 2002. With this in mind, make sure to call ahead or check their Web site before making a special trip to visit the aquarium.

Just west of Canal Park, in a slip beside Harbor Drive, sits the 610-foot freighter *SS* **William A. Irvin.** From 1938 to 1978 this steam-powered vessel served as the flagship of the U.S. Steel Company fleet, the largest flotilla of ore carriers in the world. During summer, forty-five-minute guided tours that range from stem to stern are conducted, for a modest fee, many times daily.

The sheer mass of the *Irvin* can hardly escape your notice as you enter the gigantic middle hold through a door at the top of the gangplank. But somehow it's through the smaller details of the ship's construction that the *Irvin*'s incredible size is driven home. After climbing and descending several of the sixteen steep staircases encountered during the tour, you find yourself outside the engine room on the stern deck. The links of a chain, supporting a three-ton emergency anchor nearby, weigh forty pounds each. A mooring rope coiled at your feet is almost as thick as your trunk.

To get this ship up to speed with its 14,000-ton load (11 knots was tops, 13 when running "light"), it took two 1,000-horsepower engines burning a ton of coal per hour. It also took a lot of hard work and sweat. Even in Lake Superior's cool climate, temperatures in the engine room while the ship was under way ranged from 100 to 115 degrees, with 93 percent humidity. In balmy Detroit, temperatures were 115 to 130 degrees, and the poor guys stoking the boiler had to contend with a scalding 200 degrees. Above 115 degrees, the guide explains, everyone had to wear gloves to keep from getting burned when handling the brass equipment.

It was an entirely different kind of trip for the *Irvin*'s VIP passengers in their wood-paneled staterooms at the other end of the ship. Daily activities for these major stockbrokers and U.S. Steel clients included trapshooting, driving golf balls into the lake, playing shuffleboard, and participating in an occasional game of baseball in an empty hold. Gourmet meals were prepared by a special chef and served in an elegant dining room following cocktails in the guests' private lounge. For a schedule of tours of the *Irvin,* call (218) 722–7876 or 722–5573 or go to www.williamairvin.com.

An enjoyable way to see Duluth's waterfront is aboard the **North Shore Scenic Railroad.** Day trips range in length from one and one-half hours (Lester River) to six hours (Two Harbors) and are fully narrated, providing you with piles of information about the Duluth area. You'll learn about everything from how the port was built to how to keep the seagulls away from your window at the Edgewater Motel.

In the evenings you can ride the **Dinner Train,** which features three different menus: Elegance and Romance, Buffet Dinner, and Pizza Train. The Scenic Railroad departs from the historic depot building, 506 West Michigan Street. Call (218) 722–1273 or visit www.lsrm.org for more information.

The tremendous wealth resulting from the burgeoning success of the iron-ore industry at the turn of the twentieth century is evident in two Duluth estates along the Lake Superior shoreline on stately London Road, east of downtown. **Glensheen,** an elegant, thirty-nine-room, Jacobean-style manor house set in a seven-acre wooded glen, has become one of Duluth's most popular attractions. Since assuming ownership from the Congdon family in 1968, the University of Minnesota, Duluth, has been conducting tours that focus on Glensheen's outstanding architecture, extensive handcrafted woodwork, and furnishings that date from 1908, when the estate was completed. Glensheen, located at 3200 London Road, is also available for rental. For information on rentals and for schedules of the inexpensive tours (reservations are recommended), call (218) 726–8910.

A slightly more intimate way to partake in Duluth's opulent past is to let a room for the night at **The Mansion,** a twenty-five-room bed-and-breakfast estate situated a half mile down the road from Glensheen. Built between 1928 and 1932 for Marjorie Congdon Dudley (the daughter of Chester A. Congdon, master of Glensheen) and her husband, Harry C. Dudley, a mining engineer, The Mansion has seven acres of wooded grounds and more than 500 feet of secluded Lake Superior shoreline. There are ten guest rooms in all, three in the former maids' quarters (which are moderately priced), five in the main part of the house, and an apartment that rents for a two-night minimum stay (moderately to expensively priced). All guests can enjoy the beautiful screened porch, the spacious living room, the upstairs den, and a library with a fireplace and lovely hand-carved-oak built-in bookcases lined with leather-bound volumes.

A large country breakfast is served. For reservations write The Mansion, 3300 London Road, Duluth 55804; call (218) 726–8910, (888) 454–4536; or visit www .mansion.duluth.com.

Another more diminutive, but hardly less luxurious, Duluth bed-and-breakfast is **The Firelight Inn on Oregon Creek.** Built by businessman and philanthropist George Barnum in 1910, this 8,000-square-foot house was originally designed to showcase an extensive collection of fine arts and accommodate frequent guests. It still does.

Current owners/innkeepers Jim and Joy Fischer have gone to great lengths to maintain the original opulence of this grand mansion. From the glass-enclosed veranda by the front door to the cozy sitting room with its unique arched fireplace, the entire downstairs area has a warm, friendly feeling. Five of the six guest rooms have fireplaces, and all but one room (the Woodland Suite) have double whirlpools. Three have access to a veranda overlooking a nearby ravine and brook. All rooms are appointed with beautiful antique furnishings, queen- or king-size beds, and private baths. To make reservations call or write well in advance to The Firelight Inn on Oregon Creek, 2211 East Third Street, Duluth 55812; call toll-free (888) 724–0273; or log on to www.firelightinn.com.

Duluth's historic train station, a striking 1892 châteauesque structure with steep-roofed towers and a great hall with a high cathedral ceiling, is several destinations in one. A permanent collection of paintings by Eastman Johnson is a cornerstone of the **Depot**'s several art galleries. Johnson, who was America's most celebrated artist of the middle nineteenth century, lived and painted in the Duluth area for two years. As the displayed paintings and drawings indicate, he enjoyed producing portraits of presidents, as well as of the Ojibway Indians he found on the Minnesota frontier. Also on display are exhibits on logging history and Norwegian wood carving.

A train museum in the boarding-platform area of the Depot features Minnesota's first steam engine, on display next to one of the largest locomotives in the world—the Mallet Number 227, which burned ten to twelve tons of coal *per hour* while hauling more than a hundred iron-ore cars from Tower to the docks in Duluth Harbor. Surrounding the tracks is a boardwalk with reconstructed Duluth storefronts circa 1910.

The historic Depot building is adjacent to Duluth's **Depot Theatre,** where ballet and theater performances and symphony orchestra concerts are held. The exhibit areas in the Depot, which is located at 506 West Michigan Street, are open daily for a modest fee. For information on special programs, such as the annual **All American Railroad Days celebration** each July, call (218) 733–7590 or go to www.lsrm.org.

History buffs with a taste for documents have an interesting time at the ***Karpeles Manuscript Library Museum,*** 902 East First Street. Founded by Dave Karpeles to "renew the sense of purpose our children are missing," this museum is a decidedly eclectic assemblage of historic documents and manuscripts. You'll find a page from Noah Webster's original dictionary and a stanza from Mozart's *Marriage of Figaro*. There's even a gas bill paid by Thomas Edison (suppose the rates hastened the invention of the light bulb?). The list goes on and on, with each display seemingly as random as the next. Little historical background is given regarding any of the documents in the exhibit itself, but brochures with additional information about each piece are available near the entryway. The museum is open daily year-round and is free. Call (218) 728–0630 for more information.

Lovers of old stadiums and baseball played on real grass should make it a point to see the ***Duluth Huskies.*** In days of old the Huskies (formerly the Dukes) were a Detroit Tigers farm team, and future stars such as Gates Brown and Denny McLain used the grounds of historic Wade Stadium, built in 1941, to learn their craft. Today the Huskies are one of six franchises in the independent Northwoods League. The baseball is not of Major League caliber, but neither are the prices—tickets, hot dogs for a family of four, and soft drink cost for less than $25. Best of all, the games are a lot of fun. Call Huskies Baseball at (218) 786–9909 for schedule and ticket information.

Though it's difficult to do, if you're passing through Duluth in autumn and can take your eyes off the oceanlike sweep of Lake Superior and the spectacular fall foliage along the shore, look skyward—you may well see something striking. Better yet, find your way to ***Hawk Ridge*** atop the string of hills behind the city, because, regardless of which direction you may be traveling, tens of thousands of hawks, eagles, and falcons will be winging their way

Something Different in the Arrowhead

Arrowhead offers much in the way of traditional recreation: swimming, boating, and other lake-based activities in the summer and skiing and snowmobiling in the winter. But for something different try a sightseeing trip to view the ice-coated rocks along Lake Superior, or stop at Lutsen Mountains and take a gondola ride to the top of Moose Mountain for a spectacular view of the big lake. If you want to get active, try a dogsledding trip or a lodge-to-lodge ski excursion along the Gunflint Trail, or spend a night or two in a backcountry yurt. It gets brisk during an Arrowhead winter, but you won't have to fight off mosquitoes or hordes of other travelers.

overhead in their annual fall migration. And this small nature preserve, dedicated to observing and recording this singular event, offers what some say is the best viewing site in the country.

There are several observation posts at Hawk Ridge, each oriented to a different wind direction, as well as a network of hiking trails and a bird-banding station. Volunteer naturalists on duty daily from mid-August through November can assist you in the fine art of distinguishing between the various species. On a good day—one with clear skies and a wind from the west or northwest, creating updrafts upon which the grand birds can soar effortlessly about—you may see thousands of these beautiful winged predators. More than 30,000 sightings of individual birds of the same species have been recorded in a single twelve-hour period during the peak flyover time, which is usually mid-September.

Hawk Ridge is located along the Skyway Parkway, just north of the intersection of Glenwood Avenue and Forty-third Avenue East. Admission is free, though donations for the support of the reserve are encouraged.

Each summer Duluth hosts two cultural events that attract visitors from throughout the region. The ***Bayfront Blues Festival,*** held annually over a weekend in early August, attracts major entertainers from around the country. A week later the ***Port of Duluth Festival*** features (along with concerts, jet-ski

races, and other happenings) tours of selected U.S. Coast Guard ships and giant wooden sailing ships, like the 179-foot ***HMS* Rose,** a replica of a British frigate that fought against the Bluecoats in New York Harbor during the Revolutionary War. For more information on these events, call the Duluth Convention and Visitors Bureau, toll-free, at (800) 4–DULUTH (438–5884).

Duluth's annual ***Winter Sports Festival*** in January brings several other sorts of thrill seekers out of hiding. Competitors from all over North America come to Duluth for the grueling 500-mile ***John Beargrease Sled Dog Marathon,*** which runs around the clock for four consecutive days. Large teams of powerful dogs driven by hardy mushers travel an old winter mail route from Duluth to Grand Portage and back. Not far behind them is a pack of

HMS *Rose,*
at Port of Duluth Festival

snowmobile racers who buzz through town on their way from Thunder Bay, Ontario, to the outskirts of the Twin Cities. There are snowshoe races and, moving at a more soothing pace, a parade of antique horse-drawn cutters. For more information on these events, call the Duluth Convention and Visitors Bureau toll-free at (800) 438–5884.

Lake County

As you leave Duluth driving northeast on Highway 61, you enter an enchanted realm. For 150 miles the North Shore Scenic Drive hugs the rocky, wooded, mountain-lined rim of the world's largest freshwater sea. Although there's no hint of salt in the offshore breezes and there are no tides, in almost all other respects the cold, clear water stretching blue and silver to the horizon may as well be an ocean. The moods of Superior—from its furious northeasters in late autumn to the infinite calm of August's doldrums—are just too grand to belong to a lake. The shoreline cliffs were built to the same larger-than-life scale. Even the mammoth ocean-bound freighters, which at night look like distant sparkling cities adrift beneath the stars, are dwarfed by the magnificence of this grand lake.

To help get yourself properly acclimated to the North Shore's maritime environment, a couple of shops in Knife River will fix you up with a supply of fish lured from Superior's depths. Depending on the month and the day's catch, *Mel's Fish* and *Russ Kendall's Smokehouse*—both located along Scenic Drive—carry smoked or fresh lake trout, whitefish, herring, and salmon.

Next stop is Two Harbors, whose two natural bays became an early locale for iron-ore shipping. As the staff and volunteers can tell you at the *Lake County Historical Society Museum,* which overlooks the huge ore docks from the corner of Waterfront Drive and South Avenue, Minnesota's first minuscule shipment of iron ore traveled from the Tower-Soudan mine in St. Louis County to Two Harbors in 1884. The amount of ore that passed through town that entire year—some 60,000 tons—can today be carried by a single ship.

A short walk toward the lake from the museum leads to the permanent docking site of the *Edna G,* an extremely long-lived, coal-fired tugboat that was in service at the docks from 1896 until the early 1980s, when freighters finally became capable of precise maneuvering in such small spaces as Agate Bay. The boat landing and breakwater at Lighthouse Point are good sites for watching these big ships dock and load. The museum staff can tell you which ships are coming and when.

Now then, let's say you have a question about sandpaper that's keeping you awake at night. Well, breathe a sigh of relief, because at Two Harbors's

Dwan Museum, which contains the world's largest sandpaper exhibit, the answers to your most perplexing queries about abrasives are likely to be found. This one-of-a-kind museum occupies the former office of John Dwan, a Two Harbors lawyer who in 1902 became the first secretary of an obscure company called Minnesota Mining and Manufacturing—today known the world over as 3M.

The first of the museum's two rooms gives a brief history of 3M from its formation until 1919, when company headquarters was moved from Two Harbors to St. Paul. An interesting display charts the company's growth and shows early models of some of its most famous products, including Scotch Tape and Post-it Notes. A portion of the second room documents changes in the company's logo through the years. But most of the space is devoted to sandpaper. For example, did you know that a very fine sandpaper is used to polish optical lenses? And that dentists use waterproof sandpaper to polish your teeth? And that 3M manufactures more than fifty *million* different sandpaper products for its customers around the world? For this and more impressive information, visit the Dwan Museum at 508 Second Avenue. Admission is inexpensive, and the doors are open daily in summer and on weekends through the rest of the year.

A traumatic wait ended for pie lovers in early 1998 when two residents of the Twin Cities bought ***Betty's Pies*** and saved this venerable restaurant from extinction. Major reconstruction of Highway 61 put part of the new road right through the existing building. The situation looked bleak for a while until the two new owners stepped forward and announced plans to rebuild farther back from Lake Superior. While the building and location have changed, the recipes won't, thanks to the two white knights in baker's aprons. The restaurant is located at 1633 Highway 61 East (2 miles north of town), Two Harbors. Betty's serves breakfast, lunch, dinner, and, of course, awesome pies from 7:00 A.M. to 9:00 P.M. seven days a week. Call (218) 834–3367, or visit www.bettyspies.com.

ALSO WORTH SEEING

Artist's Point, Grand Marais,
(218) 387–1400

Koochiching County and Bronco Nagurski Museums,
International Falls,
(218) 283–4316

Lutsen Mountains,
Lutsen,
(218) 663–7281

Oberg Mountain,
Lutsen,
(218) 663–7804

You'll notice the landscape taking a turn for the dramatic just up the shore from Betty's as you approach the entrance to the newly completed Silver Creek Tunnel. Beside the entrance you can browse through the locally made crafts at **Pioneer Crafts Coop** (2821 Highway 61, 218–834–4175, www.pioneercrafts .com). From here to Thunder Bay, precipitous shoreline cliffs and awesome waterfalls are regular roadside attractions.

Because of the dangers posed by this inhospitable coast, the movers and shakers of the steel industry persuaded Congress to build the **Split Rock Lighthouse** in 1909. This plan was developed following a treacherous storm in November 1905, in which thirty ships were damaged or sunk, including two in the immediate vicinity of a prominent cliff located 20 miles northeast of Two Harbors. The Minnesota Historical Society now runs the site; and, as its guides will tell you, getting U.S. taxpayers to fund the lighthouse was, in fact, a maneuver that enabled the steel barons to avoid having to institute costly safety procedures.

A beautiful interpretive center with an excellent film and exhibits comple-ments the hour-long tour of the well-preserved lighthouse and the lightkeep-ers' residences (there were a head keeper and two assistants with families). The experience provides yet another perspective on the iron-ore industry that has been so essential to Minnesota's livelihood. It also illuminates what life was like on Superior's shores in the early decades of the last century for local resi-dents and for the employees of the strictly regimented and now-extinct U.S. Lighthouse Service.

During the construction of the lighthouse, which required the assembly of a steam-powered derrick to hoist workers and materials up the 100-foot cliff face, Split Rock was accessible only by lake. Soon after the North Shore High-way was completed in 1924, however, the facility became the most visited light station in the country. By 1969 the sophistication of navigational equipment had rendered obsolete the ten-second-interval beacon and foghorn (which were detectable more than 20 and 5 miles away, respectively), and Split Rock was deeded to the state.

The Split Rock Interpretive Center, Highway 61, is open weekends in win-ter and daily through summer months, whereas tours of the light station are offered only from mid-May through mid-October. A small fee is charged and an inexpensive state park sticker is required for admission. For more information call (218) 226–6377.

A view of the lake that surpasses even the one from the top of the Split Rock tower (itself 167 feet above the lake level) can be found about 12 miles farther up the shore. Just after passing the Palisade Baptist Church on the lake side of Highway 61, you'll see an unmarked wayside parking area on the same side of the highway with a narrow, winding road leading out of sight up a steep embankment. This road leads to the top of **Palisade Head,** a spectacular 200-foot promontory that presents a vertical face to the lake and that in summer is a popular playground for rock climbers. If you tire of watching men and women cheating death on the cliff, you can also look for a nesting pair of rare peregrines—falcons famous for attacking their prey in midflight—that have recently claimed this precipitous environment as a summer home. Also, the ground cover on top of Palisade Head offers outstanding blueberry picking in mid-to-late summer.

As grand as the views from Palisade Head may be, if you really want to take your measure against the North Shore's hills, you should spend some time on the new **Superior Hiking Trail.** The rugged trail at present winds from Castle Danger to Grand Marais, connecting eight state parks in the process. Scenic overlooks punctuate the trail, as do occasional campsites (equipped with pit toilets and fire rings) and road crossings. The trail is designed so that hikers can set out for just a few hours or hike for days. When the many, many hours of volunteer labor that have been undertaken to make the trail are complete, the Lake Superior Hiking Trail will run the full distance from Duluth to the Canadian border. Trail maps are available free of charge at ranger stations and tourist information centers all along the shore. *Guide to the Superior Hiking Trail* is available from the trail association, P.O. Box 4, 731 Seventh Avenue, Two Harbors 55616-0004; (218) 834–2700; www.shta.org.

Minnesota Highway 1's winding 60-mile journey from Illgen City on the Superior shore to Ely is one of those Arrowhead roads that continuously draws your attention out the window to witness tall stands of virgin timber, sparkling lakes and rivers, and moose and deer that momentarily break from their foraging to give you a mildly curious look. A little more than halfway along its length, this highway is intersected by Lake County Road 2, very near the location of one of Minnesota's most unusual learning centers: the **Great Lakes School of Log Building.**

Since 1974, Ron Brodigan has been teaching experientially oriented courses in the basics of log construction for folks who've always dreamed of living in their own house made of trees. During the fourteen-day classes, students actually build a log structure such as the many that occupy the rustic school site (accommodations are in wood-heated bunkhouses, bathing is done in traditional Finnish saunas and solar showers, and participants provide their own food). At the end of each course, students with no previous construction experience or special strength return home with the necessary skills to undertake their own projects. Ron also offers rural-skills short courses that concern various aspects of living in the backcountry. Per-day fees at the school are inexpensive. To register or to receive more information, write the school at 1350 Snowshoe Trail, Isabella 55607; call (218) 365–2126 (evenings) or (888) 529–9582 (days); or visit www.schooloflogbuilding.com.

Cook County

As the farthest northeastern point in Minnesota, Cook County is one of the most sparsely populated as well as one of the most scenic regions in the state. Although carpeted by hundreds of square miles of thick forest and home to a vast network of wilderness lakes, Lake Superior defines the character of this area. The big lake forms the southeastern border and exerts a powerful influence on the people and landscape of the county. Major tourist attraction, producer of heavy snowfall, summer air conditioner, moderator of winter temperatures, and at times inhospitable neighbor, Lake Superior affects all who choose to live by it or visit it.

If you're driving up the shore at a pace that's suitable for taking in all there is to see and do, by now you may well have happily consumed all the fish that you purchased back in Knife River. No matter—in the tiny community of Schroeder, you can stop by the ***Cross River Cafe*** for a home-cooked meal or fresh bakery treat. If you're not hungry yet, continue north about 4 miles to Tofte and stop and ***Coho Cafe, Bakery & Deli.***

Five miles north of Cross River Cafe, you'll cross the Temperance River, which at this elevation flows within the borders of ***Temperance River State Park.*** Some sources say this stream received its name in playful recognition of the fact that it was one of the few North Shore waterways without a sandbar at its mouth. Also, among the many rivers along the shore that have impressive waterfalls—such as the Gooseberry, Baptism, and Cascade—the Temperance is distinguished for having carved a fantastic series of caldrons and spillways through the lava bedrock formation on the upstream side of the highway. A short trail winds along this section of the river, beginning from the parking area near the highway bridge.

The focal points for most of the state parks along Highway 61 from Two Harbors to the Canadian border are the rivers that tumble down from the highlands to Lake Superior. The rivers all have waterfalls of various heights and intensities, and most have unique characteristics. Grand Portage State Park has the tallest waterfall in Minnesota at 120 feet, the high falls on the Pigeon River. The Temperance River has a series of falls where the water tumbles with such fury it has carved smooth, round caldrons from the billion-year-old volcanic rock of the canyon. The Cascade River has a spectacular series of several waterfalls that drop 900 feet from the top of the ridge bordering Lake Superior. All the parks have plenty of hiking trails that follow the rivers and the shoreline of the big lake.

Each park varies in size and amenities, from the 278-acre Grand Portage State Park, a day-use-only park with no camping, to 9,346-acre Tettegouche State Park with plenty of camping, hiking trails, cross-country skiing and snowshoe trails. But even with all the camping and assorted activities available at each park, the most popular sights are always the rivers that cut through them.

Grand Marais is a focal point of North Shore recreational activity winter and summer. It is also a quaint coastal town in its own right, with a history steeped in fishing and logging traditions. When you are entering the community from the southwest, visible to your right is Grand Marais's harbor, where you'll find the North Shore's only sailboat instruction center outside of Duluth.

The *North House Folk School* offers several sailing programs, including the Lake Superior Adventure, a two-hour trip around the Grand Marais harbor and out into the big lake for an incomparable view of the Sawtooth Mountains and the North Shore. All trips leave from the Grand Marais harbor on the *Hjordis,* a 50-foot Gaff-rigged schooner. The school also offers a basic navigation and weather course, a Nuts about Knots class, and the Craft of Sail introduction to sailing.

North House offers instruction and programs to help participants learn and understand crafts of the past and present. Besides the sailing programs, courses include boat building, timber framing, shelter building, and woodworking, to name a few. For more information contact North House Folk School, P.O. Box 759, Grand Marais 55604; call (218) 387–9762; or check their Web site at www.northhouse.org.

Adventuresome souls who would prefer to explore the Grand Marais shoreline by sea kayak can rent these comfortable and surprisingly stable vessels by the day from *Superior Coastal Sports* (formerly Cascade Kayaks). Superior Coastal Sports also offers full and half-day tours, instruction, sale of new and used equipment, and multiday adventures to Isle Royale National Park, the Lake Superior Water Trail, and the waters near Thunder Bay, Ontario. For more information contact them at (218) 387–2360 or (800) 720–2809 or visit www.superiorcoastal.com.

Grand Marais's first bed-and-breakfast establishment, *Pincushion Mountain Bed and Breakfast,* is perched atop the ridge overlooking town 3 miles up the Gunflint Trail. With 15 miles of groomed and tracked trails beginning outside its door, Pincushion is perfect for cross-country skiers in winter and for hikers (the Superior Hiking Trail is also nearby) and mountain-bike enthusiasts the rest of the year; lodge-to-lodge skiing, hiking, or biking can be arranged.

The B&B is also a comfortable place to stay even if you aren't looking for such an active getaway. Scott and Mary Beattie are gracious hosts, offering their guests comfortable, modern rooms, outstanding full breakfasts, and a warm family atmosphere, all at moderate rates. For reservations write Pincushion Mountain Bed and Breakfast, Box 181, Grand Marais 55604; call (218) 387–1276 or, toll-free (800) 542–1226; or log on to www.pincushionbb.com.

Grand Marais's wilderness highway—the **Gunflint Trail**—is another Arrowhead road deserving of all the historic and romantic associations brought to mind by its name. Originally no more than an Indian footpath, the road today meanders between lakeshores and climbs up and over steep rocky ridges for 53 miles before suddenly dispersing like a river delta into a network of boat landings along the shores of Canadian-border Lake Saganaga. The Gunflint has numerous jumping-off points to the Boundary Waters Canoe Area, which borders the trail for half its length. (Boundary Waters travel information is available at the **Superior National Forest ranger stations in Tofte and Grand Marais.** Wilderness travel permits can be obtained by writing **BWCA Reservation Office,** Box 462, Ballston, New York, 12020 or by calling 877–550–6777.)

There are plenty of resorts and outfitters along the Gunflint, too, the latter providing equipment, food, and route-planning services for those interested in canoeing the BWCA's pristine waters (write the **Gunflint Trail Association,** 434 Gunflint Trail, Grand Marais 55604; call toll-free 800–338–6932; or go to www.gunflint-trail.com for a list of outfitters and resorts and for hiking, biking, and skiing information). Come winter, the Gunflint has several outstanding networks of snowmobile and cross-country skiing trails, including one that provides skiers with access to a most unusual type of accommodation: the yurt.

For centuries the people of the Mongolian plateaus have found cylindrical, peak-roofed tents, or yurts, to be practical places to live. Yurts are also much warmer than standard tents when outfitted with a wood stove, which they accommodate quite easily. Ted and Barbara Young of **Boundary Country Trekking** have established three of these dwellings an easy day's ski apart along the Banadad Trail. Each of the one-room, canvas-covered yurts sleeps four to six, with accoutrements that include bunk beds, skylights, wood stoves, and an outhouse nearby.

You can either ski from yurt to yurt or to a recently built backwoods cabin reachable only on skis. The Youngs cheerfully shuttle your gear to the following day's destination and upon your arrival prepare outstanding meals, including such specialties as roast duck, grilled trout, and the almost-mystical Mongolian fire-pot dinner. Two lodges at either end of the Banadad Trail provide more civilized accommodations, or if yurts are too luxurious for your tastes, guided ski trips into the wilderness with dogsled support can be

arranged. Prices for the yurt-to-yurt program are expensive, though they
include three meals per day, lodging, and shuttle. For more information write
Boundary Country Trekking, Gunflint Trail 67–1, Grand Marais 55604; call toll-
free (800) 322–8327; or go to www.boundarycountry.com.

Another destination along the Gunflint Trail that's well worth the effort
required to reach it is the 3.5-mile hike that will take you to the top of Minnesota's highest peak. You'll find the ***Eagle Mountain*** trailhead 17 miles northwest of Grand Marais, at the junction of Superior National Forest Roads 153
and 158 (the Gunflint and Tofte ranger stations have maps). Throughout its
length the trail winds through such dense forest that you really haven't a clue
as to where you are. Then suddenly the sky opens up and you find yourself
on the edge of a dramatic escarpment 2,301 feet above sea level that provides
a sweeping view of the forested wilderness to the south, west, and north. It is
a truly magical place to be during evening light, when the surfaces of a half-
dozen lakes down below are set on fire—though make sure you bring a flash-
light, as the hike back to the car is a nasty one in the dark.

The lure of the North Shore for those seeking a place to revel in nature's
glories is not a new phenomenon. As soon as the highway was completed from
Duluth to Fort William and Port Arthur (now Thunder Bay) in 1924, the Superior
shoreline quickly became a popular destination for the touring crowd. It even
attracted the mighty Babe Ruth, boxer Jack Dempsey, and writer Ring Lardner,
who were part of a group that banded together to build an exclusive wilderness
retreat near Hovland called ***Naniboujou Lodge.*** But perhaps the establishment's
namesake—a mythological trickster of the North American woodland Indian cultures—was a poor choice, for the project ground to a halt following the stock
market crash of 1929, with only the main lodge and dining room completed.

Today Naniboujou's moderately priced rooms attract guests who come to
collect agates on the beach or hike, ski, and fish beside the ***Brule River*** in the
adjacent ***Judge C.R. Magney State Park.*** The dining room has an even larger
clientele drawn by the very good fresh fish and poultry dishes (among others)
and the fresh-baked breads and desserts served by owners Tim and Nancy
Ramey. The setting for these moderately priced repasts is a large room whose
lofty ceiling was painted in the 1920s with a bold, colorful motif inspired by
Cree Indian mythology. Ornate paper chandeliers hang above. The huge fireplace at one end consists of more than 200 tons of native rock. Outside, the
building's wood-shingled exterior blends nicely with the sprawling grounds
that stretch down to the lakeshore. For more information write Naniboujou
Lodge, 20 Naniboujou Trail, Grand Marais 55604; call (218) 387–2688; or check
www.naniboujou.com.

The last 20 miles of Minnesota's Lake Superior shoreline take you through the Ojibway-owned *Grand Portage Indian Reservation,* one of the most historically significant and beautiful areas in all of Minnesota. After topping a steady incline that builds for several miles, Highway 61 suddenly crests at a wayside parking area with a dramatic view of Grand Portage's large natural harbor and the *Susie Island chain* beyond. On a clear day you can also see Michigan's Isle Royale National Park in the hazy distance. Rising up from the shore is a steep escarpment of hills, over which hardy voyageurs during the latter part of the eighteenth century carried their heavy birchbark canoes and many tons of animal pelts tied in ninety-pound bundles.

The white-cedar stockade and log buildings at *Grand Portage National Monument* have been painstakingly reconstructed by the National Park Service to preserve the spirit of this hub of the fur trade. Costumed guides and such special events as the annual Rendezvous and Powwow in mid-August give visitors a vivid impression of the lifestyle that reigned here from 1784 to 1803, when the North West Company used the settlement as the headquarters of its fur trade empire. Each summer hundreds of voyageurs, portaging their canoes and bearing backbreaking loads of furs from their wintering posts in the Canadian Northwest, hiked down the 9-mile Grand Portage Trail. They were met at the stockade by their counterparts, who had traveled by even-larger birchbark freight canoes across the Great Lakes from Montreal with heavy supplies of trade goods. For several weeks in midsummer, the two groups exchanged their cargoes and, with the help of local Ojibway, celebrated one of the biggest parties on the frontier. Leaving enough time to return safely to their respective wintering posts, the two groups then loaded up their canoes for the long trip home. The monument, which is well marked along Highway 61, is open daily from mid-May to mid-October; a small fee is charged. For information on special programs, call (218) 387–2788.

The dock in front of the Grand Portage monument welcomes ships from the open lake, just as it did hundreds of years ago. Throughout summer it is also the dock site of the passenger ferry *Wenonah,* which departs daily for the nearest end of Michigan's *Isle Royale National Park,* 22 miles offshore; round-trip voyages on this ferry last most of the day and are expensive. Those wishing to circumnavigate this largest island in the largest lake in the world can book passage on the *Voyageur,* which departs every other day from a landing at the northeast end of the harbor. For more information about these excursions, write the Grand Portage–Isle Royale Transportation Lines, 1507 North First Street, Superior, Wisconsin 54880; call (715) 392–2100 or (888) 746–2305; or log on to www.grand-isle-royale.com.

You'll understand why the voyageurs preferred a 9-mile hike through the mosquito-infested woods to a canoe trip down the Pigeon River, which forms the Minnesota-Ontario border, if you pay a visit to *Grand Portage State Park.* This newest of Minnesota's state parks provides parking and an access trail to 120-foot High Falls on the Pigeon River, Minnesota's highest waterfall. To find it follow Highway 61 almost to its terminus at the U.S. Customs station, where there is a small parking lot on the north side of the road.

Like the voyageurs before them, the loggers who worked the Pigeon River Valley around the turn of the twentieth century were also intimidated by High Falls. Through the mist you can see the remains of a flume that carried their logs past the waterfall without the logs being turned into splinters. Still, the river's many violent rapids were so rough that a specially low grade of lumber was developed to market boards made from Pigeon River logs.

Places to Stay in the Arrowhead Region

HINCKLEY
(area code 320)

Dakota Lodge Bed & Breakfast,
Highway 48;
(320) 384–6052

Days Inn,
104 Grindstone Court;
(800) 559–8951

Grand Northern Inn,
I–35 and Highway 48;
384–7171 or (800) 558–0612

MORA
(area code 320)

AmericInn,
Highway 65
(1877 Frontage Road);
679–5700

Ann River Swedish Motel,
South Highway 65;
679–2972

New Mora Motel,
301 South Highway 65;
679–0235

AITKIN
(area code 218)

40 Club Inn,
Highway 210 West;
927–2903 or (800) 682–8152

Ripple River Motel,
701 Minnesota Avenue South;
927–3734 or (800) 258–3734

MCGREGOR
(area code 218)

Country Meadows Inn,
Highways 210 and 65;
768–7378 or (888) 331–7378

GRAND RAPIDS
(area code 218)

AmericInn,
Highway 169 South;
326–8999

Morning Glory Bed & Breakfast
726 Northwest Second Avenue;
326–3978

Sawmill Inn,
Highway 169 South
(2301 South Pokegama Avenue);
(800) 667–7509

Seagren's Pokegama Lodge,
20648 Crystal Springs Road;
326–9040;
SEAGRENS@uslink.net

INTERNATIONAL FALLS/RANIER
(area code 218)

Holiday Inn,
1500 Highway 71,
International Falls;
283–8000 or (800) 331–4443

Island View Bed & Breakfast,
2160 County Road 139, International Falls;
286–3085 or (888) 848–8890

Sandbay Bed & Breakfast,
2065 Spruce Street Landing, Ranier;
286–5699 or (877) 724–6965

Super 8 Motel,
2326 Highway 53 Frontage Road,
International Falls;
283–8811 or (800) 800–8000

ELY
(area code 218)

Blue Heron Bed & Breakfast,
827 Kawishiwi Trail;
365–4720

Grand Ely Lodge Resort,
400 North Pioneer Road;
365–6565 or (800)365–5070

Super 8 Motel,
1605 East Sheridan Street;
365–2873 or (800) 800–8000

Trezona House B&B,
315 East Washington Street;
365–4809

HIBBING/EVELETH/ VIRGINIA
(area code 218)

Hibbing Park Hotel,
1402 East Howard Street,
Hibbing;
(800) 262–3481

Park Inn,
502 Chestnut Street,
Virginia;
749–1000 or (800) 777–4699

Super 8 Motel,
Highway 53, Eveleth;
744–1661

DULUTH
(area code 218)

Comfort Suites,
408 Canal Park Drive;
727–1378

Hampton Inn,
310 Canal Park Drive;
720–3000

Super 8,
4100 West Superior Street;
628–2241

TWO HARBORS
(area code 218)

AmericInn,
202 Highway 61;
834–3000

Country Inn,
1204 Seventh Avenue;
834–5557

Grand Superior Lodge,
2826 Highway 61 East;
834–3796 or (800) 627–9565

GRAND MARAIS
(area code 218)

Anderson's Cabins,
2 miles north of Grand
Marais on Lake Superior;
387–1814

Aspen Lodge
Highway 61 East;
387–2500 or (800) 247–6020

Best Western Superior Inn,
East Highway 61;
387–2240 or (800) 842–8439

MacArthur House Bed and Breakfast,
520 West Second Street;
387–1840 or (800) 792–1840

Places to Eat in the Arrowhead Region

HINCKLEY
(area code 320)

Cassidy's (American),
I–35 and Highway 48;
384–6129

Gathering Place Coffee Shop,
111 Main Street East;
384–7797

Tobies (American),
I–35 and Highway 48;
384–6174

MORA
(area code 320)

Country Cottage
(home cooking),
downtown;
679–2419

Downtown Deli
(bistro, coffee shop),
113 Southeast Railroad
Avenue;
679–5555

Freddies (full menu),
Highways 65 and 23;
679–2118

Wild Things Pizzeria & Deli,
downtown;
679–3346

AITKIN
(area code 218)

ADF Cafe (American),
Southgate Center–
Highway 169;
927–4500

Birchwood Cafe (American),
downtown;
927–6400

Roadside Restaurant
(homemade soups and
baked goods),
Highway 210 East;
927–2113

Rosallini's (pizza, pasta),
downtown (south of the
stoplight);
927–6412

MCGREGOR
(area code 218)

C & M Downtown Cafe
(American), downtown;
768–4311

Fireside Inn (American),
Highways 210 and 65;
768–3818

GRAND RAPIDS
(area code 218)

Air Espresso on 2,
Downtown, Highway 2;
326–8226

Bixby's Cafe
(soup and sandwiches),
1009 South Pokegama
Avenue;
326–4776

**Bridgeman's Embers
America**
(American, ice-cream treats),
331 W Fourth Street;
326–5302

**LaRosa's Mexican
American Restaurant,**
1300 East Highway 169;
327–4000

New China Buffet,
214 Northwest First Avenue;
327–0868

Pasties Plus,
20 Northwest Fourth Street;
327–2230

Sammy's Pizza
802 South Pokegama
Avenue;
326–8551

Silver Spoon (American),
18 NW Fourth Street;
326–8646

**INTERNATIONAL
FALLS/RANIER**
(area code 218)

Giovanni's Pizza,
1225 Third Street,
International Falls;
283–2600

Grandma's Pantry
(homestyle cooking, wild
rice soup),
Ranier;
286–5584

**Riverfront Bar and Grill
at Holiday Inn** (American),
1500 Highway 71,
International Falls;
283–4451

Rose Garden Restaurant
(Chinese),
311 Fourth Avenue,
International Falls;
283–4551

Spot Supper Club
(American),
Highway 53 and
Eighteenth Street,
International Falls;
283–2440

ELY
(area code 218)

Britton's Cafe
(home cooking and
baking),
5 East Chapman Street;
365–3195

SELECTED CHAMBERS OF COMMERCE

Aitkin Chamber of Commerce
(800) 526–8342

**Duluth Convention and
Visitors Bureau**
(800) 4–Duluth (438–5884)

Ely Chamber of Commerce
(800) 777–7281

**Grand Marais Chamber of
Commerce**
(218) 387–1400

**Grand Rapids Chamber of
Commerce**
(800) 355–9740

**Hinckley Convention and
Visitors Bureau**
(800) 996–4566

**Iron Trail Convention and
Vistors Bureau**
(800) 777–8497

**International Falls Convention and
Vistors Bureau**
(800) 325–5766

Mora Area Chamber of Commerce
(800) 291–5792

Two Harbors Chamber of Commerce
(800) 777–7384

SELECTED WEB SITES IN THE ARROWHEAD

Aitkin Area Information
www.aitkin.com

**Duluth Convention and
Vistors Bureau**
www.visitduluth.com

Ely Chamber of Commerce
www.ely.org

**Grand Marais Chamber
of Commerce**
www.grandmaraismn.com

**Grand Rapids Chamber
of Commerce**
www.visitgrandrapids.com

**Hinckley Convention &
Visitors Bureau**
www.hinckleymn.com

International Falls Convention Bureau
www.intlfalls.org

Iron Range
(Hibbing, Eveleth, etc.)
www.irontrail.org

Mora Area Chamber of Commerce
www.moramn.com

**Two Harbors/Lake County
Information**
www.lakecnty.com

Burntside Lodge
(American),
2755 Burntside Lodge Road;
365–3894

Cranberry's Restaurant
(American, Mexican),
47 East Sheridan;
365–4301

Minglewood Cafe
(from-scratch cooking),
528 East Sheridan Street;
365–3398

**HIBBING/EVELETH/
VIRGINIA**
(area code 218)

Hong Kong Kitchen,
1928 Fourth Avenue East,
Hibbing;
263–9398

**Iron Kettle Family
Restaurant,**
Highway 169 and Third
Street South,
Chisholm;
254–3339

La Cocina & Cantina
(Mexican),
407 Chestnut Street,
Virginia;
749–8226

**Natural Harvest Deli &
Coffee Bar,**
505 North Third Street,
Virginia;
741–4663

Rocco's Italian Restaurant,
523 Chestnut Street,
Virginia;
749–1945

Whistling Bird Cafe & Bar
(Caribbean, pasta),
101 Broadway Street,
Gilbert;
741–7544

**Zimmy's & Atrium
Restaurant**
(American,Italian),
531 East Howard Street,
Hibbing;
262–6145

DULUTH
(area code 218)

Angie's Cantina & Grill
(Southwest, American),
11 East Buchanan Street;
727–6117

Bellisio's (Italian),
425 Lake Avenue South;
727–4921

Fitgers Brewhouse
(American),
600 East Superior Street;
726–1392

Grandma's (American),
522 Lake Avenue South;
727–4192

Lake Avenue Cafe (eclectic),
394 Lake Avenue South;
722–2355

New Scenic Cafe
(international),
5461 North Shore Drive;
525–6274

Old Chicago Pizza,
327 Lake Avenue South;
720–2966

Portland Malt Shop
(ice cream—seasonal),
Superior Street next to
Fitgers;
no phone

TWO HARBORS
(area code 218)

Blackwoods Grill & Bar
(American),
612 Seventh Avenue;
834–3846

Judy's Cafe
(home cooking, American),
623 Seventh Avenue;
834–4802

Portside Pizza,
623 First Avenue;
834–6362

**Vanilla Bean Bakery
& Cafe,**
812 Seventh Avenue;
834–3714

Vietnamese Lantern,
629 Seventh Avenue;
834–4373

GRAND MARAIS
(area code 218)

Angry Trout (eclectic),
Highway 61;
387–1265

Birch Terrace Restaurant
(American),
Highway 61;
387–2215

Blue Water Cafe (American),
Wisconsin Street;
387–1597

**Cascade Lodge &
Restaurant** (American),
Highway 61 (9 miles south of
Grand Marais);
387–1112 or (800) 322–9543

Gunflint Tavern
(soups, etc.),
Wisconsin Street;
387–1563

Harbor Inn Restaurant
(American),
Wisconsin Street,
387–1191

Sven and Ole's Pizza,
Wisconsin Street;
387–1713

Roads to Take

Highway 38 from Grand
Rapids to Effie

Highway 61 from Two
Harbors to Canadian
border

Highway 1 from
Tettegouche State Park
to Ely

Highway 65 from McGregor
to Jacobson

County Road 3 from
Jacobson to Grand Rapids

Gunflint Trail (County Road
12) from Grand Marais to
Lake Saganaga

Indexes

Entries for historic sites and museums begin on page 198.

GENERAL INDEX

Wabasha Street Caves/Down
   in History Tours, 11
walking tours, Stillwater, 5
Washington County Historical
   Society, 6
WE Fest, 119
Wells Fargo Bank, 55–56
Western Minnesota Steam Threshers
   Reunion, 115
West Hills Museum, 55
West Newton, 84
W.H.C. Folsom House, 8
Windom, 92

Winnebago Historical Society, 91
Winona, 41
Winona National Savings Bank, 41
Wintergreen Lodge, 168
Winter Sports Festival, Duluth, 178
World's Largest Ball of Twine, 68
World's Oldest Rock, 75
W.W. Mayo House, 87

Yellow Medicine County Historical
   Museum, 75
Younger Brothers Monument, 94

HISTORIC SITES

Alexander Faribault House, 17, 54
Alexander Ramsey House, 10
Bergquist Cabin, 117
bison kill site, 141
Blue Mounds State Park, 95
Bunnell House, 42
Comstock House, 117
covered bridge, 34
Croft Mine and Historical Park, 137
Dodge County Courthouse, 40
Engine 201, 56
E. St. Julien Cox House, 86
Faribault House, 17, 54
Forest City Stockade, 71
Foshay Tower, 21
Frank Lloyd Wright–designed
   service station, 156
Geldner Sawmill, 88
Glensheen, 175
Grand Mound Interpretive
   Center, 160
Grand Portage National
   Monument, 187
Grasshopper Chapel, 131
Gumm House, The, 158
Harkin Store, 84
Hibbing High School, 172
Hill Annex Mine, 159
Historic Fort Snelling, 19

Hull-Rust-Mahoning Mine
   overlook, 172
Jeffers Petroglyphs, 94
Kanabec History Center, 153
Lac Qui Parle Mission, 73
Laura Ingalls Wilder Dugout, 81
LeDuc-Simmons Mansion, 19
Mayowood, 38
North West Company Fur
   Post, 153–54
Norwest Bank, 57
Old Muskego Church, 14
Oliver Kelley Farm, 129
Phelps Mill, 112
Pickwick Mill, 43
Pipestone National Monument, 96
Sandstone History & Art Center, 153
Schech's Mill, 50
Sibley House, 17
Sinclair Lewis Boyhood Home, 133
Sisu Heritage, 170
Soudan Underground Mine, 168
Split Rock Lighthouse, 181
Terrace Mill, 109
Thomas Meighen's Farm Village, 49
Volstead House, 75
W.H.C. Folsom House, 8
W.W. Mayo House, 87

MUSEUMS

About the Author

Mark Weinberger is a freelance writer who lives in White Bear Lake, Minnesota. His work has appeared in *Powder, Mountain Sports and Living, The Professional Skier,* and *Silent Sports.* He is also the author of *Short Bike Rides in Minnesota.*